DON'T MISS THESE TIME-, MONEY-, AND SANITY-SAVERS . . .

- The fifteen-minute pick-up—the house stays neat and the family works together

- The best way to handle crammed storage space . . . and decide what stays and what goes

- Using dryer sheets to freshen up more than the laundry

- Professional organizing tips for a kitchen that works . . . and the best veggie drawer liner ever

- Spring cleaning? One-room-at-a-time shortcuts to ease the drudgery

- Summer child-care options you may have overlooked . . . or just never thought of

- Valentine . . . shmalentine. Eight ways to put the fun back into your love life. The passion will follow . . .

- Ways to chill out: learn what, when, and how to freeze everything from potato chips to fine chocolates

- Eight files to simplify your record-keeping so you'll never have to hunt down documents again

- The sports mom survival kit . . . and why you should always carry garbage bags in your car trunk

- Recipe for the Frantic Woman's Cocktail . . . a relaxing libation to celebrate a job well done

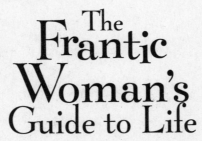

The Frantic Woman's Guide to Life

Remember: Life can't be predicted . . . but it can be planned!

The Frantic Woman's Guide to Life

A Year's Worth of Hints, Tips, and Tricks

Mary Jo Rulnick & Judith Burnett Schneider

WARNER BOOKS

NEW YORK   BOSTON

Warner Books

Time Warner Book Group
1271 Avenue of the Americas, New York, NY 10020
Visit our Web site at www.twbookmark.com.

Printed in the United States of America

First Edition: January 2004
10 9 8 7 6 5 4

Library of Congress Cataloging-in-Publication Data
Rulnick, Mary Jo.
   The frantic woman's guide to life : a year's worth of hints, tips, and tricks / Mary Jo Rulnick and
      Judith Burnett Schneider.
         p. cm.
      Includes index.
      ISBN 0-446-69059-7
      1. Home economics. 2. Housewives—Time management. I. Schneider, Judith Burnett. II.
      Title.

TX158.R85 2004
640--dc21

                                                                                2003048583

Book design and text composition by H. Roberts Design
Cover design by Jackie Merri Meyer & Brigid Pearson
Cover illustration by Meredith Hamilton

To our moms, Carol Pick and Dee Burnett: A wholehearted thank-you for shaping us into the women we are today. You made us believe we *can* do it all. Your continual encouragement enabled us to pursue our creativity and reach our goals. You have showed us how to handle the frantic life by living it first. So many of your tips have been integrated into this book, simply because you are such an essential part of us. This book is dedicated to the two of you.

Acknowledgments

There are many people who had a hand in taking our "Frantic" vision and making it a reality and we'd like to say you are forever in our hearts. To Stacey Glick of Dystel & Goderich Literary Management for believing in the project. You are the bridge that connected us to the right publisher. To our editor, Sandra Bark, for your insight, ambition, and vivaciousness, which helped create a book all of us can be proud of. To Amy Einhorn, our first reader. Your initial zeal for the project propelled the enthusiasm among the Warner staff—keep plugging in that slow cooker. To Emi Battaglia and Keri Friedman for your innovative ideas and exuberant promotional pursuit. To Harvey-Jane Kowal, Penina Sacks, and Susan Higgins for your inspired presentation and precise attention to detail. To Bryan Cronk, Theresa Dionisio, Veronica Gonzalez, Joanna Hudacko, Rebecca Oliver, and the rest of the Warner team for your invaluable input and commitment that proved to be just what we needed. To our publisher, Jamie Raab, for your excitement. You have made an impact on the frantic world.

To our Web designer Cindy Closkey for creating and maintaining the franticwoman.com site, and for your technical support and guidance. May all your wishes come true. To the woman who brought us together, Sandra M. Louden. To all of our writing workshop and retreat attendees and leaders. We thank you for your loyalty to us and devotion to the craft. To the staff at Donut Connection and Eat'nPark for allowing us to hold lengthy "office meetings" there without ever shooing us out the door.

We'd like to express a heartfelt thank-you to all the frantic women who have touched our lives over the years. We extend a special thanks to every one of you who shared a part of yourself in our book.

And we appreciate whoever created overnight mail. Being the frantic women we are, we needed this service time and time again.

Acknowledgments by Mary Jo Rulnick

A writer is only as good as the people around him or her. Through relationships, a writer can experience different perspectives and long-lasting emotions or learn a new skill. Each relationship adds a dimension to the writer's craft. There are many people along the way, from other volunteers within my community to the CEO of an advertising company, who have provided that opportunity. What I write today is due to the relationships I've enjoyed in the past. Thank you for sharing your thoughts, wisdom, and friendship.

Judy, we've hurdled a range of roadblocks, triumphed over tremendous obstacles, and conquered the distance. We've achieved a book that evokes our heart and soul to share with others living the frantic life.

To Jan and Fred Capasso and Sue and Larry Ault, thank you for your loyal understanding and unfaltering flexibility in giving me the time away from the office when I needed it (and boy did I need it). Sandy Barnett, your constant delivery of messages and other things (which we'll keep between us) were deeply appreciated. To the staff and villagers at UPMC's Beatty Pointe Village, a huge thanks for your never-ending excitement for my writing career. To everyone at Meritage Group, thanks for your faithful support along the writing path from my first article published to the acceptance of this book. To the members of Builder's Association of Metropolitan Pittsburgh's Women's Council, PA Mothers of Invention, and Women Business Network's Monroeville Chapter for your endless interest in the frantic quest.

Many thanks to *Pittsburgh Parent's* editor Pat Poshard for your foresight in giving me that very first assignment (we used it in the book, too) and your editorial advice. To Sandy Louden, your greetings opened the doors that enabled me to be in this position today. To Lori-ann Hoff Oberlin for always answering the questions I tossed your way. Mia Cronan and Linda Tomsho, your ideas inspired me, your feedback motivated me—you've accepted, never judged. To Rita Berkstein, Adrienne Fabrizi, Anica Jones, Sue Kolton, Tawnya Senchur (yes, Ton, you can have a life again), and Deanne Thomas for providing a sounding board during the past year. To the friends that I owe numerous rain checks for lunch dates, girls-only nights, and shopping expeditions, thanks for understanding.

To Beverly Breton Carroll, the miles haven't stopped our creativity from thriving, our friendship from growing, and the words from flowing. Thank goodness for e-mail. :>) To Leah Merola who stood beside me at the beginning of the frantic journey and I know stands beside me in spirit as the journey comes full circle.

To my dad and brothers, who always let me be me. You've overlooked my quirks and whims—even if I do drive all of you crazy.

To my husband, Stu. You've smiled as I danced to my own tune, you've applauded my achievements, and encouraged my dreams. Your unwavering love and support gave me the strength to reach my goals. To our children, Deanna and Josh. You've shared me with a six-hundred-page manuscript, a computer that was always booted up, and a telephone that never stopped ringing, yet you've taken it in stride. The two of you make me look good as a mother.

Stu, Deanna, and Josh, you are my foundation, the sunshine in my life, and the reason I'm always frantic. I love you.

Acknowledgments by Judith Burnett Schneider

I'm indebted to all those who have provided their generosity of spirit, knowledge, and support during the writing of this book, including:

- My coauthor, Mary Jo. We've weathered many frantic showers and storms together, and now here we are sitting atop the rainbow. Rejoice!
- My dad, John Burnett, who reads everything I write (even my thesis on the photochemistry of bicyclic aziridines) with the eye of a discerning, yet loving and somewhat biased, editor. No doubt, I inherited my love-of-books gene from you!
- My sisters, Kathy, Lynn, Trisha, and my sisters-in-law, Helen, Barb, and Ann, who together make up a wonderfully frantic flock.
- My husband's parents, Ann and Ed Schneider, who are forever on call for encouragement, support, and unlimited baby-sitting. I promise I'll be early next time!
- My writing colleagues and friends, Mary Patouillet and Janice Lane Palko, whose steadfast assurance and honesty remain invaluable. Here's to tinging the coffee mugs together.
- The writers Linda Foltz, Joanne Emrick, and my SinC group who so insightfully advised me not to order spinach salad or poppy seeds.
- Hannelore Hahn and the International Women's Writing Guild (IWWG) who encourage the personal and professional empowerment of women through writing.
- Tom Clark of Borders Books and Music who has offered input and guidance from day one, some six years ago.
- Matt and Tammy Schneider who so willingly opened their vacation home to us for brainstorming and fine-tuning sessions.
- My professors Dr. Harry Krebs at Dickinson College and Dr. Anthony Trozzolo at the University of Notre Dame, who encouraged me to blossom beyond the bud they had come to know.
- Most of all, I am grateful for the unending, unfailing strength, encouragement, and love of my husband, Timmy, and of our kids, Jacqueline, Juliana, and Timothy, who make living this hectic life so worth it all!

Contents

Introduction

Franticness has invaded all of our lives at one time or another. For some, living the hectic life is a day-to-day occurrence. For others, the scatterbrained lifestyle might come in spurts like during the back-to-school crunch and at the holidays. Sure, we've all mumbled, "If I can get through this week, life will be easier." And we *want* to believe it. Sometimes it even holds true for a few blissful days. Then, pow, another shift occurs in our well-planned agenda. That curve might involve a minor incident like a car pool mom who's stuck in traffic, leaving you to take the kids to practice—although you're already running late for a meeting. Or it might be something as unsettling and uncontrollable as a sudden illness or being laid off from work. The level of franticness and the cause are different for everyone. And yet the very existence of it remains constant for most of us.

Since we've had our share of minor and major incidents (though overall we consider ourselves to be truly blessed), we can identify with you. In writing this book, one snafu after another cropped up, adding to our frantic pace. And yes, we found ourselves repeating, "When this book is completed, life will return to normal." But did it? Definitely not. Why? Because we choose to pack as much into our days as we can—harvesting from life as much bounty as it has to offer. Though there are times when we would readily welcome five minutes of peace, on the whole, we wouldn't want life any other way.

Between us, we have five kids ranging from kindergarten to college age, two husbands with long, nontraditional working hours, two writing careers, one job outside the home, an hour's driving distance between our homes (and that's without construction traffic) so we can say, "Feeling frantic? Us too!"

From our experiences, then, we've collected the tips and ideas that have helped us get by (along with those of others who were so willing to share) and created *The Frantic Woman's Guide to Life*. Take your time, browse through the book, and pick and choose which suggestions you'd like to put to the test.

How This Book Works

In *The Frantic Woman's Guide to Life*, we've developed a system that will enable you to refer back to timely tips month after month, making a less hectic lifestyle more possible. Before you start, we suggest you obtain a notebook or a spiral-bound journal that we'll refer to as your *Frantic Journal*. Throughout the book, we'll suggest you jot ideas and answer quizzes in your journal—a book that's for your eyes only. It will contain your dreams and wishes, along with your long- and short-term goals.

Part one of this book, "Year Round," addresses the primary responsibilities of a woman's daily life—all those duties that must be accomplished every day, week, or month of the year from the swishing of the washing machine to the sizzling of the frying pan. Though many frantic women have the chance to surface-clean, the nitty-gritty, deep-down (from the closets to the garage) throwaway type of cleaning seems to escape us at every turn. Therefore, in addition to our time-tested traditional tips, we've included suggestions for adding a new twist to the old standbys that will help you zip through those mundane chores.

Part two, "Month-by-Month," focuses on every month of the year.

In chapters covering "January" through "December," you'll discover steps to help you organize life's crazy schedule and the course you find yourself taking whether you want to or not. You'll find memory joggers for everyday jobs, seasonal tidbits, and holiday reminders you might need to execute. Each month is divided into three sections starting with "Whip It into Shape." This segment deals with the organizational, hands-on process of maintaining your household. Next, you'll move into our section called "Darling Little Angels (And the Whole Blissful Bunch)," where you'll come across techniques to involve the gang in the cleaning process, to keep the peace surrounding your immediate and extended members, and to plan family fun, too. And last, but not least, is our "All About You" installment highlighting suggestions for tweaking your family, home, and work life into balance, while carving out the time you need to rejuvenate. At the end of every month, the "One-Step-at-a-Time Checklist" offers a detailed summary of what you should have accomplished throughout the month. For simplicity in tracking where you've been and what you've completed, all you have to do is mark for each task performed.

In part three of the *Guide to Life*, "A Wee Bit More," you'll read lists detailing everything from what to stock in your pantry, to what to pack when sending the kids off to camp, to the must-have necessities for a college-bound student. These lists can be photocopied and laminated for your convenience.

The final "Resources" segment provides a quick reference for the books, Web sites, software, and organizations recommended and referred to throughout the book, eliminating the need for you to search through the entire text for a specific telephone number or Internet addy (address).

We realize life will still bamboozle you—throwing zingers, obstacles, and roadblocks your way—but our goal is to provide you with the tips we've accumulated along our own frantic paths, leveling the bumps and smoothing the course just for you.

And we're off!

Frantically,
Mary Jo and Judith

Part One

Year Round

Getting Started

Taking care of the house is a never-ending job, one that demands constant attention. And if that were the only ball we had to juggle, it would be a breeze. But with the family, the pets, and work, too, daily life always seems to contain one surprise after another. If there's one thing we can count on, it's that there's always an obstacle standing in the way, preventing our days from running smoothly. Since we don't have George Jetson's maid, Rosie, to keep our households spotless, we tend to do things when they need to be done and occasionally behind schedule, too.

Though certain tasks will vary from household to household, this section highlights responsibilities you can carry out at any time during the year—most likely whenever you can. We'll cover ways to organize, approach, and complete all sorts of duties from cleaning out closets to caring for an aging relative.

As you journey through this part of the book, we encourage you to jot down notes, ideas, and thoughts as they come to mind. Write to-do lists and other such task-related entries in a notebook, a bound journal, or in your pocket personal computer (PC). Throughout this book, we'll refer to the note-taking device of your choice as your *Frantic Journal*. In addition to creative ideas and brainstorming results, we'll also urge you to answer quiz questions, complete exercises, contemplate changes in your home and life, ponder options, and so forth. All these prompts, and any you come up with on your own, can be expounded on within the pages of your Frantic Journal. It will become a sort of extension of yourself, so choose a medium you're comfortable with and stick to it. Don't worry about the order jottings follow or how the entries are organized. To bog yourself down with such unnecessary concerns is distracting and a waste of time (something we frantic women can't afford to spare). For easy reference, use small sticky tabs inscribed with key words (like "bathroom," "December to-do," or "kids' chores") to point you in specific directions, keeping your ideas within a flip of the page. You'll be surprised at how writing things down frees your mind of worry, allowing you to focus on what really matters.

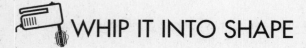

WHIP IT INTO SHAPE

Unwanted Poundage

If you tend to avoid regular upkeep in your home, the responsibilities will surely spiral out of control as quickly as your diet can. Think about it. Adding one more pound to the five you've put on can have an exponential effect. The growing list of things that need to be fixed, maintained, or replaced around the house enlarges as unforgivingly as the derriere if you don't watch out. Vow to take care of problems both inside and outside of the house as they arise so that things don't fall into total disrepair.

Instead of adding that unwanted poundage to the weight of your household burden, repair or replace items one at a time as you discover the need to do so. If a screw falls out of the door hinge, fix it rather than wait until the door falls away from the wall. Otherwise, before you know it, you're replacing stripped screws, damaged wood, and bent hinges. The time you've invested has increased from five minutes to fifty and your costs have more than quadrupled.

Although some frantics might be tempted to slough off the unwanted poundage theory, we urge you to think twice before doing so. For example, when Jody's (her name has been changed to protect her image) dream house came on the market, she wanted to place a bid on it and sell her existing residence. But over the years, her neglect of repairs had taken a toll on her house. The concrete on Jody's porch had shifted, allowing rainwater to seep quite regularly into the basement—which resulted in a separation of the porch roof outside and a warping of the game-room paneling inside. When the concrete and porch roof were detached, damage to the main roof and siding resulted. Thousands of dollars later, Jody realized that had she taken care of the shifting concrete in the first place, none of the other repairs would've been necessary.

An Inch at a Time

Keep a running room-by-room to-do list in your Frantic Journal. Write down everything that needs to be taken care of—from patching and painting to sorting through excess toys and stuffed animals. When you have a free moment or are feeling particularly productive, you won't have to hem and haw about where to begin. Read through your to-do data and pick a repair, any repair.

Think of your list as one big heap of laundry. At first glance, you think, "Ugh, I'll never see the floor again." To overcome that thought, you need to evaluate whether you're a *Toweler* like Judith or a *Tackler* like Mary Jo. The Toweler washes the stack of towels first, putting a noticeable dent in the day's work. By taking on the easy work first, Judith feels a sense of accomplishment as she scratches off responsibilities, several at a time.

The Tackler saves the easy stuff for last. By doing the darks and the hand-washables first, Mary Jo is making the job of washing the towels, underwear, and socks seem even easier. She can relax as she works because the tough tasks are behind her.

JOTS & THOUGHTS QUIZ
Are You a Toweler or a Tackler?

Sometimes it helps to understand the way in which you journey through your days. By taking advantage of your "working system," you can use wisely the time you have available to accomplish all you need to do. Answer yes or no to the following questions to determine which approach works best for you.

1. When paying bills, do you write checks for the smaller amounts first, such as cable service, then work your way up to the larger ones, like the rent or mortgage?
2. When cleaning the house, do you start with a room that you can zip through with less effort and time?
3. When running errands, do you make your first stops at the destinations where you are in and out in just minutes?
4. When de-cluttering closets, do you begin with the one in the hallway that houses bulkier towels, sheets, blankets, and quilts—and therefore contains less material to shuffle around?
5. When unloading groceries, do you stash the refrigerated items first, ending with the products that take more time to put away or with those freezer-bound items that need to be divided into smaller portions, such as ground meat, steaks, and chops?
6. When returning home from vacation, do you unload the easily stowed health and beauty products to their shelves before sorting the huge pile of dirty laundry?
7. When decorating for the holidays, do you arrange the larger decorations first, finishing up with the more time-consuming Christmas tree?

If you answered yes to the majority of these questions, then you are what we call the *Toweler*. You would rather start small, marking many things off your to-do list and working your way up to the harder tasks. By knowing this in advance, you can take advantage of your less energetic time of day to cross off all the menial chores you need to accomplish. You'll need to use a time when your energy is at its peak to do the more challenging tasks. So, plan your day and to-do list accordingly.

If you answered no to most of the previous, then you're what we call the *Tackler*. You'd rather dive right into the time-demanding or more detailed jobs first, using your energy for these and working your way down to the more mindless tasks. With the hard stuff out of the way, you can work longer and later knowing all that's left is the easy stuff. So jump-start your to-do list when your energy is high and work your way through to those tasks that you can perform on automatic pilot.

Put Things Where They Land

You've heard the cliché *a place for everything and everything in its place*. And that should be your goal. But in order to be sensibly organized, you want that chosen "place" to be convenient and easy to remember.

When straightening and ordering, don't force things to be where you think they should be, but do what we do and put them where they land. In other words, pay attention to where you set things down and make an effort to store them right there, rather than force yourself to stow things in a place that is orderly, yet illogical—at least for you.

One example illustrating how this theory can work was born on a college campus in the Midwest. After building several new complexes at the University of Notre Dame, engineers deliberately left out one important part—the sidewalks. Instead of paving them in the most logical of places, the university decided to allow students to create the paths first, traveling from building to building in the most direct routes with ease. Then, after paths were visibly worn, the corresponding sidewalks were paved.

What follows are a few commonsensical ways for you to stop trying to put things where you think they should be and just put them where they land.

- Some professional organizers might recommend hanging a key rack in your kitchen so you'll always know where you keys are. But if you're in the habit of tossing your keys on the table near the front door, then for you, there is a better solution: Skip the rack. Rather than alter your behavior, place a decorative bowl on the entry table to collect those keys.

- Instead of stuffing your wallet with everything but the kitchen sink—like seldom-used credit cards and restaurant gift certificates—place a small container the size of a No. 10 envelope in a kitchen cabinet, your car, or even your purse (depending upon how gargantuan it is). This is a practical place to store not only gift certificates and specialty store charge cards, but also insurance cards for eye and dental care, museum cards, and other such membership cards not used on a regular basis.
- The same cabinet can hold a container of often-used medical supplies such as adhesive bandages, allergy-relief medication, headache remedies, and PMS pills. Why hoard them in your upstairs medicine chest when the need for them is primarily in the kitchen, in the daytime?
- By stacking throw blankets in a basket or chest by the sofa, you're not only keeping them handy but also encouraging a comfortable home and easy cleanup.
- Do you grow green bread because no one eats it once it hits the drawer? Then make use of the unused. Put loaves in a basket on the counter. Use the newly emptied drawer for small plastic containers and loose lids that might get lost in a larger cabinet. You can always place half the loaf in the freezer to preserve its freshness (pre-slice for easy toasting).

When reorganizing and rearranging, you don't have to rush out and spend your precious dollars on gadget-y storage receptacles and the latest organizational gear. Instead, consider these options.

- Boxes of all shapes and sizes are available for free at stores that stock wine and liquor. And don't forget to retain those copy-paper boxes with lids at work. They're sturdy and they stack well.
- At the grocery store, egg cartons are unpacked from heavy-duty cardboard boxes you can obtain simply by asking.

- Plastic ice cream tubs or no-spill cups—the kind kids receive at restaurants for free—are handy for managing smaller toys and art supplies. They are durable, stack well, and are easily replaced when broken or damaged.

- Packages of paper clips, rubber bands, scissors, correction tape or fluid, sticky notes, and other office supplies store well in the minicrates from Clementine tangerines. These can also hold health and beauty and first aid items in a closet, cabinet, or drawer. These packing cases are particularly handy for such stashing because they're stackable.

- Cardboard and plastic shoe boxes are great for those once-a-year or rarely used materials like costume makeup, bow tie and cuff links, and cake-decorating utensils. Label the outside.

- A cedar chest, toy box, or wicker trunk doesn't have to be hidden in a bedroom. Situate one in a corner of the family room as a collect-all for toys, crafts, games, and puzzles. Add a cushion for extra seating.

- A child's coatrack, in addition to hanging coats and hats, can hold purses, belts, long necklaces, and bracelets. Paint or stencil it to add a unique flair.

- A plastic hamper tucked in the front hall closet provides trouble-free access to slippers and everyday shoes. Why take them to the bedrooms each night, only to pull them out again in the morning?

- As a variation, Leah Preiserowicz built cubbies in her front closet, one for each child. Now, even though the kids might stash messily in their own spaces, the room is clean and the closet is organized.

- A tie rack on the inside of a bedroom, bathroom, or laundry room door will host things you need at a moment's grasp. One inside a closet near the front entrance encourages kids to hang their own coats. Another mounted in the bedroom can hold your costume jewelry and belts.

- Small cans with lids, such as those from gourmet coffees, are stackable and perfect for holding batteries, hair bands, or extra keys.

One last bit of effective straightening advice is to heed our foolproof, one-step action plan: When you pick it up, put it away.

Even though we often make use of the containers we find around the house, now and then it's fun to splurge on those oversized rubberized storage bins to stow more valuable items such as seasonal clothes and holiday decorations. Then we don't have to worry about critters burrowing in our sweaters, dust collecting on our wreaths and wall hangings, or possible damage from pipe leakage.

Pipe leakage? That reminds us of the old cliché *don't put off until tomorrow what you can do today*. Several years ago, Mary Jo's hot water tank wore out and emptied all over the basement. Unfortunately, she had stored seasonal supplies and clothes in cardboard boxes in the same area. After spending hours cleaning up the mess, she vowed to buy more durable plastic containers. But it was one of those things she never got around to doing.

Not long after, a neighbor and her daughter stopped by for a visit. Well into the afternoon, the daughter quietly mentioned that the toilet had clogged earlier and overflowed. By the time Mary Jo was able to get the flushing under control, the water had seeped under the flooring and into the basement. Once again, she had a slew of water-soaked cardboard boxes on her hands. Needless to say, Mary Jo bought the plastic containers the very next day. *Better late than never.*

A Tisket, A Tasket

While you're busy paying attention to where things naturally land and how to store them, remember that baskets are a versatile addition to the frantic woman's home because they do so much and cost so little. Okay, we heard that groan. You've tried using baskets before and ended up in a situation we call the *masquerade cycle*. You probably started off gung ho, collecting baskets for various unorganized miscellaneous matter. But as it turns out, all you did was mask the mess by dumping it into fancy wicker containers. And before you knew it, you had a mass of messy baskets and found yourself needing to start all over again. What you didn't do from the start, however, was to consider how you wanted to use the basket initially. And then you didn't control the content for that use.

Take Serena, for example. She took the time to pay attention to where her keys and wristwatch often landed at the end of the workday. As soon as she'd walk in, she'd drop the keys, take off her watch, and make herself a pot of coffee. With good intentions, then, Serena placed a trinket basket by the coffeemaker on the kitchen counter. For the first week, her watch and keys were all that occupied the specified container. But a few weeks later, we found Serena had placed an abundance of miscellaneous items into the basket, including her nail clippers, twenty-three pennies, a spare screw, three ticket stubs, stray business cards, and much, much more. In short, Serena had lost control.

To avoid overloading those strategically placed treasure holders, here are a few useful basket-based suggestions.

- Keep a basket on your bathroom vanity to hold a blow dryer and curling iron.
- Set one on your sink for a variety of soaps and lotions.
- Try a smaller basket for toothbrushes and toothpaste and a separate one for hairclips and combs.
- Add another to the back of the toilet for spare rolls of tissue and a can of air freshener.
- If you have ever hopped into the shower having forgotten to bring into the bathroom your clean undies and bra, consider storing extras in a lidded basket, or even one that hangs from the bathroom doorknob. These make a good hideaway for such skivvies.
- Use a plastic basket—with holes in the bottom—filled with body wash, shampoo, and a scrubbie puff as a convenient shower tote. (P.S. This makes a great gift for college-bound students, too.)
- Place a basket containing paper plates, napkins, straws, and plastic silverware on the kitchen table for after-school snacking and dinners on the run. This eliminates coming home to a sink full of dishes.

- To avoid that continual search for the remote in the family room, designate a basket to catch the remote controls, program listings, and the portable phone—because it's rarely in the recharger anyway.
- Place a basket of playing cards on the coffee table to encourage family fun and one holding kids' flash cards to keep review materials at arm's reach.
- Collect those loose snapshots in a photo basket.
- Put a large basket (like a handled wicker laundry basket) in a corner of your living space for misplaced items. When full, have the kids shuffle their own things back to where they need to be. (Note: If searching for missing objects, always check this container first.)
- Place a basket at the top and bottom of the stairs, out of the way of course, or buy a contoured stair basket for items that need to be transported upstairs and down. With a little encouragement, everyone will get into the habit of toting things—helping to reduce straightening time.
- Adopt a basket-sorting technique to collect miscellaneous papers and objects belonging to each member of the family. Be clever with the type of receptacle you choose. For your teenage son, use a garbage can with his favorite team's logo on it. For youngsters, use a Barbie case, a rolling suitcase, or even a big toy dump truck. Gather CDs, handheld video games, keys, mail, books, and other out-of-place materials in them. Hand out assigned baskets to be sorted through while watching TV or riding in the car.

Filtering Bedrooms

The most effective time of year to de-clutter is when? (Did we stump you?) The answer is *always*. But how can you tackle that nagging problem of stuff continually piling up here and there? To get started in the bedrooms, for instance, don't bother with the dresser drawers or closets, at first. Focus only on what can be seen with the

HIDDEN GEM: The fifteen-minute pickup is a great way to involve the family in your daily routine. Each evening or so, set the timer for fifteen minutes or play a favorite CD. During this time, the entire family races around picking up out-of-place items. Make a game of it. The person with the most pickups gets to choose the dessert, a television program, or game for the evening. An adaptation is to do high-speed pickup during the commercials of a favorite family show.

naked eye—dresser tops, shelves, desks, floor space, and so forth. Stand in the doorway of the room and ask yourself, "How would I feel if I were showing this room to my boss or the owner of my husband's company?" Take note of where your gaze is drawn and on what it is that is catching your eye. Then force yourself to pitch, pitch, and pitch some more. Once the floor and surface space has been cleared, you can tackle the inside of closets, drawers, and that dreaded hiding space under the bed.

HIDDEN GEM: Partner up. If you can't seem to motivate yourself to sort and chuck alone, invite a friend to help. Often, just the expression on her face when you show her the knitted, holey afghan will be enough to let you know it must go. Then it's off to your friend's house to help her rid her life of clutter, too.

- Pack away all the trophies, plaques, and other dust collectors you can. If your hubby (or decorated child) insists on displaying them, offer an option. Either they're packed away or he now has the job of cleaning his favorite bowling trophy.
- As a rule, don't keep what you don't need. How many times have you heard, "Don't throw away the boxes and authenticity certificates to collectibles, or you'll devalue the items"? That's

great advice if you're going to sell them one day. But you can throw away the boxes to collectibles, such as Precious Moments or Lladro figurines, if you plan to display them for years to come.

Sort through and eliminate kids' toys. Year after year, you move the toys from one area of the bedroom or family room to another. Then one day, your little guy is heading into his teen years and it dawns on you his toddler cars and trucks are still taking up coveted space in his closet. Well, now's the time to move them out. You don't have to discard everything in his toy collection. Keep the traditional toys that never age and store them in the attic or basement (before you know it, your little grand-critters will come creeping in!).

If there's no easy way of fixing a broken toy and you can't get the parts you need from the company, then no matter how much the toy

---

HIDDEN GEM: Are the kids missing a few pieces to their favorite play sets or games? Or, for example, is the battery cover for a handheld video toy missing or broken? Don't throw it away just yet. Call the manufacturer's toll-free number and request a replacement parts list for that specific toy. Chances are, for a few dollars, you'll be able to obtain the missing pieces and the toy will be whole again (and some manufacturers will replace certain broken or missing parts for free!). How can you find the company's phone number? Often, it is printed on the bottom of the box or electronic toy. If not, you can check a new box in the store and copy down the number. The simplest way to go is to call the toll-free phone directory at 1-800-555-1212 and ask for the company by name.

---

originally cost you, it must be tossed. The same goes for toys, games, decks of cards, and puzzles with missing pieces. It's not likely that the game will be played without all the parts. If there are only a few misplaced cards, however, you can hand-make new ones to revive the game. If you don't plan on doing so, then by all means, discard.

Closets, and Shelves, and Drawers, Oh My!

It's the secret desire of every frantic woman to have clutter-free closets throughout the house. But how can you possibly put any new articles in your overstuffed closets without first getting rid of the old?

JOTS & THOUGHTS QUIZ
How Much Do You Stuff and Shut?

Do you don a hard hat before opening your closet door, knowing things will come flying out at you every time? Are you developing bulging biceps while pushing aside clothes to squeeze in just one more hanger? And are you stocked enough to supply a wardrobe for an old-time photo shop?

Answer the following simple questions in your Frantic Journal to determine the severity of your stuffing problem.

1. Do you save *everything*, like batteries that might have a little juice left and keys from your previous vehicles?
2. Do you have closets that can't be closed properly because they're stuffed full of towels, shoes, and who knows what?
3. Have you ever gone to pop in a videocassette only to find that the box for the romantic comedy contained a Disney cartoon or, worse yet, a poorly taped boxing match?
4. Do you have sports equipment stashed all over the house—hockey gear in the garage, golf clubs in the hall closet, knee pads in the kids' cubbies, and baseball gloves on the shelf in the laundry room?

If you answered yes to even one of the questions, you now know how stuffed your storage areas are. So ask yourself, "Why do I hold on to certain items as opposed to throwing them away?" Do they link you to a dream of what was or of what you hope will be again? You might cling to a pricier article, unable to bear thoughts of throwing money down the drain—even though you might never use the item again. Or you store an object for years, thinking you might need it someday. And so it goes, and the closets remain chock-full.

Imagine if you had to pick up your house and move it. And you were paying for the move per pound. The first thing you'd want to do is clear out all the stuff you don't use, need, or want—otherwise, you'll be charged to transport it. Why pay to move so much? Remember, the less your house weighs, the less it would cost. If you keep this in mind as you're sorting, maybe, just maybe, it will make the decision to toss or give away a weensy bit easier.

Because the excess stuff collected from closets, dressers, cabinets, and drawers adds a weighty burden to your life, the more garbage bags you fill, the lighter you'll feel. So heave and hurl, flip and fling. Or pack a box for donations to charity. Isn't it better to give your surplus to those who'll use it, rather than have it gather and somehow multiply in your home?

So what's the best approach for tackling those jammed, crammed storage spaces?

- To ensure a complete de-cluttering, take everything out of the closet from top to bottom. Why? By dragging out each piece as opposed to simply shuffling through the closet's contents, you'll be less likely to keep what you won't wear or use. While you're pulling everything out, empty all jacket pockets, purses, backpacks, duffel bags, and boxes.

- In looking at the array before you, decide what stays and what goes. How? Remove garments from hangers, one at a time, and try on each article. It sounds like a tedious task, but there's nothing better to motivate you to give away a pair of jeans than not being able to pull them up past your knees. Avoid the temptation to hold on to certain clothing hoping you'll lose weight. If you do shed a few pounds, you deserve a new top anyway, right? Whatever doesn't fit, place in a discard pile. Check for fading in the armpits and thinning of fabric in the rear end and at the thighs, especially for corduroy. Then toss and toss some more. As each item is cast off, remember: You're shedding pounds of house weight and unloading that subconscious burden, so force yourself to throw away, give away, or pack away.

- If you're still carrying on a debate with yourself about old favorites or expensive garments, ponder this example. The size 5 suit you purchased years ago will probably never fit again. Or by the time it does, it will be so out of style you'll look like Miss Hathaway of Beverly Hills fame. So why not pass it to a program like Dress for Success (www.dressforsuccess.org) that collects business attire for women who are struggling to build a future for themselves? (Search for such programs in your local phone directory or on the Internet.)

- Once you've emptied the contents of the closet, wipe down the walls and ceiling with a mild cleaning solution. Spic and Span is especially useful in removing black marks on walls caused by bumps from shoe heels. Do not use this cleaning solution on wood, however. Wash floorboards and doors, both inside and out, using a liquid wood-cleaning solution because dry-wiping will not remove dust in the corners and ledges of wood detailing. If your closet is carpeted, use a damp cloth to pull dust from around the edges of the floor where dirt is most concentrated. Then, vacuum.

- If better lighting is required inside the closet, add it now. For a quick and easy solution, mount battery-powered lights that you tap on and off—available at most home improvement stores. Don't forget to situate one near the bottom of the closet to minimize the possibility of wearing one black and one blue shoe.

"While getting dressed for work and having an argument with my ex-husband, my day started on a bad note," Diane Johnson says. "When I arrived at work and walked through the front door of the office, I was not prepared for the laughter that erupted. One of my coworkers told me, after she managed to get hold of herself, that the whole group watched me get out of my car and stomp awkwardly across the parking lot. I was so frenzied when I left home, I had put on not only two different-colored shoes, but also two different types of heels that made me limp when I walked!"

If you've made use of a "contribution box" and accumulated

> **HIDDEN GEM:** Keep a "contribution box" handy. Designate a box, basket, or hamper in the basement, inside a closet, or in the laundry room to gather unwanted items as you come upon them. The next time you wash your toddler's permanently stained T-shirt or the jeans that are too snug on your teen, cast them into the give-away box instead of into the overstuffed dresser drawer. Sorting as you go makes the organizing and filtering process an ongoing one, rather than a huge ordeal that must be taken on once or twice a year.

enough to fill a heavy-duty garbage bag, drop the bag off at a charity donation site or thrift shop. At times when you're entrenched in the weeding-out mode, load a bag of giveaways in the trunk each time you go out. By taking fifteen minutes before you leave to fill another bag, you'll be continually triumphing over the ongoing de-cluttering process.

Sound like too much trouble? Some veterans' organizations and other groups will come to your door to pick up donations. Often, they'll mail flyers announcing when they'll be in your area. All you need to do is call the number on the card to get on their list. Then at the predetermined time, simply place bags on the doorstep—you needn't be home when the truck arrives. For your records, they'll leave a donation receipt. Fill it out and file immediately. If you haven't received any flyers lately, check your local phone directory for contact information.

Use a deadline as a motivator. Upon calling an organization to pick up your donations, allow the date they give you to become your donation deadline. Then, you only have so much time, usually a week or so, to clear your closets. And you better hop to it. You don't want to feel guilty for asking a group to make the trip to your house for nothing, do you?

No matter what time of year you decide to gather and pitch, consider these additional routing options.

- As tempting as it is to host a garage sale, consider donating things instead. This deletes one time-consuming event from your already jam-packed agenda. By giving away, you eliminate the hassles of advertising, cleaning, pressing, tagging, and sorting articles to be displayed and sold. And the tax write-off is probably worth more than the small amount of cash you'd collect at a sale.
- If you still want to take on a garage sale but would like to share the responsibilities, ask your kids to plan and organize the sale to earn extra money. The task becomes even easier if your neighborhood hosts a community one. Be sure to remind kids that they will be responsible for setting up (although you should be prepared to lend a hand), selling, and tearing back down again. The success they'll feel and the entrepreneurial lesson they'll learn will be worth the effort, indeed.
- Try a resale store. Check your local phone directory for consignment shops near you. Most owners require you to make an appointment. They'll have a list of items they sell and at what times of year they'll take them. Checks are usually distributed to consignees on a once-a-month basis. You'll receive a percentage of the sale price, as will the owner. And if your wares don't sell, you have the choice of picking them up or allowing the shop to donate them for you.
- Don't forget to offer unwanted articles to family members, friends, or neighbors. With the high price of clothing and toys, hand-me-downs are often welcomed and appreciated. If you pass along favorite brands that wear well, your sister-in-law will love you dearly. And isn't it easier parting with a treasured outfit if you know it's going to a happy home?
- Or try an alternative—a clothing swap. Set up a neighborhood swap in which each person brings unwanted clothes and toys, cleaned and sorted by gender and size. Make up rules for the evening—such as no give-backs and no reneging. Everyone takes a turn choosing an item until they're gone. Any leftovers can go to your favorite shelter for yet another tax write-off. And if you

and your friends don't have kids close in age or size, try this swap with kitchen supplies and other household items. A friend might value the food processor you never use. And you, in turn, can scoop up her spare cracker keeper or toaster oven. Swap unused Tupperware, serving trays, pitchers, casserole dishes, and more.

HIDDEN GEM: While sorting, sifting, and filtering, don't forget to keep track of items you're giving away so you can take advantage of the tax deductions available to you. Judith attaches a clipboard and pen directly to the outside of her donation box. Throughout the year as the unwanted clothes, toys, and other discards accumulate, she writes down giveaway articles by type and brand name. Brand name? That's right. According to our tax expert, Certified Public Accountant (CPA) Tim Schneider (Judith's husband), items can be assigned a worth based on brand name by looking them up in the reference guide called *It's Deductible: Cash for Your Used Clothing and Thousands of Commonly Donated Items* by Income Dynamics (call 1-800-875-5927 for the latest annual edition). Then, come tax time, accurate values are totaled to come up with the family's annual donation deduction. Because this tax guide is rather expensive (over $100) and must be purchased annually as values are updated, check with your accountant or your main branch reference librarian to obtain donation tallies.

Making Memories from Discards

You know you shouldn't, but you have an attachment to the blanket sleeper your baby wore, your son's championship jersey, or the shirts you've accumulated on family vacations. Here's one last thought before discarding. Over the years, collect items that stir emotional warmth in a box in the attic, allocating a separate container for each child, you, and your spouse. When the box becomes full, use these

> ✷ HIDDEN GEM: Now that you've de-cluttered your closet, don't forget to separate out at least two ready-to-go outfits for times when you have a last-minute appointment or need to change in a jiffy. These outfits should be ready-to-wear, no ironing necessary, and should be stored at the end of the rack so you can grab, throw on, and go in a moment's notice. Also, put aside two "cycle" outfits for each season—for those days when you're battling PMS, cramps, and bloatedness. These are a must when you know you'll barely get through the day without suffering from tight-waist syndrome.

clothes to piece together a keepsake quilt. If you don't sew, someone you know probably knows someone who does. Or search for quilters in the phone directory or on the Internet to take on your special project. A quilt with squares from your child's or spouse's most cherished clothing makes a great graduation, wedding, or anniversary gift.

Mother of five Ann Burnett saved the T-shirts her daughter had acquired through years of participating in school athletics, including basketball, cheerleading, lacrosse, and crew. Well before graduation, Ann hired a professional quilter to make a patchwork quilt using the T-shirt emblems. She chose borders and backing for the quilt using school colors. The center square was embroidered with her daughter's name, graduation date, and a message of love from Mom and Dad. (An aside: In addition, Ann had a video made using photos from birth to senior year. She included pictures of family and friends and used her daughter's favorite songs as background music.) Needless to say, when Ann presented these memorable gifts at the graduation party, there wasn't a dry eye in the place.

Here are a few more memory-making suggestions to try before you discard.

- Use a favorite dress or shirt as matting for a frame. Trace a photo mat onto the wrong side of the fabric. Then cut, glue, and trim. For example, Patricia Kulmoski used the dress she wore to her infant daughter's funeral as background matting for framing the dried tea-rose rosary her mother gave her on that day. The framed roses still hang in Patricia's daughter's memory at the turn in her stairwell.

- As a fun option, have your child's first ballet shoes or the plaster cast from a broken bone bronzed as bookends, a picture frame, or a plaque. Search online for companies that specialize in the bronzing process or ask your jeweler for a recommendation.

Heirloom Gloom

Quit storing your heirlooms and keepsakes like your wedding gift crystal and your grandmother's china and jewelry. Instead, follow these tips for utilizing those dust-covered pieces for everyday purposes or to spruce up your decor.

- The next time you invite friends or relatives to dinner, spread out the embroidered heirloom tablecloth you've never used, toast with the crystal goblets, and set the table with the good china. "But what if it breaks or stains?" you think. It's true that by using them, you are increasing the risk of staining, chipping, or breaking treasured keepsakes. But consider this. Are they better opened and enjoyed by all or locked up in a china cabinet or, worse yet, in a box in the basement?
- If you've received jewelry as an inheritance or gift, don't lock these items away in a safe. Visit a reputable jeweler, assess whether the pieces should be repaired or reset, and then do so. Have them appraised and be sure to add them to your insurance policy. Then, don the rejuvenated jewels with pride at your next dinner party or night out on the town.
- Don't needlessly hold on to furniture that has been passed along to you. When Carol Rulnick inherited too many pieces to use or store, she knew she had to make some choices. She kept the ones that fit into her family's house and lifestyle. Then she

brought in an antique dealer and asked him to bid on several of the remaining items. By doing so, Carol sold a small bookcase to him for $200. This price was far more than the $10 she planned on asking at her garage sale.

Take a closer look at the heirlooms and keepsakes you've accumulated. If you don't think you'll use them in the near future, decide to sell, pass along to other relatives, or donate to charity.

Handling Sports Equipment

While you're rearranging and assigning closet space, designate one large storage area or a few bins in the garage for all sports equipment. Rather than scattering stuff everywhere, try one of these organizing alternatives.

- To hang sweaty sports equipment out to dry so it doesn't get that sour locker-room smell, search garage sales for an old sewing mannequin. Drape the mannequin with shoulder pads, hockey pants, shin guards, and helmets. Or purchase a sturdy coatrack or install heavy-duty hooks for such air-drying purposes.
- To eliminate balls rolling all over your house, store them in a rectangular trash can or ball rack (available at larger sports stores) that fits neatly against the garage wall, taking up less space than a round container. Or you can purchase a ball bag with a handle. Pound cut nails into the concrete wall to hang the bag. Another solution is to suspend a nylon net (like a heavy-duty fishing net) by its four corners from the ceiling. Stash balls inside.

Sparkle and Shine

Even though you've been spending valuable time straightening the house, de-cluttering, and organizing, don't neglect the heavy-duty cleaning tasks that always await your attention. The following shortcuts and tidbits will help make your scrubbing and scouring duties run more smoothly and efficiently.

- To clean your chandelier and other crystal or glass items, add one cup of vinegar to a gallon of water. Dampen a clean soft cloth (like a diaper or T-shirt) in the solution and wash the crystal. Wipe dry with another lint-free material. This solution also safely restores shine to hardwood floors.
- To clean silk flower arrangements, sprinkle a tablespoon or two of table salt in a brown paper bag. Add your silk flowers, shake, and voilà! You have dust-free daisies. Or, if you prefer, fill the kitchen sink or laundry tub with mild, soapy water. Toss in silk greens and ivy for easy cleaning. Drip-dry by hooking over a hanger or placing in a dish drainer. This is a good way to clean knickknacks, too. (Caution: When cleaning silk flowers, colors can run or fade. Be sure to wash brightly hued silks in a bucket to avoid stubborn dye stains in your sink.)
- Make daily use of ready-made dusting cloths. Or fabricate your own using leftover dryer sheets. Spray furniture polish on the sheets and store in a sealed container or zippered freezer bag.
- To keep areas smelling fresh, place dryer sheets under the mat inside the front entrance, under sofa cushions, and in drawers. The sheets also help freshen the kids' gym bags and the trunk of the car.
- Fill the tub with warm sudsy water using dishwashing liquid to clean miniblinds. If possible, soak overnight. Rinse.
- Use a feather duster with an extendable handle—a practical tool to have. It allows for quick elimination of ceiling cobwebs and dust from tops of drapery rods, a once-over for ceiling fans, miniblinds, tops of framed pictures, crown moldings, and other hard-to-reach places. Its sister duster, the flat one designed for sweeping under refrigerators, is a convenient tool both for cleaning and for rescuing tiny runaway toys.
- When laundering washable draperies and sheers, remove from

the rod, leaving curtain hooks in place. Use mild detergent in cold water and wash in the gentle cycle. Take out of the machine immediately when finished. Fluff in the dryer for just a minute. Hang while warm and damp. Tug at the bottom where each folded pleat falls and watch wrinkles disappear.

Carpets and Furniture

Figure out a time of year that would be best for you to have your carpets and furniture cleaned. Some frantic women wish to have the scrubbing done before the holidays; others prefer to wait until the spring-cleaning period. Still others clean furniture and carpets on an as-needed basis. By planning which time of year works best for you, you can watch for coupons and promotional sales to get the best price on cleaning services.

We Must, We Must

No one ever said, "When I grow up, I want to do laundry." But even so, the grubby task seems to continually nag at the frantic woman's conscience. So how can you make the laborious deed more manageable?

- Set up four hampers—for lights, darks, towels, and delicates. Have each family member sort his own laundry into the bins daily.
- Purchase a separate laundry basket for each person's clean clothes. Once you fold and fill, it's up to them to put their clothes away. If your teenaged daughter chooses to live out of a basket, so be it. But make it a rule to have baskets emptied and returned before the next specified laundry day.
- If they're not quite old enough to do it themselves, help little ones carry their baskets to their rooms and show them how to put clothes away.

- Assign a hamper, bin, bag, or specific spot for kids to deposit their dirty sports uniforms. Because they'll be within reach, you can launder these necessities before diving into the everyday loads. This saves you from having to rush around the house, digging through the clothes chute or hampers, thirty minutes before game time.
- While you're at it, train family members to place their favorite clothing on top of the washer, in a separate hamper, or in a hanging laundry bag. This way, when it's time to do laundry, these cherished articles can be washed and dried first.
- Teach older kids to do their own laundry so you can point a finger right back at them when they complain that what they want to wear hasn't been cleaned.

Before Mary Patouillet entered the hospital for surgery and a four-day stay, she typed up step-by-step laundering directions, printed them out on brightly colored paper, and mounted them above the washer. While she was gone, her teenaged son followed the instructions without fail, washing and drying his favorite T-shirts in a snap.

- If there's no room in a drawer or closet when putting laundry away, right then and there, pull out a few items to be given away. Stow them in your designated donation box. When the box is full, remember to give, give away.
- Instead of putting sports uniforms, team bathing suits, and dance leotards back in the drawer, fold from the dryer and pack directly into select gym bags or totes. Then, uniforms can always be found with knee pads and ball; the bathing suit is consistently with the cap, goggles, and towel; and the dance garb is kept in the ballet bag.
- Every now and then as you're filling the washer, tackle the mess that has collected in the laundry room. Clear your shelves, floor, and any cabinets of out-of-place items. Toss away the stained and torn clothing. Set up a new system for storing maintenance items like lightbulbs, vacuum cleaner bags, cleaning solutions,

and garbage bags. Isolate a stashing place for such household surplus as napkins and the snacks you want to hide from those ever-munching kids.

✂ **SNIPPET:** Does it feel as though you're always on your feet, running in circles, and never really getting anywhere? Well, you are! The average stay-at-home mom walks several miles a day around the house doing chores. And to boot, she spends approximately twenty-five hours a year making beds.

Is the dry-clean-only stack of dress shirts, wool pants, and evening dresses still piled high from last season? If so, what you need is a dry-cleaning drop-off system.

- Keep a box, basket, or small hamper in a closet or a corner of the laundry room for collecting dry-clean-only items. Doing so minimizes time wasted gathering dirty clothes before heading out the door. If you have discount coupons, keep those in the box too.
- Get in the habit of taking clothes to be dry-cleaned on a regular basis. If you drop them off on Mondays and pick them up on Fridays, for example, you'll always have what you need for those weekend gatherings.
- Find a good dry cleaner located near your place of work or preferably your spouse's. That way, you can pass that responsibility on.
- Look for some dry-cleaning establishments that offer a pickup and delivery service. They supply order forms and plastic bags to deposit dirty clothing. Pickup is usually at the beginning of the week and delivery at the end. This service is convenient for those pressed for time. And the cost is often only a smidgen more than drop-off cleaners.

Disaster: Are You Ready?

Disaster happens when you least expect it. Some catastrophes such as earthquakes, tornadoes, and terrorist attacks occur without much warning, affording us little time to handle the crisis, let alone prepare for it. And even though we are usually given fair notice before a flood, hurricane, or snowstorm, you might find yourself competing with the rest of your community for supplies at the supermarket or home improvement store. Will there be enough stock for everyone? Could you or should you have planned ahead?

Most certainly, you should. All the research for preparing for such emergencies has been spelled out for you at the Web site of the United States Department of Homeland Security, www.ready.gov. The site details what you'll need to make up kits full of emergency supplies and offers tips on how to make emergency plans with your family. It also highlights what might happen in the event of a biological, chemical, or nuclear attack. So get yourself to a computer with Internet access and read every page. (If you're not online at home, use the facilities at a public library.) Among other issues, the content addresses what to do if you're in a moving vehicle, a high-rise building, or away from home. Call 1–800–BE–READY (1–800–237–3239) for a free brochure.

In addition, *Are You Ready? A Guide to Citizen Preparedness* is available from the Federal Emergency Management Agency (FEMA). Request a copy by calling 1–800–480–2520 or by visiting their Web site at www.fema.gov/areyouready. Also, the American Red Cross offers tips regarding a range of concerns from food and water to preparing and stocking a shelter-in-place. For more information, stop by www.redcross.org and click on "Disaster Services" or call 1–877–272–7337 to locate a Red Cross chapter near you.

Here are nine key points to help jump-start your emergency planning.

- Determine what types of disasters might occur within your community and record all possibilities in your Frantic Journal. Once you have done so, it's time to plan your course of action.
- Obtain and read all information available to you through the pre-

viously mentioned references and any you might find on your own.

- Assemble a disaster supply kit immediately and store in a safe, accessible place.
- Discuss emergency situations with family members and make arrangements on meeting places and coping strategies for each type of potential disaster. Don't scare children by bogging them down with unnecessary details, but be sure they know what to do (taking children's ages into consideration, of course). Organize a backup plan, too.
- Find out what emergency strategies are in place at your children's school. Are you comfortable with them? Is the procedure the best it can be? If you have suggestions for changes, contact the school board, principal, or committee in charge. Study the policy and review it with your children. Inquire about putting together and safely storing emergency supplies according to the number of students and staff on site.
- Ask if a crisis plan has been adopted at work. If so, review it and discuss with coworkers. If not, find out who is responsible for putting one into practice. Prepare an emergency kit and store there, as well.
- Inventory each room of the house for insurance purposes. Use a video or digital camera to make this step easier. If you don't own one, you can borrow—or write everything down in a notebook. Include clothing, jewelry, linens, sports equipment, book and video collections, other collectables, high-tech pieces, and big-ticket items like appliances and furniture. Add model names and numbers for appliances, televisions, and computers. Don't forget to add the contents of the attic, basement, and garage. Tuck this information in a fireproof safe or your safety deposit box at the bank, or store a copy in a different location such as your office or another family member's home.
- List the contact information and account numbers for all financial institutions you're involved with—from banks to credit card companies. Every month or so, record the current balances in your Frantic Journal so as to have accurate figures close at hand.

- In addition to survival supplies, stash cash in small bills and coins both at home and at the office in case a trip to the bank isn't possible for a few days or longer.

And lastly, keep an open mind when making emergency preparations. Spend time reviewing all the modern technology you rely upon daily and plan on how you'd live without it, if you had to do so. Most important of all, don't panic. Remember: The best defense against any disaster or emergency is knowledge and preparedness. Make the time to get ready today.

HIDDEN GEM: Rather than use your expensive party candles, keep a large supply of inexpensive utility or plumbers candles and matches on hand in large coffee cans or tin containers throughout the house (keeping out of the reach of children). To understand why, consider this example. After a tornado swept through and left the Rulnicks without electricity for days, Mary Jo's daughter, then sixteen, found a way to make instant mashed potatoes. She lit six candles in a large coffee can and heated a pot of water over the flame, then added the flakes, and voilà—potatoes. It wasn't the most flavorful meal she'd ever prepared, but it sure beat the crackers and dried fruit they'd been munching on until then.

Your Decor

Do you still have olive green paisley curtains with white pom-pom balls or metallic wallpaper staring you in the face? You know your place is a decorator's nightmare, but you don't have a minute to devote to updating. Before you pull out paint and fabric swatches, let's find out where you register on our decor meter.

JOTS & THOUGHTS QUIZ
How Tired Is Your Decor?

The title says it all. Answer the following questions to test just how in need your surroundings are of some light (or heavy) sprucing up.

1. Have you had the same ornamentations decorating your tables and shelves for years?
2. Has it been more than two years since you rearranged the furniture?
3. Have you wanted to make a change in your home's decor but felt it was too expensive to do so?
4. Are you uncomfortable with the blank walls in your house?
5. Is there one color or color combination that makes you feel relaxed or comfortable, but for some reason you've neglected to use it to add accent to your home?
6. Do you buy interesting decorations and then have no idea how or where to place them?
7. Does it seem that you have no real theme running through your home?

Have you answered yes more times than you'd like? Maybe you need a bit of decor-doctoring. But don't despair. We have several simple tips that every frantic woman can apply.

Decorating Not Your Bag

If the decorating thing isn't your bag, try these suggestions to motivate and excite the Martha Stewart in you.

- If you can afford it, go professional. Professional designers can be hired for anything from a one-time consultation to managing an entire project. Remember, the pros really know what they're doing. All you have to do is give them a ballpark figure, highlight your tastes, and they'll take it from there. Be sure to go with someone who's been recommended by a reliable source—an acquaintance you respect, a coworker, a friend, or a family member.
- Look for designers who charge lesser fees for consulting on furniture arrangement—helping you to work with what you already have. They might also recommend tactful, affordable accents to be placed about.

- Consider hiring a student of interior design (a more budget-friendly method). Call schools in your area and ask to talk with the head of that department. She'll be able to recommend a student with promise who can handle the job. Just think, your room could become the subject of the next genius designer.

- Visit large department stores that have designers on hand. Pick their brains for decorating questions and concerns you might have. Between the catalog and in-store merchandise, you might not need to shop anywhere else.

- Try home improvement superstores that have staff to help with decorating options. Visit the store during a slow time, like the dinner hour, in order to receive more detailed information from a less harried employee. If you find a particularly helpful person, ask her when she'll be working again soon.

- Ask independent or franchised paint and wall-covering retailers for decorating information. Employees in a smaller store might have more time to chat and offer suggestions about what's popular in paint color and design. They're also aware of the latest and most efficient methods of applying paint and wallpaper. Some such employees do remodeling and redecorating on the side, giving them added knowledge from experience.

- Brainstorm with a friend in the real estate or home-building business. Usually, builders and Realtors keep abreast of the industry trends and can recommend the best retailers, flooring specialists, designers, and appliance dealers to work with.

- Visit model homes and condominiums that showcase what's "in"; they are almost always professionally decorated. Best of all, this method of gathering information is free. Plan a fun "girls' day out" and visit four or five new housing developments. Check out the landscaping designs and plant choices there to gather ideas for sprucing up the outside of your house this summer.

- Take advantage of guided home tours, which are valuable tools for scoping out new decorating schemes and are well worth the fee they charge. Scan your local paper or your FYI channel for such upcoming events.

Decorating Is Your Bag

If decorating *is* your thing, you probably have a flair, a knack, and a sincere interest. And while you'd still learn a few things by reading the previous section, here are some additional tips to tempt your creative side.

- Browse through furniture and department stores and visit the homes of people you know. Flip through magazines and watch home improvement shows. Make a note in your Frantic Journal concerning which accent pieces, color schemes, and furniture arrangements catch your eye. At the same time, pay attention to what you don't like and record it. Your negative internal responses tend to jump out at you and can help you focus in on what you really want.
- Don't be afraid to be a copycat—mimicking in your decor everything from the shape of the coffee table in your doctor's office to your neighbor's carpet color to your aunt's treasured knickknacks to the elaborate window treatments at a downtown hotel.
- When you begin your redecorating, take it one room at a time. Trying to re-do the whole place at once would be overwhelming and confusing. In your chosen room, focus on the carpet, the crown molding, and everything in between.

Interior designer Rose Lencher offers these inspirational ideas for decorating your home in a distinct yet practical way.

- Instead of spending excessive amounts of money on furniture that sports fabrics of popular prints and styles, invest in a high-quality, solid-colored, traditional sofa. This makes it easy to change accessories, toss pillows, and throw blankets to follow current trends. A pair of animal print pillows, for example, is far less expensive to replace than a tiger-striped love seat.
- Decorate your entire living space in color families. If all your rooms are in varying shades of beige or brown, for example, you

can move accessories around the house for a varied, fresh look without having to spend a lot of money to achieve it.

- Use things for purposes other than their originally intended function. One client chose a kitchen island unit to use as a desk in his study. It had sufficient storage and presented the touch of unique style he was seeking.

- Plant a surprise in each room. It can be as simple as a conversation piece, a striking wall paint color, or the interesting placement of an object. Examples include everything from a functioning, antique pay telephone to a metallic sculpture of a turtle peeking out from under a desk.

- When decorating a shelf, mantel, or table, don't take several small items and spread them around. It's better to group items together, especially of varying heights to give more impact. An article has more importance if it is grouped with other items rather than isolated. For example, if you have three large pieces for a mantel, place all three on one end and leave the other end bare. Allow empty space to play a part. Placing one thing on each end and one in the middle will leave a far less memorable, less effective impression.

Pushing Paper

Roses are red
Frantics are blue
Papers are piled
Bills are due.

If your heap is more annoying than this verse, the following section will help break the curse.

JOTS & THOUGHTS QUIZ
The Pressures of Paper

Is one of your greatest anxieties centered around that pile you just can't seem to eliminate from the kitchen counter? Answer yes or no to these simple questions to evaluate the level of anguish caused by the excess paper in your life.

1. Do you find yourself shuffling mail from counter to counter, not knowing where to go with it?
2. Have you ever misplaced a bill or paid it late?
3. When asked for immunization records or birth certificates, do you have trouble finding them?
4. Do you keep your relatives' addresses and doctors' phone numbers scattered here and there about the kitchen?
5. Does the pile of forms to be filled out or filed continue to grow before your very eyes?
6. Are there books, magazines, and newspapers everywhere you turn?
7. Do you like the idea of saving money, but can't face clipping and filing store coupons?

Even though every frantic woman's paper problems are unique, the number of yes answers above directly relates to how monumental your clutter challenges are. Isn't it time you searched for a solution? Well, look no further. We've got answers for you.

Post-It and Pay-It Planner

It's essential that you create a Post-It and Pay-It Planner—a specific schedule of when bills are due to be paid. On a separate calendar or in a designated section of your Frantic Journal, record due dates for credit card, mortgage, and utility payments. Include fees required for music lessons, orthodontist visits, tuition, school loans, insurance premiums, real estate taxes, and car payments. This allows you to see at a glance when to pay which bills and aids in budgeting overall monthly expenditures. You might decide to post a copy each month on your bulletin board or on the inside of a kitchen cabinet for convenience.

If you're computer savvy, take advantage of the various software programs designed for this purpose.

- Versacheck Premium Plus, available from G7 Productivity Systems, enables you to keep track of monthly bills. With its check-writing option, you never have to put a pen to a check again. Our computer techie friend highly recommends this software program, especially for financially floundering frantics.
- For the more advanced program user, Quickbooks by Intuit is another efficient program option. Although our techie warns that Quickbooks isn't as easy to use, she does admit it will accurately handle the finances both at home and at work.

These programs and more, like Microsoft Office, can be purchased in stores or online.

In addition to keeping a Post-It and Pay-It Planner for alerting you to pay bills on time, maintain a bill-paying log in a notebook with pockets or a ledger. Record the month's payment amounts, dates paid, remaining balances, and any statement discrepancies or questionable charges. You can purchase ledgers for this purpose, or sign up on certain Web sites like www.nopaperbills.com, www.paytrust.com, and www.ezbillpay.net.

HIDDEN GEM: Need a time-saving tip? When your monthly checking account statement comes in, ask the kids to put your checks in numerical order. It seems like a small task, but they'll think it's fun— and it's one less chore you have to do.

As you're paying your bills, check to see if there are any you can pay quarterly or monthly rather than yearly or semiannually. It's often easier for families to pay a smaller amount several times a year rather than one or two larger lump sums. Make sure you record any changes in your Post-It and Pay-It Planner.

On the flip side, check into discounts offered for paying tuition or other bills up front in full. Then, if you can swing it, go for the savings and write that check.

Mounds of Mail

One of the most stress-inducing sources in a frantic woman's life is the incoming daily mail. What can you do to alleviate the headaches it brings?

- Cut your quantity of mail in half by sorting out the junk mail immediately. Yes, on your way from the mailbox to the front door, divide the keepers from the castoffs. Discard company advertisements, political propaganda, and unsolicited credit card applications. Or try this suggestion. Mother of three Kathy Criniti devised a sensible method for reducing the number of those unwanted, preapproved nuisances. Rather than tossing them, Kathy opens the envelope and retains the approval request form. Across the top, she writes, "Do not send any more applications to this address. Remove us from your list." She then inserts the card in the company's prepaid envelope and drops it in the mail at their expense. As easy as it sounds, it works—as companies must honor such written removal requests. "My family receives about three-quarters less junk mail than we used to," Kathy says. "It really is a hassle-free solution."
- Discard all mail-order catalogs unless you have a specific need for them at the moment. Before you know it, more will arrive to replace the ones you haven't even had a chance to flip through.
- Sift through advertisement flyers the day they arrive in the mail. Circle the items you wish to purchase. By placing them in your purse or a file folder in your car, you'll have ready access when you're out and can stop at any time to buy those sale items for the week (preferably Sunday, before loss leaders sell out).
- Do the same for coupon inserts in the weekend edition of the newspaper. Take a few minutes every Sunday morning to clip and file. This action helps avoid excessive coupon pileup.
- As party invitations arrive in the mail, check the date. Mark it on your calendar including the location and the time in the event that you lose the invitation. Then, R.S.V.P. immediately.

If you need to call a sitter, do so at the same time. While you're at it, start thinking about what you'll wear. Then, enjoying yourself becomes a priority as opposed to the usual incessant rushing and last-minute planning. Keep the invitation with the gift and take it with you to the party to avoid showing up a day late or at the wrong location.

Don't let the following happen to you. Dressed up with gift card in hand, Mary Jo and her family headed off to a graduation party being held several towns over at a local fire hall. When they arrived and found a long line to see the graduate, Mary Jo deposited the card on the gift table with the others before standing in line. With three people in front of them, Mary Jo whispered to her husband, "I haven't seen Michael in a while, and boy has he changed."

Her husband answered, "I haven't seen Michael in a while either, but he hasn't changed that much."

Overhearing their conversation, the woman behind them asked, "Whose party are you looking for?"

"Michael Cannon's."

"Oh, his party is at the VFW, not here."

Red-faced, Mary Jo searched through the stack of cards on the gift table for the one with "Michael" scribbled on the front.

- If you've weeded out the junk mail and are still whisking daily arrivals from counter to counter not knowing where to go with the bills, letters, and forms that need to be taken care of, consider the following. As an attractive catch-all, find a picnic basket—not a large one—with a lid. Deposit it on your counter, center island, or baker's rack to house your mail until you have a moment to sort and shuffle.
- Or try a rolling cart with drawers or bins that allow you to separate papers into such categories as "To Be Filed," "To Be Reviewed," and "To Be Filled Out."
- To keep everyday files accessible, place them in a magazine rack.

But important documents like birth and stock certificates, life insurance policies, passports, house deeds, and car titles should be protected in a locked, fireproof safe or safety deposit box at the bank.

Here are a few additional organizational tips to prevent further shuffling of paper.

- Once you've become proficient in dividing and discarding incoming mail, turn to those stacks of books, magazines, and newspapers. Give away old copies you vowed to read but never did. Sort others you intend to read and alphabetize or categorize. Remember the rule of thumb: When in doubt, throw it out. You can usually get hold of another copy, if need be, though chances are good you'll never need to do so. And finally, isolate a separate shelf for favorite books and signed copies.
- Use different address books for doctor names and business numbers (like hair stylist, piano teacher, and kids' coaches), one for personal phone numbers, and one for children's friends. Mark the spine of each with a paint pen or permanent marker. Kids outgrow friends as quickly as they do clothes, so by allotting them a separate address book, you won't use up valuable space in your own. For numbers often needed, write them directly on your family calendar in the kitchen or hang a laminated list by the kitchen phone.
- Post a sheet containing the contact information of close family and friends inside a kitchen cabinet for ease of reference. Type up street addresses, telephone, fax and cell phone numbers, e-mail addys, and even birthdays and anniversaries. (Don't forget to include the phone number of your beloved clergyman.) Photocopy the sheet, laminate it, and hand it out to all listed members. Update regularly and redistribute.
- Use clear sheet protector sleeves for storing such correspondence necessities as stamps, address labels, business cards, and snapshots going to long-distance relatives.

Record Control

You're already up to your elbows in mail and other documents, files, and forms, so why not take control of your record-keeping system now? After all, it's one task you can't ignore. And although it seems tedious, once you find a suitable method, your paper-pushing time will certainly decrease.

For some practical filing suggestions, CPA Patricia Kulmoski offers concrete advice on maintaining your household records. Patricia says, "If you do nothing else as far as organizing documents at home, set aside the following eight files and update them on a regular basis."

1. *Personal:* Include birth certificates, Social Security numbers, immunization records, and education transcripts. You might want to have a separate personal file for each family member.
2. *Financial:* Store vital documents like savings bonds, stock certificates, and certificates of deposit (CDs) in a locked, fireproof strongbox or in a safety deposit box at the bank. In this financial folder, however, include statements from passbook savings accounts, checking account balances, quarterly statements from individual retirement accounts (IRAs), educational investments, mutual funds, a list of bonds owned by each family member, and other financial assets you might have. Again, you might need a separate file for each person. In addition, include receipts from paid local income tax and real estate taxes in this file.
3. *House:* Retain a record of every permanent upgrade you carry out in your home including replacing floors, water heaters, the roof, improving bathrooms, etc. Keep paid bills from contractors in this file as each improvement adds to the base value of your home when selling.
4. *Appliances:* Stow appliance sales slips, warranties, and user manuals in this folder. Include all parts and model numbers, serial numbers, and service phone numbers.
5. *Cars:* Again, you'll want to store car titles in your strongbox or safety deposit box. But here, store insurance information and receipts

from all services carried out on the vehicle. Start a separate file for each vehicle you own. This helps track how much the car is costing you to maintain and is a handy reference when selling.

6. *Donations:* Even if you give only $2 to the Salvation Army volunteer ringing the bell outside the grocery store, record this information somewhere—especially if your contributions are in cash. Scribble amounts and association names on a scrap piece of paper and drop into this file. When giving clothes or goods to nonprofit organizations ask for receipts. If you forget to do so, at least jot down each article donated. This all adds up when taking deductions at tax time. Start a new donations file each January.

7. *Receipts:* When your monthly charge card statements arrive, match purchase receipts and refund credits stored in this file with statement entries. Check for discrepancies in each case and call customer service, if necessary. Keep an envelope in your purse to collect sales slips as you shop. Use the same system for your automated teller machine withdrawals and deposits.

8. *Bills to be paid:* As soon as you receive a bill in the mail, place it in a file or basket. Come bill-paying time, you won't have to search for what remittances are due. Keep monthly voucher reminders for financial responsibilities like car payments, tuition, and orthodontist bills in here, as well.

To simplify your record-keeping tasks, remove all outdated files from your personal paperwork and store in an airtight bin. Tuck it away in the laundry room, attic, basement, or garage. Patricia advises you to retain financial records—including canceled checks, pay stubs, receipts, and credit card statements—for at least seven years.

Gift Giving

Now that you've de-cluttered and organized your closets and drawers, consider clearing some space to house birthday and holiday gifts as you purchase them.

If you have more than a few people to buy for throughout the year, adopt a gift-buying strategy. This involves writing up a master gift list in your Frantic Journal, buying and wrapping ahead of time, and keeping presents in a designated location. If purchasing items well in advance of an occasion, though, are you afraid you'll end up buying duplicate gifts, forget where you've put them, or have trouble remembering for whom you bought what? If so, follow our fail-proof plan for buying ahead and keeping track.

- Create a gift-giving log using a journal, spiral-bound index cards, a small notebook, or a specified section of your Frantic Journal.
- Design a chart blocking off four wide columns. Assign the far left one for recipient names. To the right of that, label the second and third columns for birthdays and holiday gifts. Then, subdivide the birthday and holiday columns into three smaller subcolumns. Mark headings on these six subcolumns as "bought," "wrapped," and "given" in each of the birthday and holiday categories. Record in the fourth wide column where you've stored the gift once wrapped, such as "attic," "basement," or "master closet."
- Write down all the people you buy for during the year and throughout the holiday season, listing them in groups by family, how you are associated (work, neighborhood, school), or simply alphabetically.

Why is it important to keep a detailed gift record? Maria buys birthday and holiday gifts for more than forty people and has always kept a gift-giving log, recording what was bought for whom. But she failed to keep track of when items had been wrapped and given. This minor factor wound up putting her in a major bind. Maria had purchased two identical designer purses, one for her sister's birthday and one for the school secretary. She wrapped and gave the handbag to the secretary as a thank-you gift at the end of the year. A month later, Maria went to her designated storage area to retrieve the second bag for her sister's upcoming birthday luncheon. Though she searched and searched, it wasn't there. After racking her brain, Maria realized she had wrapped and given the gift to the school secretary, not once but twice—for Easter and at the end of the year. Now, Maria's sister has no new purse and the school secretary has two. (We can only hope the secretary passes the satchel along to a friend.)

Wrap It Up

To reduce the time it takes to gather wrapping supplies, try making a gift-wrap station. Our favorite is a portable version you can put together using a new kitchen-sized garbage can or similar container. Poke two holes in the side of the bin and thread a pipe cleaner, wire, or ribbon through it. Thread ribbon rolls on the pipe cleaner or wire. Twist the ends together to keep rolls from sliding off. Poke two more holes in the other side hanging several rolls of clear tape from another pipe cleaner or wire. Slip the ties of a carpenter's apron through one hole on one side and one on the other and knot in the middle. Use the apron pockets for such items as scissors, cards, tags, and pens. Stash all rolls of wrapping paper upright in the can. Slide packages of flat paper and gift bags down the inside surface to avoid bending and wrinkling. A plastic bag stapled or duct-taped to the back of the can protects more-delicate ribbons and bows.

Store your gift-wrap station in an easily accessible place like the master closet, a spare bedroom, or the laundry room.

DARLING LITTLE ANGELS (AND THE WHOLE BLISSFUL BUNCH)

Cooking

If you're married to a chef, you can skip the following section. But, if you're not lucky enough to be living with Emeril, keep reading.

JOTS & THOUGHTS QUIZ
Your Food Viewpoint

Answer the following questions to air your cooking gripes and grievances.

1. Do you eat out three times a week or more, including fast-food runs?
2. When you finally drum up the energy to make a meal, do you open the freezer to find nothing there?
3. Do you feel guilty about not providing your family and yourself with nourishing, healthy meal choices?
4. Have you ever served cereal or toast as the main course for your family dinner?
5. Is your schedule so jam-packed that to dine together as a family, you'd have to do so at 11:00 P.M?
6. Have you ever gone to the trouble of preparing a big meal, only to have the family thumb their noses at it? And was that your husband saying, "Gee, hon, I had chicken for lunch"?
7. Do all the food preparation and purchasing responsibilities fall upon you?

No matter how many yes answers you've accumulated, you realize that too many of the duties surrounding mealtime point back to you. Let's see if we can help you do something about that.

Soliciting Help in the Kitchen

Whatever help your spouse or kids are willing to offer, accept it. Busy women often complain that their kids don't wash the dishes properly or their husbands who like to cook leave a messy kitchen. We say, look at the bright side, not only are you getting help, but with a little positive praise, you never know how much more assistance you'll receive.

Here are a few ways the family can pitch in at the kitchen counter.

- Have little ones tear lettuce for salad or pluck dressings and top-pings from the pantry and refrigerator.
- The next time your son wants to bake cookies after school and you don't feel like dealing with the mess, bite your tongue. At least the after-school snack will be taken care of for the day, and you might be able to snatch a few remainders to pack in the lunches for tomorrow. In fact, wouldn't it be a relief to have someone else bake for the next bake sale?
- Because you're more likely to grab for those recommended serv-ings of vegetables if they're cleaned, sliced, and ready to eat, ask kids to squirt off and scrub the veggies. And while you chop them into bite-sized pieces, they can mix up the dip.
- Likewise, keep your favorite choices of required servings of fruits nearby in a bowl. Why not pass the washing job on to younger ones? To rid store-bought fruit of unwanted chemicals, use soapy water or bottled fruit wash solution available in stores or online. Wash all fruit, including citrus and watermelons, because pesti-cides on the outside can contaminate the luscious inside when cutting or peeling.
- Teach your teenager how to prepare her favorite meal for dinner. Then, let her do so at least once a week. This eliminates one day of your seven-day commitment. Work on showing her adapta-tions to the recipe, too, so she'll be able to make dinner even more than once a week.
- If you find that kitchen cleanup is more of a challenge after hubby and the teens help out—especially when they burn the inside of a pot or neglect to scour the baked-on remains in the lasagna pan—don't despair. Rather than scrubbing until your arm aches, fill the pot or pan with hot, soapy water. Add two tablespoons or so of dishwasher detergent (the crystals work best), stir, and soak overnight. In the morning, stuck food and stains will wipe clean.

> **SNIPPET:** Still reluctant to allow kids to roll up their sleeves in the kitchen? You might want to think again. Because that's exactly how child chef Justin Miller got started. He went from rolling stuffed cabbage in his kitchen at home to rubbing elbows with David Letterman in New York. *The Guinness Book of Records* twice featured Justin as the World's Youngest Chef. Might you have a budding talent in your house?

Family Meals

Mixed-up schedules and irregular work hours don't always allow for family meals to be eaten together. And though you're tempted to say, "Dinner is at six o'clock and if you miss it, too bad," there are still mouths to feed, no matter what time of day it is. So why not put the following solutions to the test?

- Consider making nutritious meals that can be eaten on the run. *I have no time to cook* and *I never know who's going to be home for dinner* are two of the excuses frantic women use when they find themselves stuck in a fast-food rut. Let's face it, "driving through" *is* easier, cheaper than a sit-down restaurant dinner, and better than skipping a meal. It is fast, convenient, and most of all, on the way to wherever you're going. So, how can you overcome this habit? On the night of art class and swimming, Judith and her children are in the car from 3:45 until 7:30. She packs the kids each a boxed lunch with a deli sandwich or a hamburger on a bun wrapped in foil, prepackaged snacks, a piece of fruit or carrot sticks, and some cookies for dessert. She also includes bottled water, a pouch drink, or a thermos of milk. (P.S. This is also a money saver when going to the pool, park, or beach.)
- Try serving a full meal rather than a snack after school, before

everyone has to run back out the door. Then, you might be able to convene over a bowl of cereal or warm soup later in the evening.

- If Dad works late on certain nights, have the kids eat their bedtime snacks while Dad eats his dinner. Although not quite a family meal, this helps keep the lines of communication open and sure beats watching the tube while munching.

Sparking a Renewed Interest in Cooking

If you can't bear to fill your trusty pots using the same old recipes, try one of our recipe-reviving ideas.

- *Plan a recipe swap.* Talk about and share recipes with friends, coworkers, or teammates. Ask what dishes others prepare that are gobbled up and appreciated. Share your preferred menu items, as well.

> **HIDDEN GEM:** Ask a friend to double her favorite recipe the next time she makes it. She can give one pan of that gooey vegetarian lasagna to you and keep one for herself. Then, when you're making those porcupine meatballs she loves, send over a batch for her crew. While this trick works for everyone, it is an especially doable way in which single moms can help each other.

- *Rediscover old favorites.* Recently, Judith and her sisters dug out recipes they'd not made since parties of yesteryear, such as green olive spread, Swiss cheese dip, ham barbeques, spinach salad, and peach cobbler. They prepared these selections for a slew of family birthday parties. The retro-recipes were enjoyed by all, as was evidenced by the lack of leftovers.

- *Try this tactic with drinks and punches, too.* Remember how refreshing that melon ball tasted or how punchy a sip of a sea breeze felt? (Find these retro-recipes and more in "A Wee Bit More," part three.)
- *Record favorite recipes.* In a special card file, folder, or in an isolated section of your Frantic Journal, jot down recipes you have enjoyed. Then, when you can't come up with any fresh ideas to delight the family's palette, flip back to the old standbys and know they'll be well received.
- *Prepare a new dish once a week.* The recipe can be recently discovered from the daily paper or a Web site, but don't forget the ones you cut out years ago and never tried. Or perhaps you'd prefer to splurge by selecting from a new cookbook.

Designate a time, like Sunday afternoons, to do the grocery shopping for those weekly sale items listed in store ads and flyers. If you wait until midweek to shop, stores might be sold out of loss leaders. As mentioned previously, to make grocery shopping even easier, presort coupons for weekly sale items in a separate envelope. On the outside, jot a list of stores, items needed, and current prices. Tuck the envelope inside your purse or place in a file folder in your car for quick access and handy reference. (See "Mounds of Mail" section, this chapter.)

Successful Freezing

Are you profiting from all your freezer has to offer? "Most women aren't," says Ruth Wiltman, our freezing expert. The key to successful chilling is all in the timing. One of the biggest mistakes inexperienced consumers make is to allow too much time to elapse before deciding to freeze an item, thinking they'll use the product within a day or two after they buy it. Four or five days later, they stash the product in the old subzero compartment. "And that's too late," Ruth says. Freeze bagels, bread, muffins, baked goods, and even packaged cookies the day you purchase them, and not a moment later.

Another important factor in preserving a food's freshness, according to Ruth, is double insulation. Often consumers will remove food from the package and place it in a freezer bag or container. Rather, if you place products in a plastic bin with a tight-sealing lid, *without* removing the store packaging, you're providing at least two layers of insulation that will lock in taste and keep unwanted air and odors out. For additional protection, lay a sheet of foil or plastic wrap over the opening of the container before sealing the lid. This technique not only ensures freshness but prevents unwanted frost buildup, too. It even works for ice cream.

In deciding what to freeze, Ruth suggests you go beyond the usual meats, vegetables, and breads to just about anything you can squeeze between the shelves. She freezes fine chocolates directly in the box, in a larger plastic container, the day she purchases them. You can do the same with individually wrapped bulk candy. Ruth even places bagged salty snacks like potato chips, pretzels, and Doritos in two plastic grocery bags, ties them shut, and puts them in the freezer. Sound strange? Ruth says, "Once you've tasted a crisp frozen chip, you won't want to go back to eating them at room temperature." After all is said and done, how does she thaw her frozen goodies? In the evening she removes what she wants to use the next day and places it in zippered plastic bags on the counter. That way, your bagels, bread, or chocolate truffles will be ready to munch come morning.

On the Road with Kids

More often than not, extracurricular activities throw a kink into your already topsy-turvy lives. So how can you control the chaos surrounding these activities while still trying to enrich your child's upbringing? Let's look at an example.

After her divorce, author Loriann Hoff Oberlin found it necessary to limit the activities in her household to approximately two per child at any given time. In researching her book *Surviving Separation and Divorce*, she discovered an unexpected dilemma. When Mom has primary custody and Dad is awarded visitation on weekends (when many sports meet), you might very well have signed up and paid for all sorts of activities in which the child will be unable to participate. "If you're fairly sure your ex won't be willing to take the kids to sports, church activities, whatever," Loriann says, "then you'll save yourself money and unnecessary frustration by limiting the number of activities per child." If you opt not to do so, not only will you be out the expense, but your child could find himself trapped between parents' opinions. Loriann suggests it's better not to get the child's hopes up for commitments that just won't work.

What else can you do to keep your sanity as you rush about carting kids from one commitment to another?

- Remember to take snacks or toys for your toddler while waiting for your older child to finish her instrument lesson or sports practice. Keep an extra diaper bag or snack and toy bag packed at all times and store it in your car, hall closet, or kitchen cabinet for easy access. By prepacking, you'll be ready to keep your toddler happy, even at those unexpected times when you run into a friend in the mall parking lot.
- Apply the same tactic for older kids. Pack a snack and something to do such as a handheld game, books of mazes or word searches, sketchpads, playing cards, and portable CD players with headphones.
- Keep quick-grab snacks in the car for any age child (and for yourself!). Place trail mix, nuts, dried fruits, cheese crackers, dried beef, and protein or cereal bars in a zippered plastic bag or shoe box–sized container. As you restock, vary the contents so kids don't tire of the same old stuff.
- Pack the trunk at the beginning of each season for whatever activity lies ahead, whether it be baseball, soccer, horseback riding, or water polo. You'll need collapsible chairs, a cooler, a blanket, a large umbrella, and outdoor toys like Frisbees, balls, and skateboards for nonparticipating kids. Don't forget to stash coupons in the car for local pizza or ice cream shops for days when everyone deserves a special treat.
- Add a postgame change of clothing for when you might have to scurry from one place to another before heading home.

- Keep a case of bottled water and sport drinks in cooler weather in the trunk or in the back of the van.
- Keep half-filled water bottles in the freezer in warmer weather. Fill the empty portion with water before you head to the park or beach. Frozen water bottles will act as an ice pack in the hot weather in addition to providing a drink later in the day. (In winter, freeze bottles that are only one-quarter filled, as they will thaw more slowly.)
- Store insect repellent, sunscreen, and sunglasses in the glove compartment to quell any difficulties that might occur with pests and summer sun.
- Don't forget the first aid kit. Add Benadryl liquid and Benadryl cream for immediate response to allergic reactions, rashes, and bug bites. If necessary for your family's needs, add bee sting anti-serum and steroid inhalers for asthma.

Former soccer mom Linda Bellini suggests parents keep large garbage bags in the trunk of the car. When kids are playing sports in the rain and end up covered in mud, have them step into the bag and bring it up over the clothes before sitting down in the car. (Hint: Depending upon the size of your kids, you'll probably want to stock trash bags that are at least forty-eight inches long.)

HIDDEN GEM: Ever get in the car with just enough time to reach the away-game field, only to find the gas tank's on empty? This is especially true if you're guilty of stopping at the station and putting in $5 or $10 at a time. Instead, try filling the tank on payday to eliminate frustration when time is of the essence—which is just about always. It helps, too, if you can get in the habit of filling up when you notice the tank is about half full. By doing so, you'll almost never put yourself behind by having to stop at the pump before a game or activity.

Keeping It Cost-Effective

Everything involving the kids seems to be so expensive—each needing $10 here and $20 there. And if you have more than one child, you can often be found looking on with empty pockets. So how can you keep activity costs within a reasonable limit?

- Avoid the tendency to keep up with the proverbial "Joneses." If all the kids in the neighborhood are taking tae kwon do or competitive dance lessons four days a week, and it's costing them an arm and a leg, don't consider this option. Be careful not to be drawn in just because everyone else's kids are doing it. Have the courage to say no in order to better live within your means. By the way, you don't have to tell people (even your kids) why you aren't participating.
- Consider youth groups, scouts, school activities—such as yearbook or chess clubs—or other church activities that might better fall within the realm of your monthly budget.
- As previously mentioned, limit the number of activities each child participates in, thereby keeping costs in check, as well.

Family Bond

It's not often that the frantic family gets to relax together, enjoy quiet conversations, or explore one another's true feelings—all essential in strengthening the family bond. So what can you do to stay connected?

- If you have teens, pay attention to what type of music they like, and learn something about the groups they follow. Keep your eyes open for articles about their favorite artists and cut them out. This will require little effort on your part, but will go a long way in the eyes of your teen.
- Focus on taking an active role in cultivating your child's interests—like art, science, computers, or fashion—as another way to

stay connected. Something as simple as reading the same book can spark stimulating conversations that are open and meaningful.

- If your child loves a particular sport, get involved by helping him or her practice. Pick up the basketball and toss a few in the hoop together for fifteen minutes or so. Or make a game out of how many shots he can put in the basket while you snag the rebounds. In addition, you can pitch and catch baseball, tend goal for soccer, volley the tennis ball, or even roller blade together. Swing a golf club or hockey stick and hop on the trampoline to show them just what Mom is made of. A few minutes together, here and there, can remain in your child's heart forever.

- Help your son collect baseball cards or your daughter find unique thimbles at garage sales or at online auction sites, if hobbies are their preference. Imagine how many good memories will warm her as she peers around her room, recapping how you helped bring pieces to her collection.

- Think of ways to spend time together that will be fun for all. Here's an example. Temporarily throwing practicality to the wind, Mary Patouillet decided to treat her family by having a hot tub installed. As a registered nurse, she knew the therapeutic benefits her teenaged son would reap, soothing tense muscles and achy joints after sports practices. What she didn't know was how the act of relaxing in a swirling pool could encourage such honest interaction—an open exchange of ideas that helped to promote the warm family environment she longed to hang on to. "The hot tub has kept us all in touch with one another. My sixteen-year-old is actually interested in what my husband and I have to say," Mary says. "Especially when we're soaking rather than rushing around."

- When you have children of varying ages, don't forget to direct attention to the older children. The younger ones need transportation to activities and help with their homework, even assistance in pouring a glass of juice—so you're still part of their lives. Take, for example, Dee Burnett, mother of seven. She believes the presence of a parent in the older child's life is vital to the child's sense of security. "And that security is the root of their well-being," Dee adds. So be sure to show you care by stocking their favorite snacks, lending an ear, or often just by being there. Take something to your teen's room while she's doing her homework. Or unload the dishwasher while he's preparing a snack. By finding a reason to be in the same room together, you're subtly encouraging casual conversation. And as Dee well knows, if kids don't talk with you about the little things, they'll never open up about the bigger issues.

- Use your time in the car for one-on-one discussions about friends, school, or individual interests, thus keeping the lines of communication open on a continual basis.

- Take advantage of alternate forms of communication such as the following. During a critical time in her daughter's life (because her good friend was seriously ill and hospitalized at length), Ellen e-mailed brief notes to her daughter. She typed how proud she was of the young girl's efforts to remain a part of her sick friend's recovery. With a simple click of the "Reply" button, Ellen's daughter was able to express her concerns and ask difficult questions.

- Link the generations by inviting other family members to join in strengthening the bond. For example, for the past four years, seventeen-year-old Travis Senchur pedaled his bicycle weekly to his Grandpa Schrecengost's house a few blocks away. Now, he's behind the wheel of the car "Pap" helped him rebuild. Yes, rather than sit and sip lemonade, the twosome visited junkyards, bought automobile parts, and fixed the family's extra vehicle. At fourteen, Travis had dreamed of having his own car to work on, and that wish came true with the help of Grandpa.

I'll Be There

The pressure of keeping in touch with those near and far takes its toll on us for sure. How can you strengthen the ties that bind when time is so limited? Develop a memorable long-distance relationship with those whose absence has been gnawing at your conscience by giving one or more of the following a try.

- On the first Monday of each month, write out a card to those relatives whom you think about often but can't seem to find the time to contact. You'll be surprised at how this simple gesture lifts the spirits of all who receive your greetings—and at how good it makes you feel.
- If writing's not your thing, pick up the phone on a Sunday evening and call a distant relative. The effects of a ten-minute phone call can last a week or even a lifetime.
- Write a progressive card or letter that each family member adds to and mails to another relative he hasn't spoken with in a while. Try to keep it going as long as you can.

Get-Well Wishes

What can you do to fight that sense of helplessness when someone you care for is under the weather, having surgery, or threatened by a fatal disease? You want to help. You want to do something.

- Send letters of hope, prayer, and encouragement; they mean a lot more than you might think. Judith's mom wrote letters regularly to Kristy Warren, a family friend who was stricken with cancer. Each note told of prayers said for Kristy and contained inspiring words about finding strength and hope. The letters were read over and over and cherished by Kristy, her husband, and her two daughters.

  Faith Kachurik sent a card a day to her friend while she was going through surgery. One time, Faith sent a Christmas card in the summer because that was all she had on hand. She jotted, "You'll be up and about by the time Christmas comes round." Her friend appreciated the gesture, regardless of what the card looked like.

When a ladies-only trip was canceled due to a friend's declining health, Mary Jo planned a Niagara Falls party at home instead. The gals flipped through postcards, photos, and tourist information while appreciating one another's company.

- Send a photograph as a postcard. Don't do anything fancy—just turn the photo over, draw a line down the middle, and write the address on the right and a brief note on the left. Affix a stamp and mail.
- Send a calendar with a saying like, "Look how many days you've made it through since the surgery." Or for a child, write, "Only three more weeks until the cast comes off!"
- Mail a deflated balloon with a message printed on it.
- Write a note on a piece of paper, cut it into eight to ten pieces, and slip them into an envelope. Write on the back of the envelope, "Put together for a *pieceful* message."

Special Needs

If you're the parent of a child with special needs, listen to the insightful advice of Cindy Hatcher, mother of two, whose older daughter faces the physical challenges of having cerebral palsy. "From the time of Lauren's diagnosis," Cindy says, "we have treated her like a normal child first. And then we look at the disability." This has helped Lauren to grow up in a healthy, positive environment.

Here are a few tips from Cindy on how to go about giving your child the best of opportunities and the healthiest of surroundings.

- Include your child in regular activities, as long as her abilities allow her to participate safely. Remember to let her be a kid. My husband and I encourage Lauren to participate in many of the activities other children do, such as playing outside in the neighborhood, taking beach vacations, and shopping at the mall.
- Sign up your child for special needs activities, too. These are helpful, especially when the means of doing them are adapted for her. For example, Lauren takes horseback riding lessons that

are geared to kids with physical disabilities. The horses and staff are trained to work with such children, making it safer than taking Lauren to stables not equipped to do so.

- Be aware of limitations before you put your child in harm's way. Prior to allowing Lauren to try something new, I experience it first for myself. For instance, I rode several of the rides at Walt Disney World before Lauren did, to test whether Lauren was strong enough to ride safely. I found that some of the harnesses were stable enough and others weren't.

- Don't drag your child around from doctor to doctor or clinic to clinic in search of a miracle cure. It is best to provide her with top-rate medical care, then help her to adapt in any way necessary.

- As a couple, sit down and divide up the duties that revolve around your child. Now that Lauren is getting taller, my husband handles most of the physical responsibilities, including lifting and exercising, while I manage the schoolwork and personal grooming.

"One of my friends made an observation that Lauren is so well adjusted," Cindy says, "that she doesn't even view herself as a special needs child. And I guess she's right."

May all children be blessed with such wonderful parents. Good job, Cindy!

Elder Care

The responsibility of caring for aging relatives hits most of us sooner or later. With all that's involved in scheduling appointments and shuffling your sick or elderly relative to the doctor, you sometimes find you're neglecting your own life and home. Taking care of an aging or ill family member is exhausting, both physically and emotionally. Here are some ideas to reduce the stress associated with such demands.

- Designate one or two days a week to run Mom or Grandpa to the store, the doctor's office, or the hair salon. This frees up three or four other weekdays for you to take care of your own errands and chores. Otherwise, the newly added duties continually loom over your every move and cause you to be "on call" 24/7. When you have an assigned time to tackle the situation, somehow it's more manageable and you feel more resolved.

- On these assigned days, plan on crossing a few of your own errands off the list, too. If the doctor appointment is a time-consuming one, and you'd be in the waiting room for an extended period alone, skip out to return library books or to pick up the dry cleaning. On your mom or grandma's beauty shop days, make an appointment to have your own hair done (or the kids') to kill two birds with one stone.

- Accept the knowledge that when caring for the sick or elderly, problems will arise unexpectedly like unplanned hospitalizations or emergency doctor visits. During these critical times, something must give. You'll probably have to skip the regularly scheduled activities because you're needed by your loved one's side. Your best bet is to admit this up front, soliciting other school moms or friends to cover for you at your daughter's lacrosse tournament or son's class pizza party.

- Share the care, like sisters Laverne Rieger and Mary Ann Marty did for their aging mother. Rather than place her in a professional facility, each had a room set up in her home just for Mom. And every month, she'd move to the other daughter's house. Mom loved living with both families, especially enjoying the grandchildren, while neither daughter had to totally disrupt the structure of her family for any extended period of time.

If you suddenly find yourself in the position of having to offer more daily assistance for an aging or ailing relative, how do you go about it? Pat Eyerman, a provider of home health care for more than twenty-five years, shares these suggestions.

- *Be patient and compassionate.* When you first enter the home of a person newly in need of help, give them time to accept your assistance. The adjustment period will vary from person to person—but it can require as long as a couple of weeks. Remember, you're entering their domain, so don't rush it.

- *Don't be overbearing and controlling.* Imagine how they'd feel if you burst through the door like a whirlwind, rushed through their chores, and then twirled back out in a flash. Rather than dictate what's to be done, ask them what they'd like you to do and how they ordinarily go about it. They'll begin to relax and, depending upon their capabilities, will take pride in helping you get the job done.
- *Be respectful of their needs and wants.* Allow your "patient" to do the talking and the decision making, if possible. This lets her know you respect her ways and affords her the necessary esteem and self-worth that she might feel are slipping away.
- *Show trustworthiness.* Even if you are a family member, this person is used to functioning on her own. And at first, she might feel vulnerable and protective of her things. Don't take offense at accusations of food, money, or other items that she thinks have been lost because of you. Be patient and explain. It's all part of the adjustment.

"It gives me a deep sense of satisfaction to take care of the sick," Pat says, "knowing I've made a difference at a difficult time in their lives."

The Next Step

At some point, the aging process takes over and the time comes when your loved one is in need of more help. But how can you be sure? Ask yourself these questions to aid in your decision.

- Is declining health the main reason for your loved one's loss of independence?
- Has a doctor suggested a lifestyle change for him?
- Has a spouse passed away and the burden of running a household alone become too much?

- Can she no longer cook or keep house for herself?
- Does the distance between your home and his make checking in on him impossible?
- Is she lonely?

If you've answered yes to more than one question, you'll need to help make a change in your relative's living situation.

The Transition

If a family member has recently moved to a senior citizens' care facility, Sue Ault, senior living services manager, recommends these simple tips to help smooth the transition.

- Visit the facility during a special event or activity to make her feel important. A number of places host dinners and evenings of entertainment. Make it a point to check the facility's calendar or newsletter for such occasions.
- Schedule a service for the loved one such as a weekly hair appointment or a dinner outside of the building. It's amazingly refreshing for residents to look forward to and enjoy such outings.
- Be sure you feel comfortable and secure with the staff and population of the building your relative will be calling home.
- Choose a facility near your own residence, enabling you to make frequent visits or to arrive quickly in case of an emergency.

The best way you can help an aging relative is to stay involved in her life and her medical care, letting health care providers and facility managers know that your family member is an important part of your life. Your presence, inquiries, and concern show staff members that your relative is loved and will be checked on regularly. This will help to keep her from becoming neglected and lost in the health care shuffle.

Additional Assistance

If your elderly family member is a military veteran, make sure he or she is taking advantage of VA benefits. These include inpatient and outpatient hospital care, prescription coverage, and extended care services. Most of these offerings are entitlements and are not based on need. For more information, contact the Department of Veterans Affairs at 1-800-827-1000.

Quality improvement organizations are usually government-funded establishments whose job it is to make sure senior citizens are getting quality-of-life care. The program is designed to protect seniors from being released too soon from the hospital, in addition to ensuring they receive good care if residing in a health care facility. To find out more about a quality improvement organization near you, contact Medicare, the Social Security Office, or the Department of Aging in your area.

Check with the local Department of Aging for additional services that are available, too. For example, a list of local facilities and contact names can usually be provided.

Family's Best Friend

Whether or not you're an animal lover, the dog, cat, or even the hamster adds one more responsibility to be taken care of by none other than you. And all is well until the pet chews your shoes, knocks over your coffee, or messes on your imported wool rug (and the vet bills, well, we won't approach that subject). Even so, dogs and cats and other pets still need to be properly cared for—their nails trimmed, their coats brushed, and their ears cleaned. If these tasks aren't in your job description, professional dog groomer Sharon Fitzgerald recommends you take the initiative to visit a trained expert. "Pets are like kids," Sharon says with a smile. "They behave better for strangers, making professional bathing and grooming easier and safer for you and your pet."

Sharon advises that you get to know the needs of your breed, including vitamin supplements, variety and amounts of food, and skin type. For example, you don't want to bathe a collie as often as you would a small long-haired dog, because it can dry out his skin. You also want to keep up with shots and license renewals, of course coupled with a medical checkup, which must be done on an annual basis. Don't make a habit of feeding table food to pets, either. "Not only will you be depriving them of nutritional needs," Sharon says, "but you might just find yourself with the additional burden of preparing special dinners just for your pets."

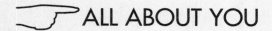 # ALL ABOUT YOU

Interoffice Memo: Go the Extra Mile

Have you felt somewhat stagnant in your daily work routine? If so, ask yourself, how can I go the extra mile? What can you learn on the job to further your knowledge and position? How can you help others while broadening your horizons and improving your professional image?

Deanne Thomas, an activities coordinator for a retirement village, found a way to assist the facility's marketing director while benefiting her own department at the same time. She planned monthly events for her residents that were also open to the public and advertised through the marketing department. The expenses for such events were coded as "marketing" rather than being charged to Deanne's department. The residents enjoyed a day of entertainment without the funds coming out of their activities budget.

Jewels and Other Adornments

Diamonds are a girl's best friend, says the TV commercial (the guys can keep the dogs). If you want to preserve them "forever," care for your jewelry the right way. Find out more by taking this quiz.

JOTS & THOUGHTS QUIZ
A Jewel of a Questionnaire

Finally, after hours of browsing, you've found a dynamite necklace to complement the knockout dress you just had to buy. You're a bit reluctant, though, because the chain is costume jewelry and, in the past, you've never had luck in preserving their luster. A little T.L.C. will go a long way in keeping all your accessories, both costume and genuine, in tip-top shape.

Answer true or false to determine just how much jewelry-care knowledge you have.

1. Use hair spray and perfume after you put on jewelry.
2. Fasten necklaces in the front to save wear and tear on the clasp.
3. Humidity will not cause discoloration of your costume pieces.
4. Clean your jewelry with diluted vinegar.
5. Keep chalk in your jewelry box to draw out moisture.
6. Wipe off your necklaces, bracelets, and rings after wearing to remove body oils.
7. Use toothpaste to clean your gems and jewels.

Give yourself one point for each right answer.
1. False   2. True   3. False   4. True   5. True   6. True   7. False

6–7 points: Congratulations! Your jewelry will last longer than it will be in style. You probably even know to clean that delicate string of genuine pearls in mild, soapy water.

4–5 points: Well, it could be worse. Eventually, you will have a bracelet without the matching necklace since you've sprayed it one too many times or cleaned it with the wrong cleanser. Keep in mind that jars of liquid jewelry cleaner are made for the more durable 10k, 14k, 18k, or 24k gold pieces, as well as platinum. Jewelry with gold overlay will not hold up to such strong ammonia-based solutions. Be careful not to dip softer stones like opals and emeralds in these cleaners, either. Their more porous compositions are subject to clouding.

1–3 points: It's time to gather and count your spare change. You'll need every bit of it to replace the items you've cleaned with the wrong products, the chains you've left in the bathroom to discolor, and the clasps that have broken because you've reached around the back of your neck instead of the front. But cheer up. Now, you've learned a few simple jewelry-care tips to help preserve those sensitive pieces in the future.

Insurance Reminder

If you're lucky, a beautiful piece of jewelry enhanced one of your recent celebrations. But every time you draw it from the jewelry box, you're reminded it hasn't been insured yet. And you might have other pieces that need to have the prongs or stones checked. The next time you go shopping, drop the items off with your trusted jeweler to be cleaned, inspected, and appraised. Then, pick up the phone, fax the appraisal, and change your insurance coverage.

Time Alone for Single Moms

Some of the difficulties you face as a busy woman are magnified for the single parent. All emotional stresses aside, one of the biggest physical changes after a divorce or the death of a spouse is that it seems you never have an hour of peace or a free moment to get a few things done. Remember that feeling you relished, when the garage door would go up at 5:30 or 6:00 P.M.—just in time for help to arrive during one of the most stressful times of the day, the dinner hour? But now, you must take matters into your own hands. So how can you find the help you need? Ask neighbors, friends, and nearby relatives to pitch in with car pools and baby-sitting. You'll be surprised at how willing others are to lend a hand if you just ask.

You might even opt to do what single mother Alison does. She hooked up with another young mother who had a husband with a demanding job. The two women wanted to take courses at a local college. Together, they worked out a schedule in which each could watch the other's child while class was in session. They studied at the same time and shared meals, thus lightening the load all round. And needless to say, the two toddlers truly benefited from the pint-sized companionship that accompanied the arrangement.

Take Five: You and the Gang

Two mothers, Pam and Amy, stood with their pack of children under five years old, waiting for a table at a casual restaurant. When the hostess asked how many they had in their party, Amy responded, "Eight with three high chairs." Within minutes after being seated, one child fell off a chair while another waddled up to the buffet and grabbed a handful of red beets and threw them. Still another never made it to the table, distracted by the candy machines near the door. The two mothers struggled to strap everyone in and finally sat to sip a soda. How much fun were these two frantic women really having? How could they have better spent their afternoon together?

- Have lunch at a fast-food place that has a children's play area. Though it might not be your first choice for dining, you can be sure kids will be entertained, leaving you more time to chat and catch up.
- Develop a baby-sitting co-op with friends and neighbors so you can alternate going out without the kids. This is a special treat for single moms who well deserve a day out with adults.
- Meet weekly with friends at each other's homes. Often kids will look forward to the novelty of playing with another child's toys. Likewise, the host children enjoy a renewed interest in what they have, as other kids introduce new methods of play. If you can manage, plan a light meal or snack and a craft or activity for the kids.
- If you can afford it, hire a sitter for one day a week as a permanent part of your routine. You can plan outings or luncheons, run errands, or schedule doctor appointments for this block of time. If you're a working mom and/or are single, arrange for a sitter at least

one night a week, no matter what. As simple as it sounds, this tactic can be a major stress reliever in the frantic woman's life.

No matter which alternative you choose, be forewarned that there *are* times in your life when many of the previous options will fail. For example, Judith and a friend met regularly for a time, bringing four preschoolers together while the women attempted to read and critique their manuscripts. The last time they convened, one toddler flushed a Matchbox car down the toilet. The women then decided to halt their weekly meetings, restarting them when the youngest was in kindergarten.

ONE-STEP-AT-A-TIME CHECKLIST

At the end of this section and at the end of each chapter in part two, we'll feature a checklist highlighting every tip and task we've recommended. As you complete your responsibilities, one by one, mark the date in the space provided. If one of our suggestions isn't applicable for you, write "not applicable" or "n/a" in the date column. By tracking tasks using our plan-of-action checklist, you'll find that the mission of maintaining some semblance of order in your household (and your life) has become that much easier. So say good-bye to the frantic pace and welcome the satisfaction of knowing where you've been and in which direction you're headed.

Date completed Or N/A	Task
_____	Take care of home repair problems as they arise.
_____	Make up a room-by-room to-do list.
_____	Shift where you store things so that you're putting them where they land.
_____	Make use of boxes, hampers, tie and coat racks for organizing and storing.

_____ Use baskets here and there for placing items at arm's reach.

_____ Sort through bedroom contents including clothes, toys, and games.

_____ Organize and clean closets, shelves, and drawers.

_____ Set aside a donation box with a clipboard attached.

_____ Donate items or have a garage sale.

_____ Keep track of donated items in a journal.

_____ Make a memorable gift from old T-shirts (or start collecting favorite clothes to do so).

_____ Quit storing heirlooms and start using them.

_____ Take control of sports equipment by storing on shelves and air-drying on mannequins.

_____ Make use of our sparkle-and-shine cleaning tips.

_____ Have your upholstery and carpets cleaned.

_____ Try a few of our laundering suggestions.

_____ Place soiled sports uniforms in one place for immediate cleaning.

_____ Designate a spot for dry-clean-only clothes.

_____ Prepare supplies for an emergency.

_____ Spruce up your decor.

_____ Create a Post-It and Pay-It Planner.

_____ Take control of mail clutter.

_____ Sort through books, magazines, and newspapers.

_____ Start separate address books for doctors' names, business numbers, and kids' friends.

_____ Sort important papers using eight essential files.

_____ Write up a master gift list in your gift-giving log.

_____ Make up a gift-wrap station.

_____ Ask family for help with the cooking and kitchen duties.

_____ Spark a renewed interest in cooking by planning a recipe swap or purchasing a new cookbook.

_____ Try freezing something new.

_____ Pack snacks, toys, and other essentials to be kept in the car.

_____ Evaluate the cost of kids' activities.

_____ Cultivate the family bond by talking with teens or playing ball with your youngster.

_____ Keep in touch with loved ones near and far.

_____ Involve your special needs child in regular and special activities.

_____ Offer loving care to your elder family members.

_____ Give some attention and grooming to the family pet.

_____ Go the extra mile at work by reaching out and trying something new.

_____ Have valuable jewelry cleaned, checked, appraised, and properly insured.

_____ Single moms, ask friends and family for the help you need.

_____ Find a less stressful way to get together with friends.

Part Two

Month-by-Month

January
February
March
April
May
June
July
August
September
October
November
December

Organizing

J anuary. The very word stirs a brew of emotions in all of us. We feel relief that the hectic holidays are behind us. We mourn the fact that another year has passed too quickly. (Or we're glad it's gone, if it wasn't a good one.) And we anticipate what tomorrow will bring. Regardless, the beginning of a fresh new year should encourage you to take hold of your life, starting with a clean slate. So prepare to de-clutter, organize, and make some serious changes. When planting a foot on this New Year's path, what's a woman to do but forge ahead? So let's go.

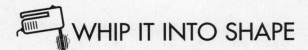 WHIP IT INTO SHAPE

Second Chance: De-Decorate

This is your second chance to de-decorate the house and store items until next year. While you're in the attic stashing, toss any decorations you didn't use this year or last to make room for the newer, more appealing ones you'll be purchasing from the clearance table.

One Step Ahead

While packing away extra holiday greeting cards, light sets, wreaths, and ornaments, Janice Lane Palko jots a list of the supplies she'll need to make next year's celebration run more smoothly. "I write down how many new strings of lights to buy," Janice explains, "including the size, color, and length." She also notes how many boxes of cards, ornaments, or wrapping paper she must replace. "I shop the after-Christmas sales and check as many things off as I can," Janice says. Then, once she's exhausted all the possibilities for now, she follows up by flipping ahead and attaching the unfinished list to her October calendar. Later in the year, to kick off the holiday season, Janice purchases the rest of what she needs when a fresh variety of items hits the shelves. Rather than wait until unpacking the holiday stuff and rushing out to pick up what's missing, she can purchase replacement supplies well ahead of time.

Give It Some Thought

Once the holiday decorations are down and tucked away, pull out your Frantic Journal. Brainstorm the reorganizing and remodeling projects you've been longing to tackle and rewrite those outdated to-do lists. Prioritize your wants and write your favorites on a sheet of paper, sticking them smack dab in the middle of the fridge door as a blatant reminder.

Later in the month, decide upon which remodeling project—large or small—you'll work on first and determine whether or not you'll need to hire a contractor.

Planning your projects no less than one season ahead is restoration and renovation specialist Alexandra Sabina's rule of thumb. She reminds us, "The contractor's job is only to perform the work. It is up to you to educate yourself on current trends and innovations." If you do not have the time to educate yourself, expect to pay for the service provided by architects, designers, decorators, and full service contractors. It will be well worth the investment. (Not all contractors are full service. Most only have the capability of providing you with labor.)

Alexandra suggests these ways to minimize the possibility of cheating yourself out of enjoying your home remodeling experience.

- Consult with local building inspectors for local building code prerequisites.
- Educate yourself, as best as possible, about materials and work that you wish to be performed.
- Build a team of specialists you can count on to provide you with the information that you need to make creative and informed decisions.
- Create a working criteria list of specifics. Make sure the contractor incorporates your specifics into her contract. (Specifics include size, color, location, times, dates, quantities, and brand names.)
- Conduct business only with contractors that can articulate their intentions explicitly, in legal form, such as a neatly typed and presented contract.
- Make sure all contractors and workers carry full liability insurance applicable to their job and your project.
- Check all warranties, both from the manufacturers of products and from the contractor's warranty on their craftsmanship.
- Last, but not least, never sign a contract that does not read "specifically" the way you want it to read. Make sure the items on your criteria list appear in the contractor's contract.

Get Organized

Over the next few weeks, most stores will advertise housewares and white sales. Take an inventory at home of what you need to replace and purchase. Buy hangers and storage bins in various sizes for your ongoing organizational process. Replace sheets, pillows, blankets, comforters, linens, bathroom rugs, and accessories that have seen better days. Or buy new ones and store for a bride-to-be or a graduate you know who will soon be heading off to college. Fill in the houseware items you've lost or broken while entertaining during the Christmas chaos. Or, for once, break down and buy yourself that countertop grill, espresso maker, or handheld steam cleaner you've always wished for but didn't want to fork over the money for.

Shift and Sort

Have family members sort out the Christmas gifts they will not use or have duplicates of. Encourage them to organize new items in drawers and closets, pulling out and replacing old gear as they go.

If you or your teen received an excess of toiletries, lotions, soaps, and other personal supplies, for example, load the surplus into a few spare makeup bags or handled caddies (those plastic, two-sided toolboxes with a handle in the middle), rather than have them scatter along the shelf each time you reach for a bath towel. Place the container of extras in a bathroom cabinet for easy access and ready use. Then, there'll be no more "discovering" such treasures still packed in gift bags come March. Also, by inventorying your surplus bin every now and then, you can efficiently replenish what you need when products go on sale.

While making use of handled caddies, consider positioning various sizes in cabinets and closets throughout the house for gathering health and beauty products, over-the-counter medicines, loose change, and lost-and-found items. These inexpensive organizers come in handy throughout the house—from the attic and toy room to the laundry room and garage.

Return, Return

Don't delay in returning unwanted gifts and surplus merchandise you've received and accumulated over the holidays. If you're lucky enough to have the receipts, you can wait a few days until the lines disappear. If not, you'd better get out there and face the crowd or you'll be receiving mere pennies back on every dollar spent.

$peaking of ale

While you're around and about, scan the after-Christmas sales. Look for things you can use year round like paper products and plain-colored gift wrap. Silver, gold, or metallic blue paper, for example, can be used to wrap wedding, shower, and new-baby presents the whole year through. It's also a good idea to shop for any January and February birthdays on your list. By the second week of this month, prices are just about as low as they'll go with selections still being in the fair-to-good range.

Other useful sale items to look for include tablecloths, runners, placemats, stadium blankets, china and crystal gifts, picture frames, photo albums, candles, candlesticks, baskets, scarves, wallets, jewelry, and discontinued toys.

Holiday Wear

Sort through your holiday wardrobe and eliminate seasonal clothing and outdated footwear you didn't use this past year. Then, have fun purchasing drastically discounted holiday-wear basics like sweaters, socks, and accessories including belts, handbags, and costume jewelry. At the same time, pick out the formal attire you need for an upcoming dinner party or wedding at prices you just can't afford to pass up.

Winter Clothes

So, you're in the groove, separating your holiday clothes and gifts, but what's next? Sort through winter clothes and shoes and toss all the weathered items you've been hanging on to for no good reason. Discard that argyle sweater you bought in Scotland or the red satin jacket from Vegas that you never wore (thank heaven). The memories are in your heart, not in the souvenirs you've stashed away. If you feel you really can't part with something, put it on and snap a picture. Then, you'll still have a tangible remembrance without having to store the cherished, yet no-longer-needed article.

Tracking Expenses

Buy accordion file folders that allow you to deposit paid bill statements in selected slots. Keep two check-sized accordion folders for receipts from personal and work-related expenses. Label your tabs "January" through "December" and drop slips in the corresponding sections. Mark the year on the outside of the folder. Remember, filing each day keeps the IRS away.

CPA Tim Schneider reminds us that it's worth the effort to maintain files of living and working expenses in order to evaluate your potential to itemize (which is a good thing) on your federal income tax return. Track expenses and save receipts from the following categories.

- *Medical:* Save receipts from all medical, dental, and optical expenses including doctor visits, prescriptions, and doctor-recommended remedies for medical purposes—for example, the installation of special air filters or air conditioning equipment for relief of respiratory problems. This also includes such doctor-prescribed therapies as exercise and a specified diet regimen.

- *Taxes:* File proof of state and local income tax payments, as well as real estate tax receipts.

- *Home mortgage:* Before the end of this month, you'll probably receive an annual mortgage statement that will indicate interest and points paid, both of which are deductible expenses. Note, however, that if you recently refinanced, the deduction for points is limited.

- *Investment interest:* Interest paid on money borrowed to make investment purchases can also be deducted. Save your bank and brokerage statements showing interest amounts in this file.

- *Charity:* Both cash and non-cash donations need to be substantiated in order to be deductible. Record the name of the charity, date and location of the contribution, a description of the contributed property, and the fair market value of the donation, including your method for determining it. Insert receipts obtained from charitable organizations in this file, too.

- *Business:* Any time you spend money on something you won't be reimbursed for by your employer, save the sales slip. On a separate piece of paper, record the merchandise purchased, when, and for what purpose. Staple the note to the receipt for clarity, and file. Refer to this data when reporting nonreimbursed business expenses on your income tax return.

"While this might seem like a burdensome process," Tim says, "a few minutes of record keeping a month can amount to substantial savings come tax time."

Taxes: Keep Your Eyes Peeled

Watch your mail delivery for tax-related documents over the next few weeks. Put all tax stuff in the same place. A file folder in your mail basket places important papers at your fingertips the minute you need them.

Quarterly Taxes

As if we haven't said enough about the dreaded dues, we want to remind you about your quarterly income taxes. If, for some reason, you don't have withholdings deducted from your paycheck, or if you are self-employed, you'll need to pay federal and state income taxes on a quarterly basis. These are generally due on the 15th of the month following the end of the quarter. But for whatever reason, the quarters are "irregular." So these taxes are to be paid on or before January 15th for the fourth quarter of the prior year, April 15th for the first quarter of the new year, June 15th for the second quarter (which is shorter), and September 15th for the third.

Similarly, local wage taxes must be paid on a quarterly basis to your municipality. These are, by and large, due on the last day of the month following the close of the quarter (but inquire locally to be sure what's expected in your area). You'll need to pay these taxes, also called penny taxes, on or by January 31st, April 30th, July 31st, and October 31st.

This month, adjust your budget to cover federal and state income tax payments due by January 15th, and local wage taxes due January 30th. We'll send reminders your way throughout the year about which taxes are due to be paid and when.

> **HIDDEN GEM:** Here's a tip for self-employed people with children from CPA Tim Schneider. If you own your own business and have children, it's a good idea to place your kids on the payroll. That's right, put them to work and compensate them for it. Kids can run errands, file documents, prepare promotional materials, sort through supplies, restock shelves, enter data into computers, and much more. By encouraging your children to earn, you're not only instilling responsibility and independence, but you're affording them the benefit of having an earnings history. This will help when they apply for college loans or other types of credit. In the long run, offspring on the payroll can help you, too. If they weren't receiving a paycheck from you, that money would have been taxed at your rate. Of course, children ages fourteen and older who bring home over a certain dollar amount still need to pay taxes, but more than likely their rate is significantly lower than yours, thus saving you money.

DARLING LITTLE ANGELS (AND THE WHOLE BLISSFUL BUNCH)

Birthday Calendar

Make up a birthday calendar for the year. Mark the names on the actual dates of your kitchen or office calendar, daily planner, or pocket PC. When you check your weekly schedule, you'll know at a glance whose birthday is coming, alerting you to buy the gift or send the card to arrive on time. Kiss your scatterbrained side good-bye as you highlight anniversaries, weddings, graduations, new-baby due dates, and other important events, as well.

Or you can make it even easier on yourself if you're someone who checks e-mail on a daily basis. Wouldn't you love to have a personal assistant to remind you of special dates and parties? Say no more. Not only can you have an instant reminder by the day, week, or month, but it's free. You can customize your chosen program to give you a nudge before the holidays, too. Sign you up? Visit www.evite.com to design your own personal assistant that will send you a reminder via e-mail. And guess what? It's easy to do.

Vacation Fun

If you want to land the vacation destination and accommodations of your choice, the time to make plans and reservations is now. Research online the area you'd like to visit, the ideal week (or weeks) you'd like to go, and the lodging choices that are available to you. If you're not connected to cyberland, use your library's Internet service or leaf through the travel section. Visit a travel agent and request brochures.

Booking summer vacations well in advance will give you the advantage of choosing from a range of vacation rental homes, condos, or hotels. If you wait, your choices will narrow to the pricey oceanfront mansions or the lodging that reminds you of the old saying "Don't let the bed bugs bite." So if you want to book a beach house with a private pool to share with another family, doing so now will afford you a wider selection of homes in your price range. You'll also be able to satisfy your preference of proximity to the beach and number of bedrooms. Don't limit yourself by waiting until April or May to decide. Since you're spending your precious dollars and time, why not get exactly what you want, where and when you want it?

But how do you begin? On the Internet, go to one of the larger search engine home pages like google.com or dogpile.com. Type in the city name and state of your choice destination. Click on the site that lists lodging, restaurants, and an events calendar. From there, you can further link to real estate agencies and rental properties by owner (if they have individual Web sites). Keep a listing in your Frantic Journal of what sites you visited, starring those you especially liked. Otherwise, you might decide you want to put money on a place you discovered in yesterday's cyber-explorations, only to spend the next three days trying to figure out where it was that you found it.

Search on the Internet for hotel rates, too. To find the best deal, double-check the cost per night by calling the toll-free number. Then, triple-check by directly phoning the specific hotel using the local number provided on the Internet. (If the local number isn't listed online, ask the toll-free operator for it.) Always request AAA (American Automobile Association) and AARP (American Association of Retired Persons) discounts, if applicable. And look into any corporate or government reductions available to you. Do the same for restaurants, too. There are some eating establishments in high-traffic areas that offer AAA discounts nationwide. The Hard Rock Café is one of them. So flash that membership card and remember, it never hurts to ask.

> **HIDDEN GEM:** Keep this tip in mind for upcoming trip needs. According to AAA, travelers often stop in for maps on Mondays after making travel decisions over the weekend. Thursdays and Fridays are also busy with vacationers grabbing TripTiks before they depart after the workweek. To avoid an extended wait, then, plan to drop in for all your travel needs midweek.

A cautionary note: Before you book a package deal, tally up the prices of the individual options that are included and compare with the total package amount. When Mary Jo was planning a surprise trip with her mom, one five-star hotel offered a quote for an overnight special that included accommodations, a breakfast buffet for two, and a riverboat ride. But when she broke down the individual costs and added them up, the package totaled $30 more than it would have been had the add-ons been purchased separately.

If you're a good-deal hunter by nature, consider these five tips for booking Internet air travel offered by seasoned bargain seeker Linda

Johnson Tomsho, author of *Walt Disney World for Cheapskates: 125 Money-Saving Tips.*

1. Before you begin, research standard round-trip fares for the route you're considering by calling airline reservation lines. That's the only way you'll be able to determine a bargain when you see it.
2. Visit the airlines' Web sites. Fares are almost always discounted 5 to 10 percent from those you'll be quoted by a reservationist over the phone.
3. Get on the e-mail lists of airlines that fly from your city to receive notification of special fares and discounts.
4. If you have a little flexibility, experiment by varying your travel dates by a day or two in either direction. You might find that a difference of one day in your itinerary will grant you substantial savings.
5. Once you've sealed the deal on the best price, check back every now and then to see if a new, even better special has opened up. Read the fine print of the particular fare you booked to make sure there are no penalty fees for changing rather than canceling your flight. But don't try to switch reservations on or near your departure date—that will end up costing you. However, if you've booked nine months in advance and find a more deeply discounted rate three months later, by all means, inquire about the change. Your savings might far outweigh the penalty, if there is one.

Have fun surfing because the right bargain is only a click away—just look at the following example.

Mary and Tom Wills of Florida purchase airline tickets over the Internet on a regular basis. Because Tom is originally from the West Coast, they travel cross-country several times a year to visit family and friends. They prefer shopping online because not only can Mary and Tom opt for the cheapest ticket price, but they are also able to select the time of day they'd like to travel, whether they want to fly direct, and what airline they prefer. Gone are the days of picking a ticket price and getting stuck with whatever airline and flight time travel Web sites assign.

Of course, you'll want to check out several Web sites and compare prices. Don't forget online contacts for travel agencies like www.aaa.com (the Web site of the AAA Motor Club). Sometimes you're still better off calling the airlines directly, so cover all bases before you hand over that credit card number.

By the way, while you're on the Web, check out the Transportation Security Administration's site at www.TSATravelTips.us for tips on how to expedite the screening process at airport baggage and passenger checkpoints.

Football Time-Out

Super Bowl Sunday—you either love it or you'd love a "blackout" to fall over your hometown. If football isn't your favorite, you need to readjust your thinking. What better time to pay back all those invites you owe from the previous holiday season? And to top it off, with a swig of the cold stuff, the football party menu is a cinch. Spread a buffet table with manageable foods, soft drinks, beer and wine, simple snacks, and you're all set. And you don't have to worry about occupying guests since the television is the obvious focal point. This has to be one of the easiest and cheapest ways to entertain.

> **SNIPPET:** Thirsty Americans spend approximately $25 billion each year on—you guessed it—beer.

Here are some ideas to make this your best bash.

- Move your party invitations into the twenty-first century by saying good-bye to addressing and licking envelopes. Not only will you save time, but you'll be able to keep the usual postage costs in your pocket. Announce your party by sending your guests invitations via www.evite.com. Customize everything from graphics to messages with the easy-to-use template in less than ten minutes. The site will even track R.S.V.P.s online and offers an option for guests to see who else is coming. What more can you ask for? And for you noncomputer people, we wish we had an alternative to offer. Guess you'll either have to go through a friend who's connected or start licking and stamping.

- Ask guests to wear team-related clothing. Gather extra items you might have in your closet so no one will be left standing on the sidelines. Slip extra jerseys over kitchen and dining room chairs, or make a football dummy to greet guests as they enter.

- Decorate by displaying pennants, flags, pom-poms, etc., throughout the house, the front door, and entrance. If you have a chandelier or accessible light fixture, hang a banner from it. Scan through the kids' toy boxes for footballs, helmets, and shoulder pads that can be utilized. Do you know anyone who has a Little Tykes football toy box? If so, borrow it and fill with canned drinks and ice. (Make sure you line it with a sturdy trash bag first.) Buy a length of indoor/outdoor carpet grass at a home improvement store to use as a tablecloth for real AstroTurf your fans will love. To take it one step further, paint the yard lines on it. Draw, paint, or glue team logos on a garbage can and place near the munchie table.

- For party day, keep the refreshments simple. You want to stay out of the kitchen rather than be penalized for not coming out of your zone. Use slow cookers to make spicy vegetarian chili, hot dogs and kielbasa, and potato and cheese pierogies—a local "delicacy" in some areas. (See "A Wee Bit More," part three, for description and recipe.) Borrow extra slow cookers if you don't have enough. Keep a variety of cold and finger foods for the guests to nibble while watching the game.

- Set up more than one TV area. A place for the littler fans or non-football followers to celebrate would be ideal.

- For favors, make pom-poms for everyone using tissue paper and dowel rods. Take several sheets of standard-size tissue paper in team colors and fold in half. From the open end, cut one inch strips toward the folded end, leaving about one-and-a-half inches uncut at the fold. Lay one end of an eighteen-inch dowel rod (about the width of a pencil) on the folded end opposite the cut strips. Roll, wrapping the tisssue around the rod. Use a stapler, cellophane tape, or rubber bands to attach the tissue to the rod. Rah, rah, rah!

- Involve everyone in a football pool to keep the day interesting. Reward winners for first quarter, half-time, third quarter, and final scores with small prizes.
- Make folded footballs with sheets of loose-leaf paper, just like the ones you made in school. Set up a card table with plenty of paper footballs for impromptu games.
- Design scorecards for rating the legendary Super Bowl commercials. Have guests vote for the commercial they think will be rated the best of the bunch. Read the newspaper the next day to see who was right and mail the winner an inflatable football for the fun of it.

SNIPPET: The Snack Food Association and the National Potato Promotion Board state that 11.8 million pounds of potato chips were consumed during the 2001 Super Bowl. Now, that's a lot of crunching and munching!

Holiday Happenings: V-Day

Make Valentine's Day plans for you and your partner (see our February chapter for specific suggestions). Hire a sitter now before every teenager you know is booked. Buy gifts and cards for those you love. Token presents such as red socks or tees will delight the little cupids in your house.

Even though the upcoming February 14th holiday brings thoughts of romance, even non-romantics love to receive Valentine's Day greetings. It's a good time of year, then, to let elderly relatives and friends know they're thought of and loved, now and always.

Rubber-stamp your way to Valentine's Day greetings. What could be better than receiving a handmade card? Collect a variety of rubber stamps and ink pads and keep them in a shoe box for easy storage. You and your kids can make Valentines from colored paper or card stock by stamping an image and shading it in with markers or colored pencils. Let the creativity flow as the family makes a supply to keep on hand year-round. Stickers work well for your younger ones. (P.S. Using a decorative ribbon, tie together six stamped greetings with matching envelopes to create a charming, useful gift to uplift those close to your heart.)

Kids and School

Half of the school year is over, so why not evaluate how your student is doing? Have you talked to your child's teachers lately? Should you make an appointment to touch base with any of the instructors to keep your child on track? Have you neglected to find a tutor or specialist who was recommended months ago? Now that the hustle-and-bustle season is over, it's time to figure out what your kids need in order to further themselves in school.

Warning Signs

As if keeping the kids on the right homework track isn't enough for one lone woman, do you sense a bigger problem lurking? If so, what can you do? Before you jump to conclusions, scrutinize this checklist. If you answer yes more times than you're comfortable with, then your child might benefit from additional outside instruction.

- Are grades lower than you or your child would like?
- Does one subject seem to be more difficult than another?
- Are you concerned that he's below reading level?
- Does the class move too fast for him?
- Is it difficult for you as a parent to give him what he needs in the way of help or time?
- Does he study for hours before a test yet still score poorly?

- Do test questions confuse him when paraphrased?
- Does he have trouble comprehending what he reads?
- Has the teacher pointed out a deficiency in a specific subject?
- Are you seeing the same snags crop up year after year?

Armed with the observations triggered by the above points, is it time for you to seek professional help?

Finding a Tutor

Finding a tutor whose instructional method matches your child's learning style is of utmost importance. Think about your child's personality. If he is shy, an unfamiliar environment might not be the best place for him. So consider having him tutored in your home. If your offspring happens to be easily distracted or will require a formal environment to focus, then the tutor's home or a learning center might be a better option.

Here's what to consider in finding a tutor.

- What are the tutor's qualifications and is she able to handle learning disabilities, if necessary?
- Why did the tutor get into the business?
- Does the person have experience with your child's age/grade level?
- Will pretesting or an evaluation be performed? Is there an additional fee for testing?
- Will a plan of action be mapped out for you?
- What curriculum materials will be used? Are the supplies up-to-date?
- Will the tutor work with your child's regular schoolwork and teacher?
- Will a certain progress or reading level be reached?
- Does she have statistics of past clients including their ages and records of improvement?
- Will she give you the contact information of previous clients as references?

- If so, ask references these questions: What are the tutor's strengths and weaknesses? Did the student show a steady improvement? Were the parents satisfied? Would they solicit help from the tutor again?

After several tutoring sessions, assess the following areas of concern.

- Is the tutor patient and prompt?
- Are you and your child comfortable with the tutor's attitude and personality, as well as the location of instruction?
- Does your child resist the tutorials or not mind going?
- Have you noticed changes in your child's attitude and ability?

To make the experience triumphant for your child, you must have total confidence in the person or place you are hiring.

A Little Help

Perhaps your child needs only temporary assistance. Or maybe she can't quite comprehend the current math lesson, but she's never had a problem before. And try as you might, you haven't been able to help her understand it. In this case, test these simple solutions.

- Approach her teacher. Sometimes teachers will offer after-school or lunchtime help to students who are having trouble with a current lesson, chapter, or assignment.
- If that isn't a possibility, contact local college counseling centers. A college student majoring in your child's troubled subject area might be just what your child needs. Since students are always looking to earn some extra money, this could be a great bargain for your budget. Offer a fee that you are comfortable paying. If the college doesn't have a formal tutoring program, stop by the administration building and obtain permission to post a notice with phone number or e-mail flaps. This will give you a number of people to interview before selecting one. Be aware of the fact that you'll probably be responsible for tutor transportation.

- For another available source, consider a local senior citizens center. The center's director will know the abilities and former occupations of its members, such as retired librarians, teachers, engineers, and business owners, who might be ready and willing to help.

Help for Homeschoolers

For you homeschoolers, Barbara Page suggests that planning ahead can save the busy woman hundreds of dollars. How? By finding out what homeschooling conferences and curriculum fairs will be held in your area this spring. Publishers and suppliers provide significant discounts on materials at these events.

Barbara also says some states insist upon achievement testing at certain grade levels and by specific dates. It might be necessary for homeschoolers to arrange their own assessments and other notifications required by their individual state laws or regulations. Check out your state's assessment requirements with the National Home Education Network or your state-level Home Education Association. These specifications must be anticipated, scheduled, and budgeted for. Barbara warns that some assessment providers will try to sell things to homeschoolers that are not required by state law or regulation, so protect yourself by knowing the law. Thanks, Barbara!

Enticing Family to Do Their Share

Give kids responsibilities for the new year and add a fun family reward. But how do you know what jobs to assign to them? Pinpoint one area in which each family member has some interest. If your husband is a whiz with numbers, give him control of the record keeping. If your son likes to arrange his sports equipment a certain way, hand him the responsibility of managing all sports paraphernalia. Pay attention to who moans the least when doing a certain task. If your daughter doesn't mind taking recycled products to the bin in the basement, let that become her job. And now for the compensation, start a new family tradition. Add events as simple as milk shake night or hot chocolate morning. For the teens, make it a night of pizza, popcorn, and plenty of pals.

Working Around the Kids

Are you having trouble finding ways to work around young children at home? Being a single parent and the mother of a child with special needs never stopped Loriann Hoff Oberlin from finding creative strategies to get her job done. While writing *Working at Home While the Kids Are There, Too* and other books, Loriann couldn't afford to constantly hire sitters, nor did she want to rely upon family and friends. Loriann's kids became accustomed to what she did for a living. They'd accompany her on trips to the library, bookstore, and copy center. "It just became a part of our existence. And even now that I'm remarried and they are a little older, they still joke about our weekly trips to libraries and bookstores."

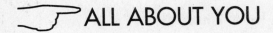 ALL ABOUT YOU

Interoffice Memo:
Compute the Commute

Take time to look into the specifics of your commute, including where you park for work, the route you take, and the time you begin each day. Look into ride shares, flextime, and monthly bus passes, as well as freeway and parking passes. By making your commute more efficient, you'll ease a bit of the tension associated with the home-to-work transition and vice versa.

For example, the Pennsylvania Turnpike and several other state toll roads have what is called an *E-ZPass* system that allows drivers to zip through a specific booth to pay the toll. The pass is electronically monitored and calculated so drivers don't have to stop when coming and going. They no longer wait in long lines during rush hour, thus saving travel time. How does it work? The pass electronically tabulates the fare owed and automatically deducts it from the driver's total reserve amount.

When funds drop below a certain figure, a new minimum is withdrawn directly from the driver's checking account or charged to his or her credit card, which in turn shows up on the next monthly statement.

To-Do, To-Do

Make separate work-related and personal to-do lists in your Frantic Journal and vow to start crossing things off.

Write down one task each week that you've been pushing to the back burner. This could be anything from reorganizing your computer and e-mail files to beefing up your dinner selections. For example, if you need to jump back into the workplace, check into programs available at your local college offered free of charge to job hunters. Or if your financial picture needs some focus, find money-related workshops specific to your needs and convince your spouse or friend to go with you.

Boot Camp

Some frantic women out there have been able to successfully incorporate exercise into their schedules to preserve their health and especially their sanity. Others, however, have spent many hours worrying and wishing they could find the energy and motivation to work out and win.

Mother of four Mary Lou Gramelspacher has isolated time in her busy schedule to work out on a daily basis. Even though her children are involved in numerous activities and she works twenty-five hours a week or more, Mary Lou has made exercise a priority in her life. She joined a tennis league and swimming pool at a local community center, putting her on the court or in the lap lane seven days a week.

JOTS & THOUGHTS QUIZ
Flexing the Procrastination Muscle

Check the following "distractions" that come between you and your rowing machine.

- ☐ Time
- ☐ Money
- ☐ Kids
- ☐ Your not-so-tip-top shape
- ☐ Ability
- ☐ Lack of pleasure
- ☐ Lack of enthusiasm
- ☐ Mental block
- ☐ Negative attitude
- ☐ Slow results

Too many checkmarks might mean you don't really want to work out. You know you should but, with all your time-consuming commitments, you tend to let exercise take a backseat to just about everything else. And there's always something else that needs your attention.

We're sure you can relate to Happy Barber's dilemma. She tells us about one of her busy weeks. "I made four dresses for a wedding. Angel's birthday was the next day. Our anniversary was two days later. Mandy's birthday and Maddie's birthday followed. I am about to feel that things are becoming more manageable, but I'm tired. And on top of all that, I have to figure out how to exercise."

So what can Happy do? According to personal trainer and mother of two Kim White, Happy is not alone. "Many, many people out there have clothes draped over their treadmills," Kim says. "So the key is not to feel guilty." Just as you've heard before, Kim tells us it's all in the motivation—motivation that, of course, must come from within.

The following tips can help you to de-clothe that treadmill and dust off those sneakers.

- *Find a support system.* People often don't have the support system they need to get started in an exercise program and/or to keep at it. Some women tell their spouses or coworkers that they want to adopt an exercise regimen and the reply is a glum, "Yeah, yeah, I've heard that one before." So where can you find the support you need? Ask a friend, coworker, or supportive spouse to join you three times a week for a morning walk. Or sign up for a class that meets at a regular day and time. If it's one-on-one encouragement you need, by all means, find a personal trainer who's right for you.

- *Stop blaming stressful situations.* If you're living in a stressful situation and keep waiting for it to go away before you start to exercise, hear this. "Stressful situations usually exist over a longer period of time," Kim says. "And often, they drive you into certain habits." For instance, Kim talks about a mom who rarely eats dinner until her young children are tucked into bed. That leaves her eating her largest meal after 9:00 in the evening—and we all know that's not a good thing. And because the kids won't be leaving the nest in the near future, this mom can't wait for her life to change. So don't let the situations that everyday life presents become an excuse. In other words, stop the buck here.

- *Follow the thirty-day (or more) rule.* You've heard it before, but as a general rule it takes at least thirty days to break a bad habit. And Kim believes the converse is true, as well. That is to say it'll take thirty or more days for you to incorporate daily exercise into your normal routine—and to have it *feel* normal. In fact, for some, it can take up to six months. So get started and be patient.

- *Don't be so hard on yourself.* Often, women come down too hard when something happens to interfere with their workout routines. If they miss a training session, they throw in the towel. It brings them down and they view themselves as failures. "But don't get discouraged," Kim advises. "If you skip a day or two, you don't have to start back at day one. Just keep it up for a few more weeks and, before you know it, daily exercise will be something you crave rather than a task you dread."

- *Give yourself a break.* There will be weeks when you just won't be able to exercise as much as you'd like—because you have to visit a close family member in the hospital every day, for example, or a special project at work requires you to be there after hours. That's okay. If you're feeling a bit under the weather or have outside stresses that are taking their tolls on you, allow yourself to take a few days off. More than likely, within a week, you'll be craving the uplifting feeling that regular exercise brings, so you'll hop back to it in no time.

"Many times, my clients start off with such energy and enthusiasm," Kim says. "But it is short-lived." And within a few weeks, they're telling Kim that they *had* to eat junk food and miss their workouts because they were on the road, or because other life situations wouldn't allow them to do what they were committed to doing. To that Kim says, "Life's situations are never going to be ideal. So don't let them become an excuse for you to neglect giving your mind and body the care they require and deserve." That's the best advice yet, Kim. Thanks!

SNIPPET: Wondering why you have jeans anywhere from a size 6 to 12 hanging in your closet? It might not have as much to do with your gaining and losing weight as it does with inconsistencies in what manufacturers offer. *Consumer Reports* scientists evaluated size consistency within the same label. Tabulated results showed notable differences in the same size, style, and brand of jeans—as much as two inches! The good news is you don't need to suck in your stomach anymore. For a better fit, just try on a different pair. Certain manufacturers are also participating in what they call vanity sizing. This involves expanding the fit of the garment so that women who actually wear a size 12, for example, can slip on and purchase a size 10 instead. That's why in some stores you reach for an 8 and, in others, a 6—or even a 4—fits like a glove. It's been said that Marilyn Monroe was a size 12. But, in today's designs, she'd likely be wearing an 8 instead.

Take Five: New Year's Options

If resolution making has your insides tied like a New Year's pretzel, try creating what we call "New Year's options" instead. Why? Usually,

the resolutions we take on add extra height to the mountain of responsibilities we already have. Our resolutions might be pie-in-the-sky
goals or ones that force us to bite off more than we can chew. Often,
too, instead of being flexible with our resolutions, we stop trying and
shatter them completely. Or we forget about them as our days zip by
like a roller coaster.

Try making smaller target goals you can actually achieve. Rather
than vowing to lose twenty pounds, if that is your goal, work toward
losing the first three or four. By adding physical reminders in your
home and workplace—an inspirational saying on the fridge, a reward
chart by the treadmill, or a smaller-sized outfit on the back of your bedroom door—you'll keep your goals within your grasp.

Be sure to set a limit for yourself or things will spiral out of control.
Imagine riding the upside-down rides at an amusement park several
times in a row. Is your stomach quivering at the image? For example, if
you love to read as we do, this simple pleasure could turn your household upside down. How? Have you ever read an entire book from
beginning to end, then scurried around the house trying to catch up on
all the things you should've done? Don't let something you enjoy transform from a pleasure into a pressure. So, go ahead and set your goals.
Jump on the upside-down rides if you please but, in order to catch your
breath, you'll want to climb on the carousel—taking it more slowly
every now and then.

JOTS & THOUGHTS QUIZ
Getting to the Root of Things

Take a look at the obstacles that are present in your life, today and
in the past. Write down what it is that stands between you and your
dreams. Don't think of anyone else but you.

1. What regret(s) still haunts you?
2. Do you have a fear you might never have confessed? What is it?
3. Can you pinpoint a void that exists in your life, be it large or
   small?

Now that you've written down three main obstacles in the Jots & Thoughts Quiz, what can you do with this information? We call it "activating hope." Turn that hope into a reality by taking that first step to making a change in your life. Use your regrets, fears, and voids as a driving force for you to achieve.

For example, when Judith was up to her elbows in diapers and strained carrots, her mother had read about a writers' conference and encouraged her to attend. During one particularly inspiring session, Judith looked across the aisle and noticed an older woman, possibly eighty-five or so, taking notes. "That'll be me," Judith thought. "If I don't give this writing career a try now, I'll be ninety and wishing I had."

Similarly, you don't want to wake up one day and realize you're ninety years old and haven't done what you've always wanted to do. Take action now. Try anything from learning Russian to rock climbing to shopping the flea markets. Find a course that's right for you.

Take a moment to ponder how you'd like to expand and change your life. Remember, don't put off until tomorrow what you can accomplish today.

ONE-STEP-AT-A-TIME CHECKLIST

As you did in part one, mark the date of completion (or n/a for not applicable) next to each task on the following checklist. You'll feel like a new woman when you glance down your list and see all you've accomplished.

**Date
completed
Or N/A**

Task

_____ De-decorate.

_____ Write next year's holiday supply list.

_____ Write and prioritize a reorganizing or remodeling to-do list.

_____ Purchase housewares and bins. Replace small appliances.

_____ Make use of handled caddies throughout the house.

_____ Return unwanted gifts.

_____ Shop the sales for items to be used all year.

_____ Purchase holiday wardrobe basics and formal wear.

_____ Sort and discard weathered winter clothes and shoes.

_____ Buy accordion folders to maintain personal and business expenses.

_____ Create a tax-related folder for incoming documents.

_____ Pay quarterly taxes if you don't have them deducted from your paycheck.

_____ Make a birthday calendar.

_____ Research and map out family vacation.

_____ Plan Super Bowl party and activities.

_____ Purchase Valentine's Day cards and gifts. Make plans.

_____ Evaluate kids' schoolwork and progress.

_____ Check whether children need more help with studying.

_____ Find a suitable tutor.

_____ Use less costly means to provide help with schoolwork.

_____ Homeschoolers: Plan to attend an upcoming conference.

_____ Assign kids new chores and add a family reward.

_____ Discover ways to work around the kids.

_____ Compute specifics regarding your commute.

_____ Make separate work-related and personal to-do lists.

_____ Start a regular exercise program.

_____ Create a New Year's option just for you.

Connecting

In the beginning of February, retail store windows, magazine ads, and TV commercials are littered with love-related goods galore including everything from sealed-with-a-kiss boxers to heart-shaped Jacuzzis. This month is overflowing with symbols of love—engagements and weddings, as well as hearts, flowers, and candy. But don't shortchange yourself by relating only to your partner. February is also a time for you to reconnect with anyone who has added meaning to your life, whether it was yesterday or several years ago.

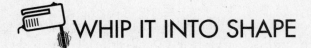 ## WHIP IT INTO SHAPE

Tax Time

If you're planning on preparing your own tax return, obtain any tax forms you might need from your local IRS office, at the post office, or online at www.irs.gov. Some public libraries also make forms available for your convenience. Don't delay filing. If you have a college-bound student come fall, make tax preparation a top priority. When filling out financial aid applications for grants and scholarships, use the actual adjusted income amount rather than estimated figures. This saves you the hassle of verifying income on yet another form later.

If going the professional route this year, make an appointment with your accountant now to have a better choice of what time slot best fits your schedule. Later, the mad rush will be on and you'll have to take whatever appointment you can get.

Certified Public Accountant Patricia B. Kulmoski says to keep this in mind. If you've had a busy year financially—including receiving an inheritance, buying or selling property, undergoing a divorce, death of a spouse or child, changing jobs, moving from state to state, seeing a significant increase or decrease in your investment income, winning the lottery (don't we all wish?), and other major changes in your financial status—you might want to consider professional preparation. Professional accountants are trained to handle these special situations. "People end up paying more taxes than they need to," Patricia says, "especially when the filing becomes more complicated."

Financial Aid

Come August, will your once-little, now-grown-up child be heading out your door and into the upper echelons of the academic world? If so, you'll have to undergo many preparations before he sits within the house of knowledge. By now, you might already know what school he'll be attending. Or at the very least, his list should be narrowed down to a final few.

This month, concentrate on filling out financial aid applications. Before you attempt the process, let us help you to get ready. Purchase an expandable plastic folder with dividers. Make sure it's large enough to hold a file folder and the many brochures, handbooks, scholarship applications, and so forth, you'll receive. Next, make a personal data file for quick reference in the future. Slip in a copy of your year-end tax record, Social Security numbers, and earnings income figures for you, your husband, and child inside the file.

Contact the institution and ask about financial aid seminars available to parents. Most schools offer at least one or two such workshops that are usually free of charge. A popular one teaches how to fill out the FAFSA form (see the following paragraph). If the intended facility doesn't offer such options, call other universities near you. You want to glean as much information as possible on the subject. Since attendance is usually on the low side, take a list of questions with you for one-on-one feedback. As an added bonus, free gifts are often passed out with, believe it or not, no strings attached.

The most important document you must complete is the Free Application for Federal Student Aid form, also called FAFSA. This one is used for both federal and state grants. Note that state and federal deadlines might not be the same. Apply by completing the standard paper application available through your high school guidance counselor, the college, or by calling the U.S. Department of Education toll-free at 1-800-4-FED-AID. For computer-savvy folks, apply online at www.fafsa.ed.gov. Whichever method you choose, fill out the application only once. Check for the current cutoff date and send it in as soon as possible. Be sure to make a copy before sealing the envelope. (If you're divorced, it's best if the custodial parent handles the filing process.)

A month or so after you've sent out the FAFSA, you'll receive a Student Aid Report (SAR). Correct any errors and resubmit. You can always check your current filing status online. Keep a copy of the completed form and the SAR in your personal data file.

Now that you've accumulated everything you need, the financial aid filing process will be a bit less draining—less so than your soon-to-be dwindling bank account, anyway.

Tuition Reduction

Will you be sending your child to a private elementary or high school next year? Inquire about financial aid, scholarships, work-study programs, or other discounts offered to defray educational costs.

In cooperation with local retailers, some schools have partial tuition reimbursement plans. Schools are invited to purchase gift certificates to certain stores, restaurants, and shops at a discount. The schools, in turn, sell the certificates at face value, making a profit of 1 to 18 percent. Some institutions pass the savings on to enrolled families. If the school doesn't offer any such programs to lower tuition rates, consider inquiring about starting one.

What's Cooking

Did you know that February is National Canned Goods Month? And if you're thinking, "Ugh, what can I make that's different with a bunch of canned vegetables?" we have a recipe for you. Cook up a batch of our tasty meatball soup that'll warm your family's insides on a cold February evening.

✦ Georgia's Meatball Soup ✦

INGREDIENTS

2 pounds ground beef
2 eggs
1 cup soft bread crumbs
1 (15-ounce) can beef broth
2 (15-ounce) cans stewed tomatoes
1 (15-ounce) can corn
1 (15-ounce) can green beans
1 envelope onion soup mix
6 to 8 sliced carrots
¼ cup celery tops
¼ cup parsley
4 or 5 diced potatoes
¼ teaspoon pepper
¼ teaspoon oregano
2 beef bouillon cubes
water
salt

Step one: Combine ground beef, eggs, and bread crumbs. Shape into meatballs about one-half inch in diameter and bake at 400 degrees F for 10 to 15 minutes. (To save time you can substitute ready-made frozen meatballs.)

Step two: In an eight-quart pot or large slow cooker, combine beef broth, stewed tomatoes, corn, green beans, onion soup mix, carrots, celery tops, parsley, potatoes, pepper, oregano, beef bouillon cubes, and 5 cups water. Salt to taste. Add meatballs. Bring to boil and simmer for 5 to 6 hours. For Crock-Pot cooking, heat on low for 5 to 6 hours. (This yummy, nutritious recipe is provided in memory of Georgia Colonna who so kindly shared it with us years ago.)

Stockpile

After the love-related holiday passes, some stores will have a surplus of red and/or white paper products. When prices are 50 to 70 percent off plates, napkins, and tablecloths, stock up on these supplies for the patriotic and Christmas holidays later in the year. Or keep them on hand to use now and then, when you're in a rush and don't have time to wash the dishes.

DARLING LITTLE ANGELS (AND THE WHOLE BLISSFUL BUNCH)

Holiday Happenings: Lovers' Delight

Confirm your Valentine's Day plans. If you haven't made any yet, we're giving you a second chance to squeeze in some fun. Try something new—and be creative. While dining out constitutes a typical Valentine's Day celebration, why not go for something nontraditional like scheduling a sleigh ride, going cosmic bowling, or spending the evening aboard a heated riverboat cruise? Would viewing the city from an observation deck be a romantic treat? Or how about visiting one of your old hideouts or participating in a favorite activity you haven't tried since you were dating?

If money's running short, take the time to write your sweetheart a juicy love letter or silly poem, rent a romantic comedy, or throw a few steaks on the grill, even if they are tube steaks (a gentler term for hot dogs). Relive past memories by snuggling together on the sofa with a bottle of wine, chocolates, and photos of the early days. You can either include the kids in your plans or ship them off to Grandma's house.

✂ SNIPPET: The next time you pop the cork, let this vintage fact flow: The date on a bottle of wine indicates the year the grapes were picked, not the year of bottling.

If you don't have a loved one to celebrate with, venture out with single friends for a night of woo-woo woman-hooding. Or invite them over to play an old board game like Mystery Date, if you can grab hold of one. Share stories about your first kiss, your worst nightmare date, and how long it's been since you last went "out." Award prizes like a furry "lips" pillow, bifocals for better foresight, and a juicy romance novel.

Toast each other by tinging goblets filled with silky smooth sips of the Frantic Woman's Cocktail created especially for us. Here's the recipe.

✦ Frantic Woman's Cocktail ✦

INGREDIENTS
½ ounce Frangelico
½ ounce vodka
½ ounce amaretto
cream

Fill a highball glass with ice. Add Frangelico, vodka, and amaretto. Top off with cream and stir.

Sip, don't gulp, or you'll be the first asleep and vulnerable to silly slumber party antics.

Summer Camps

Would you like to send your little darling to camp, but the monumental task of finding one to satisfy you and your child has forced you to put it on hold? Don't wait any longer. Now is the time to do the research, both online and locally, for the various summer camps available.

Decide whether your child is going to camp just for the fun of it, to socialize with others, to learn a new skill, or to improve an old one. Take your child's ability and personality into consideration. Are you interested in introducing him to a new sport or in boosting him to a more competitive level? You wouldn't want him to attend a program designed for active or advanced campers if he's passive or a novice. Likewise, you don't want him to be bored with the basics when he's more than ready for a bigger challenge. Either way, such an experience would be more torturous than pleasurable. And that's not what you want for your youngster.

Scan school district, college, and community bulletins for camp offerings. If you're looking for something in particular, such as a craft, acting, or instrumental program, ask the art, drama, and music teachers for potential contacts. The same idea applies when trying to find a sports camp. A physical education teacher, coach, or former high school player might have a few leads for you. Sporting goods stores, health clubs, recreation centers, and athletic associations are other possible resources. If cold calling makes you nervous, recommendations from other parents or your family physician will ease concerns when searching for a camp.

In addition, check regional newspapers and magazines for listings. The publications' bulletin board or community calendar notices usually feature camp offerings. Many times the sports section will include schedules of upcoming baseball, basketball, or soccer camps. The papers' health segments advertise those related to certain diseases or disabilities, such as Camp Huff 'N Puff, geared toward those individuals who have been diagnosed with asthma. To find out more about this camp, call 724-772-1750 (or Pennsylvania residents can call toll-free at 1-800-220-1990).

Online, you'll find camps hosted by such big-name companies and organizations as Nike, Boy Scouts of America, and Girl Scouts of the USA. Not sure where to begin? Click on to the American Camping Association (ACA) Web site at www.acacamps.org. This nonprofit organization has a database of more than two thousand camps that have received ACA accreditation for camp procedures, policies, and practices. When searching on the Web, keep your Frantic Journal at your side to record your favorites for ease of reference later. Otherwise, you might not remember which soccer camp it was that you liked the best.

While online, check out www.KidsCamps.com for more selections. Or better yet, visit the sister Web site called www.GrownUpCamps.com to research tempting getaway options for yourself.

After the type of camp is decided on, you'll want to find the best one to suit your child's needs and to quell any parental anxieties that are beginning to surface.

Beverly Breton Carroll, author of *The Confident Coach's Guide to Teaching Basketball*, and her husband, Celtics basketball coach John Carroll, are the founders of All-Star Basketball Camps in Waltham, Massachusetts. They've furnished these suggestions for choosing a sports camp.

- Check the ratio of campers to coaches. How many kids does each coach teach? Each individual sport has its maximum number. For instance, in basketball, if a team has more than ten to twelve kids on it, that's too many.
- Find out who runs the camp. Is the director a figurehead or actively involved with the camp throughout the session? Does the person running daily operations have adequate background and experience in the sport for the level you're seeking for your child?
- If possible, check into the talent level of the campers as a group. Ask behind the scenes to discover how competitive the games are to make sure the skills level is a match for your child.
- Verify the safety of the camp. Ideally, you want a certified trainer available for the campers at all times who is equipped to handle any type of injury.

- For overnight camps, be clear on all the logistics. What kind of facilities or dorms are the children staying in? How are they managed? How is security handled? How well supervised are the campers when they're moving around from dorms to dining halls to sports facilities? How much downtime do they have?

"Get some references," Beverly says as a final note. "Talk to someone who's gone to the camp in the past."

SNIPPET: If you view camps as small potatoes, look again. According to the American Camping Association, more than ten million youths annually attend summer camps. That's almost double the entire population of Ireland.

Summer Child Care

Cold winter months make it hard to imagine the hot summer days that are just around the corner. But before you know it, your little ones will be singing "School's Out for Summer." And as much as you might want to, you can't ignore the fact that they'll be home—round the clock—so day care arrangements might need to be made.

Though countless books on the market offer sound advice for choosing child care, we're going to focus on making the process as trouble free as possible.

Before you make any calls, inquiries, or decisions, ponder these questions.

- How old are your children? Age makes a difference in deciding what type of care will benefit the little ones. A center with crafts, games, swing set, sandbox, and storytelling would be sufficient for younger children. As the kids near junior high age, they'll want something more challenging with plenty of action. Plus, the older the kids get, the more active and pickier they become. Is there enough room for them to play, run, and release their natural energy? Will they have access to their favorite hobbies? Some centers have swimming pools and tennis and basketball courts.

- Will they need rides to and from their extracurricular commitments? This is especially important for children involved in athletic programs when games are scheduled during the daytime hours. If the provider cannot drive the kids to a designated destination, is she close enough that you can carpool with another family? Keep this in mind if you plan on signing the tykes up for sports or any classes such as art, computers, or summer school.

- What type of care would you prefer? Family-style day care offers supervision in the provider's home environment and has a minimal number of enrollees. A franchised or corporate center has a larger facility with more children present. Are you looking for a place where the kids can socialize with others or where the attention will be more individualized? Whereas younger kids love being the center of attention, older ones are easily bored and would rather hang out with their peers.

- Do you want the facility to be closer to home or work? Who will transport the children? If you and your spouse are taking turns dropping off and picking up, your best bet is to have a place close to home. Take into account what will fit into your lifestyle. If you'd prefer quiet time to adjust from the workplace to the home front, consider day care close to home. This allows you the opportunity for a few minutes of peace to gather your thoughts before jumping from corporate world to your dwelling place. On the other hand, if you'd rather spend every minute you can with your little ones, select a location closer to work. By choosing this route, you'll have the luxury of lunching with the kids, too. On the trip home, take advantage of the car time for focused conversation before reaching the front door and the oodles of responsibilities that await you there. In addition, any prolonged stops won't put you into a tizzy if unforeseen circumstances, like a traffic jam, cause you to be late.

The next step consists of finding a good match for your family. Before you hire someone, here are a dozen questions to ask.

1. What is the ratio of children to adults?
2. Are they licensed and trained in first aid and CPR?
3. What's on the daily agenda? Are there planned activities? Free time?
4. Are the children ever taken away from the property for any reason, such as field trips, activities, or errands?
5. Are snacks and lunches included in the rates?
6. What is the policy regarding absent days due to illness or vacation? Do you still pay or are you given a credit?
7. How do they handle discipline? Naps? TV time?
8. Can you stop in during the day for a visit?
9. Are telephone calls welcomed or discouraged?
10. Are there restrictions on what your child is allowed to play with and where he is allowed to venture?
11. Will staff be permitted to smoke on the property?
12. For in-home care, are there pets and/or firearms on the premises?

These are questions and answers to contemplate before signing on the dotted line.

If you're looking "outside the sandbox" for day care options, however, here are a few ideas from other frantic mothers.

With four preteens between them, Wendy Joy and her neighbor hired a high school student for the summer. Each week the kids and sitter would alternate between the two houses. Not only was the change of surroundings good for all involved, but the system supplied built-in friends all summer long.

Colleen Prokopik was hired by a working mom who belonged to the same swimming pool as she did. Even though the kids weren't the same ages, weather permitting, all five went to the pool every day. Colleen found the kids became more responsible because she assigned everyone a certain duty to handle, from toting inflatable toys to accounting for shower necessities.

While chatting with another mom, Karen Joos, a preschool aide, was enticed by a grand-slam opportunity. Her friend, a work-during-the-summer mom, needed to find a suitable sitter, and hiatus-bound Karen wanted a summer job. With her high school sons working full-time, Karen wasn't looking forward to lonely days in an empty nest. The simple conversation concluded with the perfect solution for both women.

Hiring your own clone (though desirable) is an impossible feat, but finding someone you and your child are comfortable with isn't. Planning, asking questions, and knowing what type of person you want to handle the job when you're not able to, gives you the peace of mind you deserve when it comes to caring for your precious children.

Family Togetherness

As this is the month of improving relationships and togetherness, clean out or rearrange an area in your home—making it work better for cultivating a positive family environment. Will clearing the basement offer a good place for teens? Do you need more seats in your family room—encouraging all of you to be together more often? Could you use a designated space where kids can nestle into a comfy chair with a book, magazine, or headset? Or would a place with enough elbow room and art supplies entice them to indulge their creative sides? Focus on improving at least one family area in your home.

You might be able to make room in the den or an extra bedroom for just this purpose. Furnish with casual fun furniture or add a few throw pillows to what you already have in order to update the look, making it more inviting for kids and their friends. As you know, it's always better to have them hanging at your house than wandering in places you wish they weren't.

Eight Ways To Rediscover
Your Loved One

Cupid's arrows, candy hearts, and hand-dipped chocolates are in abundance everywhere you look. So it's a great time of year to remember the warmth and strength of your love. But who has time or energy? Most mushy-gushy recommendations from those relationship Web sites or lovey-dovey magazines offer crazy fixes for adding passion to a fizzling relationship. Passion is only one part of the puzzle; it's the day-to-day communication, respect, and contentment pieces that help to complete the overall picture.

Did you ever wonder why some relationships seem tighter than others? There are probably more reasons for this than there are Hershey's chocolate kisses. One thing's for sure, though. If you don't find, maintain, or create a common thread in your relationship, you're bound to unravel and drift apart. And wouldn't that be so easy to do with all the responsibilities and commitments most of us encounter on a regular basis? Sure, it is! By the time dinner dishes are washed and put away, who feels like discussing the day's events, let alone future dreams that now seem light-years away? The possibility of snuggling together in front of a cozy fire, toasting each other with soft music playing (and without your darling little angels yelling, "I need a glass of water"), only happens in the movies.

To our knowledge, there isn't a magical love potion to guzzle when your relationship falls flat, so we've decided to help you take a realistic approach to reigniting the old flame or making it burn even brighter than before. How? By interweaving a common bond with your sweetheart—not just at special times, but throughout daily life. Remember, it's the little things you do that pull a partnership closer together.

What follows are eight simple suggestions for tightening the weave on your "I do" blanket.

1. *Start a hobby together.* Are you feeling as if you never have a chance to do or share something, anything, together? Commit to one new recreational interest for just the two of you. It can be stargazing, wine tasting, museum touring, or movie reviewing. Or you might try an activity as simple as reading two copies of the same book at the same time, forming your own mini-discussion group.

2. *Laugh together.* Did you ever notice how much fun kids have

throwing a snowball, turning the hose on one another, or bopping each other with a pillow? Well, maybe the kids know something we don't. Or maybe we've just forgotten. Laughing together lightens the mood, allowing us to let our hair down and have a good time to boot. So, pick up a snowball, the garden hose, or a pillow and take aim. Fire!

3. *Set up an environment conducive to gaining each other's undivided attention.* Wouldn't you love to chat with your honey without competing with the TV, the telephone, or the demands of the kids? Well, the next time he shaves, plop down on the toilet seat lid and chat. You'll have at least ten minutes of his attention before he hops in the shower.

4. *Utilize his television time.* While watching the tube, does your hubby sit on one sofa and you on another? Well, honey, move on over. You don't have to like what he's watching, just cuddle beside him with a book or magazine. And it's a definite that the kids will take comfort in seeing you nestle together.

5. *Start lively conversations.* Do you need some prompts to get the conversation started? Try politics. Yes, watch the local news or your township meetings together (some local cable channels televise them). Granted, you might have different perspectives, which adds to the controversy, but the room will be filled with chatter, and you might learn something new about your partner. Again, too, it's healthy for kids to hear friendly debating— teaching them how to express and support a point of view.

6. *Get involved.* Once a month, or every three, volunteer together. It could be something as simple as helping out with your child's sports team or as involved as building homes with the organization Habitat for Humanity (www.habitat.org).

7. *Build a dream.* What were the goals the two of you shared when your relationship was but a budding bloom? Work toward building them together again. If the dream is impossible, adapt it to fit into your lifestyle today.

8. *Start a united tradition.* Whether it's stopping for cappuccino after church, reading the Sunday paper together, visiting the library

weekly, washing the car over the weekend, or enjoying Friday night movie time, join together to create and discover a united tradition.

The goal is to intertwine your lives together in order to make the bond stronger.

Here's how real estate agent and multi-million-dollar producer Linda Foltz keeps the lines of communication flowing in her marriage.

"Believe it or not," Linda tells us, "when I'm not climbing the corporate ladder, chauffeuring kids to their endless activities, cooking well-balanced meals, disinfecting the house, squeezing cantaloupe in the grocery store, or washing the self-perpetuating pile of stained laundry, I'd like to spend some quality time alone with my husband. But more often than not, by the end of the day, I'm sound asleep before the kids—talk about a formula for disaster!

"Seriously though," Linda continues, "this is my second marriage, and I'd like it to be my last. So I want to make time for my husband— one of the few men patient or crazy enough to marry a woman with four kids. It would be just my luck that the kids will finally leave the nest and I'll look around to find that he's been gone for years, but I was too busy to notice.

"Every evening before dinner, regardless of how hectic the surroundings are, the two of us sit and talk over a glass of wine or a cup of cappuccino," Linda says. "It works at this time of day because the kids are usually finishing up homework, getting ready for an activity, or taking a break in front of the television. If we waited until later to make time for each other, it would never happen—because I'm too tired and it seems that the kids just never go to bed."

SNIPPET: Remember what it felt like to fall in love?

If not, grab some chocolate. Chocolate contains phenylethylamine (PEA), a natural substance that is reputed to stimulate the same reaction in the body as falling in love.

Charity Begins at Home

February is the time to keep *all* the relationships in your life growing, not only the romantic ones. Show children how to reach out by having them do something charitable within the family like writing a letter or an e-mail message to a distant relative. Or why not have your daughter visit, call, or shop for an older family member no matter how much homework she has? Not only will the child gain insight into various cultures and past ways of living, she'll become rooted in a greater sense of family and learn the importance of compassion. In addition, she'll be forced, at least for the moment, to look beyond the narrow world that revolves around her.

You can also use the experiences of visiting elders as a way to work through problems, bridge gaps, or simply share valuable time together.

☞ ALL ABOUT YOU

Interoffice Memo: Broaden Your Horizons

While you're strengthening the bonds of friendships and family, enhance your professional relationships, too, by networking in your field. Reach out by registering for a conference, attending a special meeting, or organizing an informal one yourself by asking a renowned speaker or expert in your field to visit your company as a guest lecturer. Not only will you gain insight and a fresh perspective, but you might even climb up one more rung on the corporate ladder. At the very least, the program will provide a break in the monotony of everyday work life.

Want to know more? Contact organizations that provide a speakers' bureau, such as Women's Business Network, Inc., Business and Professional Women, Association for Women in Communications, and the YWCA. Inquire with the personnel department at your local newspaper. Some daily papers list writers and editors who will speak on topics related to their field for a minimal cost. Keep an eye open regarding lectures or workshops offered by up-and-coming authors and well-known personalities in your area. Some presenters will come for free if you allow them to sell their books and related merchandise.

Interoffice Memo: Relationships

And now, how can you improve relationships with coworkers, your boss, and/or your subordinates? Suggest a regular breakfast, lunch, or coffee gathering for at least once a week or month. This is a fun way to explore the personal side of those people you spend so much time with and have never really gotten to know.

Friendship Month

Remember to honor your friends during National Friendship Month. Rekindle friendships from the past and celebrate those you currently cherish. An afternoon tea is fun and easy to plan. Serve flavored tea, tea sandwiches, scones, and a few scrumptious desserts. Or for a trip out, plan a "girls only" day by touring a former plantation, restored mansion, or Victorian house.

For long-distance friends, locate several photos showing your happy faces from the "good old days." Scan the pictures into your computer or make color copies at a nearby office supply store. Create a "best friend" card with these memorable photos and include captions such as "Remember when we had time to chat?" "Wishing we were as close now as we were then," or "And we thought deciding what to wear was our biggest dilemma." Or tuck in a tea bag with a little note saying, "I wish we could share a pot of tea. Enjoy this cup and think of me." If you do nothing else, dig out your class list and e-mail an old pal, today.

JOTS & THOUGHTS QUIZ
From Social Dud to Shining Star

When it comes to socializing, are you a Star, a Filler, or a Social Dud? Answer yes or no to the following questions.

1. Do you call others before the party, chatting, stirring excitement, debating on what to wear, making it almost like a preparty affair?
2. Are you the first to arrive, ready to greet everyone with a cheerful smile, not wanting to miss a moment's chance to chat?
3. Do you scan the crowd checking to see who else was invited?
4. Do you work the room, mingling as you go?
5. If your partner is waylaid while getting drinks, do you strike up a conversation with those around you, then venture off to the buffet?
6. Are you the type of person who boogies onto the dance floor with the first good song of the night, not caring that you might be the only one dancing?
7. Are you one of the last to leave, making the host nearly push you out the door or having the valet hand you your car keys with a reprimanding glare?

6–7 yes answers: Strike up the band, you are a Shining Star and any hostess would love for you to be a guest on her list. She can always count on you to keep the party from getting stale.

3–5 yes answers: You're what we call the "Filler guest." You add numbers to the party, possibly good conversation, and an extra pair of hands in case the hostess needs you. However, if you want to move from Filler to Star at the next bash, circulate more and open your mouth. But skip the weather bit. Ask yourself, "What do I want to know about this person?" The answer might give you the opportunity to add someone new to your social circle.

0–2 yes answers: Sorry to say it, but you're a Dud standing in the reserved pothole. You need to dig your way out of there and move into the Filler position. After that, Star status is just around the corner. Before the next party, find out who will be attending and pick up the phone. Chat about the party, place, and yes, what you will be wearing. Then, arrive early. By showing up on time, the crowd will be thin and you won't feel overwhelmed. This gives you the chance for chitchat with each new arrival cushioning your comfort zone, which sure beats walking into a mass of hyper bodies and loud noises.

Looking for Love

For single women, finding someone to build a relationship with isn't easy. Make an effort during February to connect with someone new, whether it be romantically or simply to further a friendship. And if you're thinking you just can't face the bar scene, keep reading to see how some other singles stumbled upon their sweethearts.

After Melissa's husband passed away, she never thought she'd remarry. And running a grocery cart into a good-looking guy at the supermarket wasn't her bag, even though several magazine articles recommended it as a way for a woman to meet the man of her dreams. With two teenagers, she figured most men wouldn't want a three-for-one deal. Tapping into her love of country music, Melissa and a friend began attending a country line dance held at a local center every Sunday evening. At first, Melissa stayed in the background like the typical wallflower. Then one night, she tried learning the steps to a particular dance by watching the guy in front of her. He noticed, slowed his pace, and gave Melissa simple instructions. Afterward, he struck up a conversation with her and, as they say, the rest is history.

Divorced after nine years, Jamie met Mr. Right at her class reunion. In high school, she had considered him Mr. Completely Wrong. Back then, she admits, he wasn't her type. But that night as the conversation flowed, Jamie found him to be compassionate and intriguing. Despite her preconceived notion, this time around, he was just what she was looking for.

Where else can single women meet potential partners? Join a co-ed volleyball or golf league. Go to lectures, discussion groups, community sporting events, or even charity bingos.

Want to try Internet dating? Web designer Cynthia Closkey offers an introduction to and ten tips for online dating.

Cynthia informs us that the banner ads for dating Web sites are tempting: just a few clicks to find your perfect match. But will they work for you?

Online match services are like personal ads in newspapers, except that they allow you to search for matches easily and anonymously. The bigger sites are generally best, because they have the largest pools of potential matches and are typically well run. Most sites allow you to search initially for free, so you can check whether there are many registered members in your area before subscribing.

Here are ten suggestions Cynthia recommends you follow.

1. Try it. Don't worry about whether people will recognize you. It's like any other dating—you're making yourself available, checking out all avenues.

2. When describing yourself, highlight what's unique about you. Lots of people enjoy long walks along the beach and want someone who is honest, so skip the obvious stuff and talk about your love of opera or passion for Three Stooges trivia. Unusual profiles are more interesting and memorable.

3. Stay in the positive. Talk more about what you do and what you're looking for rather than about what you're hoping to avoid.

4. Include a recent photo, preferably in color. The photo should be clear and, if possible, should show you smiling. Avoid glamorous shots, which look too polished. A nice vacation photo is perfect. (Make sure there are no previous boyfriends in the picture, obviously.)

5. Use the dating Web site's online message system—it will provide privacy. Don't offer your personal e-mail or phone number until you've exchanged a few messages and feel confident that you've found someone you want to meet in person. Some people try to avoid paying for the e-dating service by sneaking their e-mail or Web addresses into their write-ups. But if you write to prospects directly, you lose anonymity.

6. Don't play Ping-Pong with e-mail. One response per person per day is plenty. If you write back the instant you get a message, you aren't giving yourself the chance to think about it, and you can seem desperate (or just geeky). Wait a day before responding—and know that if someone is interested, there's no need to rush.

7. Don't feel pressured to write back to people who don't fit you.

There's little you can say that would make them feel better and often responses can be encouraging when that's not your intention.

8. Don't drag things out too long—you'll probably have a gut feeling after about three e-mails whether you're interested in meeting someone. It's easy to misunderstand what's meant in an e-mail message. Better to meet in person within two weeks of the initial contact, so you don't get emotionally involved with someone who you like online but not in person. (This does happen, strange as it may sound.)

9. When you decide to meet someone in person, select a public place. Coffee shops are great. Bars aren't quite as good, because alcohol can muddle your thinking. Don't go straight to a dinner date—expectations on both sides will be too high, and it'll be harder to get past initial nervousness.

10. If things don't work out with one person, keep trying. Be proud of yourself for extending and trying to connect with new people.

Cynthia says, "The rest is just dating."

Negative Relationships

More than likely, some people you talk to on the phone or in person make you feel exhausted or even crabby. Eventually, you come to recognize it as a pattern. Now, we're not suggesting you cut this person out of your life, especially if she is a neighbor, colleague, or relative. Instead, keep your contacts with her to a minimum. When you know you have to call her for some reason, do so five minutes before you're headed out the door. Then you won't be tied up long enough to have her negativity rub off on you. You can also call from your car on your cell phone (using a headset or earpiece)—planning it so that you arrive at your destination a few minutes later.

As a practice, minimize the time you spend with negative people and in not-so-positive situations—that can readily zap you of precious energy.

> **HIDDEN GEM:** Adopt a favorite song as your pick-me-up theme. Whatever music puts a swing in your step, keep it on hand for those days when you need it as a quick mood booster. And though it might sound frivolous, buy extra copies of the CD so you'll have one for your car, one for the portable CD player, and, of course, one for your home sound system. If music causes you to smile, your high spirits will be contagious, making others want to be around you.

Second Chance: Boot Camp

We're giving you a second chance to add exercise to your life. Consider doable, affordable options like walking, biking, or hiking. How often have you watched televised exercise shows—while sitting down? Well, toss aside the bonbons, tie up the cross trainers, and shake your bootie. Shoot to implement this plan once or twice a week. Then, as you increase your activity and progress, let the endorphins kick in and do the motivating for you.

Rather than adding the expense of child care while you work out, do something invigorating *with* the kids such as bowling, open gym, swimming, or ice skating. This works especially well for single moms and those with traveling husbands. Check local high schools and community centers for programs. If you can, make this a healthy, weekly addition to your schedule.

Take Five: A Breather Just for You

Even though you're busy connecting with others this month, take a breather and soothe yourself. Delve into a nonfiction book or explore a new Web site related to what's important to you: your inner self, the workplace, and family. The list of recommended reading is limitless. For example, the book *Write It Down, Make It Happen* by Henriette Anne Klauser encourages you to uncover what you want in life and shows you how to achieve it. Books like *Dare to Change Your Job and Your Life* by Carole Kanchier help you develop an action plan to take control of your career. And the Main Street Mom Web site (www.mainstreet-mom.com) features an interactive cyber community and informative articles for raising a family with traditional values.

Fortify yourself by escaping into the world of words that can offer you a fresh perspective on the sometimes-overwhelming roles we assume.

ONE-STEP-AT-A-TIME CHECKLIST

Date completed Or N/A   **Task**

_____ Obtain tax forms or make an appointment with your accountant.

_____ Prepare a data folder to hold college financial aid forms and personal information.

_____ Inquire about school tuition reduction programs.

_____ Make Meatball Soup.

_____ Stock up on reduced red and white paper products.

_____ Make Valentine's Day plans.

_____ Explore summer camps for kids.

_____ Research summer child care options.

_____ Cultivate a positive family environment by giving a small section of the house a makeover.

_____ Rediscover your other half.

_____ Have children reach out to older or distant family members.

_____ Attend a work-related conference or organize a workshop.

_____ Schedule a breakfast or lunch with coworkers.

_____ Celebrate Friendship Month with friends near and far.

_____ Single ladies: Make it a point to meet someone new.

_____ Minimize time spent with negative people.

_____ Add an exercise program or incorporate an invigorating activity into your schedule.

_____ Take a breather by delving into a nonfiction book or exploring a new just-for-you Web site.

Spring-Cleaning

As spring draws near, we're shedding our bulky layers of winter clothes for fresher, lighter ones. Since this puts us in the mode of switching gears, why not utilize the seasonal change to clear out needless clutter and mounding dust bunnies from our homes? In the purging process, your household will become more organized, therefore alleviating some of the franticness in your days.

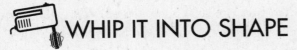 WHIP IT INTO SHAPE

We Must, We Must

As the winds of March blow through, so storms in the traditional task of spring-cleaning. Now, don't groan. You know it must be done—and just think of that satisfied feeling you'll have when all the scrubbing and scouring is behind you. We know the frantic woman can't spring-clean the way past generations did—polishing from top to bottom until the job is done. She's just too busy. Instead, she needs to chip away at the boulder before her, a little at a time.

First off, we've outlined a few methods to help shed your household of clutter, making what we call the ridding-out process a bit less painful. Fortunately, if you've cleared and sorted as we recommended in part one, you've relieved some of the clutter problem, making spring-cleaning that much easier. Here are a few more tips to alleviate the angst.

- If you tend to postpone dry-cleaning winter coats because you're expecting one last snowstorm, skip the task for now. Have them cleaned at the beginning of the winter season, instead. Sift through pocketed items before dropping coats off. (Don't worry. We'll remind you about this later in the year.)

- Start sorting through kids' winter clothes. If certain pieces barely fit your growing kids, don't hang on to them. It's safe, too, to give away any trendy colors and styles that probably won't last. Undoubtedly, something bolder and better will hit the stores by fall.

- If your stuff is not categorized, take the time to assign one drawer or shelf for one type of item. In the bathroom, start by placing toiletries on one shelf and first aid supplies on a different one; bath towels in one spot, washcloths and hand towels in another; and so on. In the bedroom, separate casual tops from workout clothes, assigning them different drawers. It sounds simple and logical, but how often do we think we're saving time by taking the clean pile of shirts and stuffing them into the same drawer? By segregating like this, the next time you're looking for your bathing suit, for example, it won't take you hours of searching— only to find it stashed among the sweatshirts and sweaters. This system of sorting works anywhere in the house, from attic to kitchen to basement.

- If you do have designated shelves, drawers, bins, or closets for certain categories of stuff and you're still brimming over the edges, eliminate unnecessary duplicates. You only need half a dozen sweatshirts, for example, not twenty. And how many baseball hats does one husband or son need? Toss the excess in your donation box and marvel at all the fresh, clean space you've created.

- Use selected spots as a limitation. When the shelf is full of DVDs or videos, for example, don't overflow onto another shelf. Give some away to libraries, preschools, or senior centers so that all the movies still fit on one allotted shelf.

Sparkle and Shine

Okay, we've put it off long enough—the hands-on cleaning. But who wants to spend her day dressed in old clothes, surrounded by an array of rubber gloves, chemical cleaners, and visions of Carol Burnett doing her one-woman act? We don't. However, cleaning doesn't have to be a dreaded chore you put off until it's nearly impossible to pull off. Shortcuts like these will aid in shrinking the strife.

- As you clean, carry a light box or empty laundry basket to collect misplaced items as you go. Yes, you've heard it before but probably neglected to follow through with it. Instead, you find yourself in a frenzy by taking an out-of-place item to another room, then straightening in that room before finishing the first. By gathering items in the basket, you can remain in one room at a time, allowing you to work in a more productive, orderly fashion.
- When you enter a room, hang a small plastic grocery bag on the doorknob. As you encounter broken items, garbage, and throwaways, you'll have a convenient place to pitch them.
- Start in one corner of the room as you're wiping and polishing, and work your way around. As you go, scrub from top to bottom in each section so you're not pushing dust from dirty areas to clean ones, making them dirty again. This helps to control backtracking and allows you to sweep through the process in no time flat.
- Clean ceiling fans with a damp sponge to soak up the dust rather than have it fly all over the room.
- Use a new sponge mop dipped in a bucket of warm water containing a tablespoon of baking soda per half gallon to wash down walls. For a quicker, drier wall-wiping approach, use your mop-

in-a-box contraption with replaceable dust cloths such as Swiffer or Clorox Ready Mop.

- To get rid of the edging of dust that collects on the rug around the room's perimeter, while you're wiping the baseboards, take another damp cloth and brush the indentation where the carpet and woodwork meet, pulling the dust out to where it can be vacuumed away. This saves you from bending over a second time, looking like the Hunchback of Notre Dame.
- Vacuum the dust from the fireplace bricks with a Shop-Vac.

Kitchen Sparkle and Shine

Take the time to clean the kitchen cabinets, drawers, and pantry.

- *Cabinets:* Sort through dishes, cups, glasses, pots, pans, and trays. Get rid of all dishware you don't use like logo-mugs, take-out cups from restaurants, and gas station glasses that tend to accumulate over the years. Take all stockpots, party trays, and serving platters you use only a couple of times a year and store in a covered box or bin in the basement or garage. Empty all contents in each cabinet, rather than just shuffle them around. When you're actually holding that bulky, archaic food processor in your hand, you'll be more likely to give it away. If you feel leery of tossing perfectly good appliances and dishware, donate the items. Soup kitchens, senior centers, fire halls, and shelters appreciate such donations. Sort through your cookbooks, too. Pass along the newer ones you haven't used, and probably never will, to a new bride, first-time apartment dweller, or college student. The older volumes can be contributed to a used-book sale at your branch of the public library. Once the debris has been thinned out, wash cabinet shelves and doors, inside and out, then restock, placing infrequently used items at the back and favorites in the front, of course.
- *Drawers:* The same goes for the drawers in the kitchen. If you

find you're always rearranging junk in the gadget drawer just to get it to close, it's time to eliminate some of the bulk. Remember, you need only two or three spatulas and rubber scrapers. Store oversized barbeque grilling tools elsewhere, rather than have them take up valuable space in the kitchen. A good place is in a rubberized, waterproof container near the grill. Now is the time to get rid of that potato masher and flour sifter you never use, too. Again, offer donations to nonprofit groups or charities hosting flea markets. Now on to the cleaning. Ever try to wash out a drawer, only to trap all those stubborn crumbs in the far back corner? If cornered crumbs cause you trouble, vacuum each drawer with your vacuum cleaner attachment hose first, before getting the crumby matter wet. Then, just as you did with the empty cabinets, wash the drawers both inside and out, wipe dry, and restock.

- *Pantry:* When you open your pantry, are you looking at boxes of stuffing mix and instant mashed potatoes that have been there forever? Have you hoarded all sorts of imported *this* and gourmet *that* that have gone unprepared for some time? Sort through and throw out those miscellaneous cans of whatnot or donate them to a food bank if not expired. And if you're worried about Murphy's Law slapping you in the face with the need for one of those items soon, not to worry. Tell yourself you can repurchase a fresh supply of whatever you need with one quick trip to the grocery store, if that time *ever* comes.

Don't forget to apply these tactics to the bottom drawer of your oven and the top of your refrigerator, if you store in these areas.

Professional coach and organizer Barbara Schwarck offers these kitchen organizing tips just for you. "Feel free to play," she says, "and make sure that you make them work for you."

- Group and store like items in categories, near where they're used.
- Cover the back (inside) of the cabinet doors with cork tile. Keep

your grocery list, freezer inventory, coupons, take-out menus, and/or messages here. This frees the fridge of clutter.

- Put cup hooks on the back (inside) of cabinet doors. (Be careful not to screw through the door to the front side!) The hooks are great for hanging smaller items like measuring spoons and cups.
- Separate baking sheets, wire cooling racks, and other flat pans to make it easier to grab just one. A plate rack (the type that stands the plates on end) works great.
- Don't stack mixing bowls too high. It's a lot of trouble to unstack them to grab the middle one, if that's the one you use most often.
- When stacking casserole dishes, turn the bottom one upside down, then stack the next size on top of it. It's easier to remove a dish this way than if you had to un-nest them.
- Wrap a kitchen towel around a section of newspaper and line your refrigerator veggie drawers. The paper will soak up any moisture, keeping veggies crisp.

Barbara continues with several more general tips for keeping yourself on track. "Many of us would like to be more organized," she says. "Yes, even the people who are *way more* organized than life itself would like to be more organized." Barbara believes that wherever you are on the scale, there's always room for a better, faster, and more efficient way to run your life. Why? Because being unorganized can be draining and often it is a waste of time. And, while you are filing things over and over again or feeling bad about the garage, you could be doing something else. You could focus on goals you want to achieve or just have more time to play. Being organized is a self-esteem booster.

Here are Barbara's nine basic steps to help you become more organized:

1. Pick a small project and make a date with yourself.
2. Set aside at least half an hour, but no more than two hours, for the first session.
3. Work on it several times a week in small increments (between twenty and sixty minutes).

4. Find a support person to do this with.
5. Create a vision and a plan for the area.
6. Decide what needs to happen first (de-clutter, organize, maintain).
7. Come up with criteria for "releasing" things.
8. Think about what kinds of systems you may need and what will work for you.
9. Create a plan to maintain your systems.

HIDDEN GEM: Need some extra money? Reach into the back of the freezer and pantry and use up what's there. For one week, maybe two, you might not need to buy groceries other than milk, bread, and fresh fruit. During this same time period, skip those regular fast-food stops, too. Try this tactic before you roll up your sleeves and get dirty in the kitchen. Not only will you diminish the surplus, but you can spend the leftover grocery money on yourself. And wouldn't that be a surprising change?

Now that the excess has been weeded out from all your kitchen storage space (and you have a handle on how to take an organized approach), here are several more cleaning tips to help you wash and wipe with ease.

- In the kitchen, make up a 25/75 solution of bleach and water and pour into a marked spray bottle. Use on your countertops and table, especially after handling raw chicken, meat, or eggs, all of which can carry bacterial dangers. Run through the dishwasher all plates, knives, and cutting boards that come in contact with these foods, as well. (Caution: Keep this solution out of the reach of children and pets.)
- Keep dishwashing liquid in a pump dispenser by the faucet next to your antibacterial hand soap. That way, you're not bending and searching in the cabinet beneath the sink several times a day

when preparing to wash the dishes. Some brands of dishwashing liquid are sold in such pump containers. If the types available don't happen to be your favorites, purchase a decorative dispenser separately and fill with whatever brand you choose.

- Use cotton swabs to clean the crud from the narrow vent slats of the microwave.
- Dip the fan filter above your cooking range (found underneath your built-in microwave) in sudsy water and rinse well. Air-dry before replacing.

SNIPPET: Speaking of cleaning solutions, take a wild guess what you'd use if you had to bathe an elephant. Give up? Murphy's Oil Soap is the product most commonly employed to wash elephants in captivity. That gives new meaning to the phrase "tickling the ivories," doesn't it?

As you're thoroughly cleaning the kitchen, and you're stuck there for most of the day anyway, take advantage of our double-duty suggestions.

- Toss a roast in the slow cooker with some chopped potatoes, carrots, onions, celery, and beef stock.
- Simmer chili, spaghetti sauce, or soup stock on the stove.
- Roast a turkey or turkey breast in the oven.

Start these self-simmering dinners before you begin your one-woman act. By performing these double-duty tasks, not only will you have an organized kitchen, but you'll enjoy home-cooked meals for the rest of the week.

Bathroom Sparkle and Shine

Now that the kitchen is in tip-top shape, it's time to snap on the rubber gloves and hit the bathrooms.

- If after you scrub the shower walls you find them covered in soap scum two days later, try tossing that bar soap out the window and switching to liquid bath gels. Then for cleanup, all you need to do is spritz down the walls with a shower cleanser and wipe clean. Even if you have grout and tile, there's no more scrubbing, honest.

- To make chrome fixtures in the bathroom gleam shiny and bright, use a solution of Spic and Span to wash off soap scum and toothpaste stains. Then, rinse and wipe dry.

- Pull out all of the contents from your medicine cabinet and vanity. Wipe down the inside and the shelves of both. Discard outdated items. Organize contents into caddies or bins (if you haven't already done so) before you stow them away again.

- Take the cover off of the bathroom's exhaust fan. (Usually, you can just unscrew this, but make sure it is turned off first.) Clean the accumulated crud off of the blades, around the outside of the fan, and on the inside of the cover.

- Pop the shower doors out of their tracks and place standing upright on an old towel. (If weather permits, take them outside for easier cleaning.) Use an old toothbrush or a small dish brush and clean the inside track on all four sides. Scrub both sides of the shower doors and all the metal trim.

- While the shower doors are off, now is the time to replace the caulking on the tub. Remove the old caulking first. (Once you find a loose piece, you can pull the rest until all of it is off.) Apply new caulking, according to the manufacturer's directions, around the tub, showerhead, and faucet. Make sure you wait the recommended period of time before you turn on the water. Replace shower doors afterward.

- Clean and polish vanity door handles.

- Check the bolts around the bottom of the toilet to see if they might need to be replaced.

- For the toilet that wiggles a bit when bumped or jerked, replace the wax ring (available at home improvement stores) under the unit. What happens if yours needs to be replaced but you decide to let it go for a while? Well, how should we say this? Look out below!

- While you're checking out the bathroom fixtures, don't forget to replace washers on the faucets, too.

Warm Weather Preparation

As we take in the warmer breezes of spring, we must prepare our abode for the upcoming outdoor season.

- Clean window and door screens by removing them and scrubbing lightly with a brush using mild soapy water. Squirt screens with a hose and allow to air-dry before repositioning them in the window frames.
- Pull out or uncover and clean patio furniture and grill.
- Rake stray leaves left over from late fall to ensure that grass will grow in evenly.
- If you can afford to, have the lawn professionally aerated or rent an aerating machine. Share the cost by obtaining one on a weekend when friends or neighbors can aerate, too. Then everyone can benefit from the process, giving the grass roots more room to expand and allowing for the spreading of the nutrient additives that will help produce a healthy, green lawn.
- Till the soil in your garden and the mulch in your landscaping beds to allow the spring growth to sprout.
- Edge landscaping beds by hand or using an edging machine to preserve that manicured look you paid so much for. Too often, frantic homeowners will allow a year or two to go by without edging and, as a result, the once crisp, clean border of the landscaping bed becomes a sloppy, floppy uneven groove.

By preparing for spring with the first sprouting crocus, you'll be able to relax and enjoy those sun-filled days ahead.

A Splash of Freshness

As a bonus for all that hard work your little patch of earth brings you, would you love to add a fountain, waterfall, or healing pond to your backyard decor but don't know how to go about it? Mother of four Tammy Schneider and her husband, Matt, turned their average backyard into an exotic wonder. "I was looking for a unique way for all of us to enjoy the yard," Tammy says. "The water is soothing to look at while sipping my morning coffee. And after the kids wake up, I love watching them scramble all around it—and sometimes *through* it." Tammy says that the change gives her home a more relaxing sense despite her usual frantic pace.

The couple used a professional pond designer to do the job, but there are many do-it-yourself diagrams and kits available at home improvement stores and on the Internet. All you need is a little money and a big willingness to get the job done.

Tax Time

Gather forms, receipts, and other information needed to fill out your annual income tax form. Complete the process yourself or, as discussed in the February chapter, make an appointment to have yours prepared professionally.

Reminder Alert

Flip your bed mattresses today or else you'll be sleeping in a groove in months to come. And that'll only add to your frantic woes, introducing you to a new expense—chiropractor bills.

🕊️ DARLING LITTLE ANGELS (AND THE WHOLE BLISSFUL BUNCH)

Holiday Happenings: Spring Flings

In the first week of March, plan your St. Patrick's Day celebration, making sure everyone has something green to wear—even you honorary Irish recruits. Then, work on Easter or Passover gifts, festivities, and attire. Assemble the family's holiday outfits, from socks to jewelry for each occasion. List in your Frantic Journal any items that must be purchased. To save time, gather all needed goods in one trip to the store, rather than drag the task out over the next several weeks. While you're shopping, pick up the necessary party foods, gifts, and Easter basket stuffers.

Do you need a few nonperishable filler ideas for the Easter baskets? Delight kids with these on Easter morning.

- *For younger tykes:* miniature cars and dolls, bubbles, jacks and ball, jump ropes, sidewalk chalk, inflatable pool toys, and sand pail and shovel.
- *For older kids:* shampoo, deodorant, brushes and combs, lip gloss, nail polish, fast-food and movie gift certificates, CDs, prepaid phone cards, stationery, stamps, wallets, and disposable cameras.
- *For all ages:* art, craft, or school supplies, flower/herb seeds and pots, books, bookmarks, magazines, videos or DVDs, novelty toothbrushes, flavored toothpaste, bath gel, fun socks, T-shirts, fancy shoelaces, flip-flops, hair scrunchies and clips, sunglasses, and baseball caps.

Maple Syrup Festivals

Maple syrup festivals take place in March and early April when sap is harvested and turned into a velvety, sweet topping. Kids love to participate in this back-to-nature event. To find locations, dates, and times of festivals near you, search on the Internet using one of the larger sites like google.com or dogpile.com. Type "maple syrup festival" in the search box and delight in all the festivities you'll find.

Craft Time

Some women love to buy or make crafts, while others hear the word and cringe. Whatever your preference, National Craft Month will go on with or without you. But why not use it as an incentive to dig out that project you started eons ago? You probably came across it while you were cleaning closets. If not, consider doing something that will enhance your decor like the latest method of painting walls using plastic bags, feathers, or sponges. If you can, turn it into a family venture.

If you'd rather attempt a smaller assignment, check out a specialty store near you. Many craft retailers across the country sponsor special classes, demonstrations, and "make it then take it" projects for adults and children throughout the month. Some stores advertise a new theme each week to highlight a different craft category—featuring projects to interest just about everyone.

The National Craft Association (www.craftassoc.com), Hobby Industry Association (www.hobby.org), and I-craft.com (www.i-craft.com) offer contests and post calendars complete with ideas and instructions. Are you interested in earning extra income from that hobby of yours? The Hobby Industry Association offers a free arts and crafts newsletter, membership kit, and informational booklet called *How to Turn Your Arts and Crafts into Cash*.

While you're cutting, gluing, or sewing, why not get a jump-start on the holiday season by making Christmas presents and thank-you gifts? Yes, it's early, but if you start now, you won't be as overwhelmed with the task later in the year. To motivate yourself, ask a friend to join you in the endeavor. You can meet weekly, for example, at a pre-arranged time, working together and enjoying each other's company while accomplishing something productive.

Or for those of you wanting to raise funds for a local organization, arrange an old-fashioned quilting bee. For instance, if you walk into Ann Breton's formal dining room, instead of fine china and goblets decorating the table, you'll see the latest community project. Ann and her friends gather weekly to work on a handmade quilt that, upon completion, is auctioned off for charity. The quilting friends have raised more than $2,000 per quilt for local communities and schools and have shared a bond that goes far beyond gossiping over the back-yard fence.

☞ ALL ABOUT YOU

Interoffice Memo:
Work Sparkle and Shine

Spring-cleaning shouldn't stop when you leave home. At the office, purge piles from your desk and filter through files, too. Don't know how to begin? Try these suggestions to get you started.

- Staple business cards to index cards with ample room to jot notes and dates of discussions. Arrange alphabetically in an inexpensive file holder.
- Remove all outdated files from your work space, desk, or filing cabinet and place in an appropriate container. Keep in a designated storage space assigned by your employer. While sorting, toss all newspaper and journal articles you've saved as relevant to your work. Chances are good that, by now, there have been more current studies outdating your accumulated information anyway. And with the Internet at most everyone's fingertips, such paper piles are deemed unnecessary.
- Type information from business cards directly into your pocket PC or computer address book as soon as you receive it. Don't wait until you have fifty cards to enter. Once the data is saved, resist all temptation to store the stack in your Rolodex or drawer. Toss the cards to reduce redundancy and desktop clutter.

Take Five: Massages,
No Longer Frivolous

Since it seems like all you've been doing lately is clearing out, systematizing, and cleaning, treat yourself to a rubdown. Better yet, have a massage party. Invite three friends over for a chair-massage get-together. Don't shake your head at this as an extravagance. Often, massage therapists will offer a discount when visiting a home or office for more than one person. To boot, there are other perks to having your muscles kneaded.

Physical therapist Jen Komorowski shares these five health benefits. Professional massage therapy . . .

1. Increases circulation.
2. Decreases muscle spasms.
3. Relieves pain.
4. Reduces inflammation.
5. Stimulates lymph glands—the workhorses of the immune system.

"Massage really gets the healing juices flowing," Jen says. "It's a therapy that's no longer just for the elite or the disabled. It's a healthy practice available to everyone."

Under the Umbrella

Did you know that March is National Umbrella Month? How many times have you been caught in the rain without one of those nifty contraptions? Or are you embarrassed with every downpour because of your stained, bent, or broken "umbie"? Now is the time to make sure you have a decent-looking, working umbrella in the car, in the foyer closet, and at your workplace. You might even decide to toss a small, collapsible bumbershoot in your briefcase or purse.

Why is it important to inspect your umbrellas? No one knows better than Eleanor Mrozowski. One Saturday morning, Eleanor decided to treat herself to a day of browsing in the exclusive downtown shops. With a gloomy sky and rain in the air, she reached for her umbrella before heading to the metro. When the bus stopped in front of the shops, she popped up her umbrella as she exited. And there she stood in horror facing the entire Rolex/Gucci crowd. Why? Because her young son's Scooby-Doo undies had dropped out of the umbrella and onto the pavement in front of her!

ONE-STEP-AT-A-TIME CHECKLIST

Date
completed
Or N/A   **Task**

_____ Sort clutter and designate drawers, shelves, and closets
for specific items.

_____ Scrub each room from top to bottom.

_____ De-clutter, scour, and organize kitchen cabinets, drawers, and pantry.

_____ Scour bathrooms from top to bottom.

_____ Prepare yard. Clean screens and outdoor furniture for
warmer weather enjoyment.

_____ Add a bonus such as an outdoor pond or fountain.

_____ Gather tax data and file your return. Or make an
appointment with your accountant.

_____ Flip your bed mattresses.

_____ Plan St. Patrick's Day, Easter, or Passover outfits and celebrations.

_____ Attend a maple syrup festival.

_____ Start a new craft project.

_____ Clean out your desk and work files.

_____ Treat yourself to a massage.

_____ Replace damaged umbrellas.

(Note: See our "Spring-Cleaning Checklist" in "A Wee Bit More,"
part three.)

Meeting Deadlines

April brings lots of showers, so the old saying goes. But for most of us, it delivers downpours of deadlines. Yes, it's the time of year to hand over your dues to Uncle Sam. This month is all about meeting those designated due dates with an organized approach, if not a smile. Follow the tips in this chapter to keep you on track when spending your refund check, confirming summer child care, and giving of yourself through volunteering.

 WHIP IT INTO SHAPE

Central Air

Have your central air conditioning system professionally checked and cleaned. Change disposable air and furnace filters. Or squirt the dust off with a hose and air-dry if you have the permanent ones. Adjust the humidifier setting to a lower level for the upcoming summer season.

Tax Time

This is your last chance to fill out income tax forms before the April 15th deadline, unless you want the IRS to come knocking on your front door. If you just can't make it, file for an extension.

Tax adviser Tim Schneider reminds us, "If you aren't ready to file your taxes, you must estimate your liability as best you can." How? Tim suggests you compile your sources of income for the year, then schedule your deductions to come up with a close estimate of taxes due. Send a completed extension form (available at your local IRS office, the post office, or online at www.irs.gov) and a check for the approximated tax amount to the IRS on or before April 15th. "If you neglect to send in your estimated tax on time," Tim says, "be prepared to pay the IRS a huge chunk of change."

Quarterly Taxes

For those of you who have to pay your taxes quarterly (if you don't have them deducted from your paycheck), pull out your checkbook now. Your federal and state income taxes are due by April 15th, and your local wage tax is probably due by the 30th.

JOTS & THOUGHTS QUIZ
Your Financial Self

Have money worries creased your forehead lately? Is this an ongoing concern or a new one for you? Find out whether you're a "Moneybags," "Change Jingler," or the "Empty Pockets" type by answering the following questions with yes or no. Let's see if you're in the black, red, or green.

1. Do you feel financially frazzled, never knowing if your money is here, there, or everywhere?
2. When you write a check, do you cross your fingers hoping there's enough in the account to cover it?
3. Are you never quite sure of the current balances on your credit cards?

4. Do you need to curb your spending but just can't seem to change your ways?

5. Have you ever been caught without enough money in the checkout line while onlookers try to offer you their spare change?

6. In general, do you buy things you can't afford and certainly don't need?

7. Do you periodically remind yourself that you are in dire need of setting up a budget?

0–1 yes answers: Step right up, Moneybags. You could moonlight giving others financial advice. You're one of the gifted who balance their checkbooks monthly and never get socked with a late fee. You're the envy among your friends.

2–4 yes answers: Stop riding the fence, Change Jingler. You're one of those people who has some spare change, but not dollar bills. You're rolling your pennies several days before the next paycheck comes around. Unfortunately, those "too good to pass up deals" have made a dent in your budget. Make a decision now to jump on board the financially wise train and chug away from your money-draining habits.

5–7 yes answers: Slow down, Empty Pockets, or your family will never be able to throw you a retirement party. That's right. You'll look like Rip Van Winkle toting your briefcase as you hop on the bus on your ninetieth birthday. Hopefully, you'll be able to flash the senior citizen discount card. But, if you start using one or two of the tips listed in this chapter, within months you'll be moving into the Change Jingler position. Then, follow the rest of the tips, and it won't be long before you'll be able to claim the first-place title of Moneybags.

Where's the Money?

If you're one of the unfortunate ones who owe Uncle Sam, do you know how you're going to come up with the funds? Are you concerned about how to stretch your paycheck, in general? Does it seem to go out the door more quickly than it comes in? Well, let us help you discover new ways to recapture some of the cash that's silently slipping through your fingers.

Some of your spending habits might have originated because you work outside of the home or are continually rushing from one errand to the next. These practices might be costing you unnecessary money loss—money you could be spending on something you need, or want, or better yet, you could be saving it for a more secure future. But how can you stop senseless spending? Pinpoint your daily buying habits by writing down where every single penny goes for just a week. If you can, encourage your husband and kids to participate by handing them a pocket notebook or computer-generated chart. "I've heard this before," you say. Yes, we know you have. But did you actually attempt to carry it out? Well, today is the day to hide the wallet and pull out the pen.

Once the week is up and the data have been gathered, examine how much money is going to what outlets. Categorize them as "Necessities," "Entertainment," and "Miscellaneous." Are you paying late fees for library and video rentals? Are you buying treats and small toys for the kids on your way home from work because you feel guilty being away from them all day? Do you make daily stops at the local coffee shop for muffins and coffee? Or are you in the habit of eating lunch out several times a week? Do you give the kids money for vending machines rather than packing drinks and snacks for the car? Every wasted dollar, two, or three should instead be put toward paying Uncle Sam, getting that much-needed home improvement, taking a vacation, or padding your savings account.

What, it's only a dollar, you say? Well, in a few days' time, those dollars become twenties, and by the end of the month those twenties are hundreds! A two-dollar cup of coffee a day grows to $730 by year's end. So fill your to-go mug from the pot at home—and savor the savings as you sip on the run.

Now, scan your broader financial picture. Take a look at your credit cards, loans, and home mortgage. If you carry a balance, what interest rate do you have? When have you last checked the costs of long-distance telephone calls, cable or Internet service, and insurance premiums? Do you have a choice of utility providers? By doing your own detective work, you might not have to scrape and scrounge come next April 15th.

Financial Aid Deadline

As we discussed in the February chapter, the financial aid application deadline for college students is just around the corner, so don't wait. Gather the information you need (or pull it from your designated accordion folder), fill in the blanks, and drop it in the mail, today.

HIDDEN GEM: Have you been pitched so many options regarding saving for your kids' college years that you feel like one of those bobble-head dolls? Upromise Inc., based in Needham, Massachusetts, has an easy answer for you. The company has solicited manufacturers and merchants to contribute a portion of your everyday purchases to your child's higher education. After you register, each time you use a particular credit card or grocery store's frequent shopper card and buy certain products, funds will be credited to your Upromise account. In addition to the more than one hundred chains participating in the Upromise program, other retailers including gasoline stations, long-distance telephone companies, booksellers, and restaurants are also joining in—most offering contributions of 1 to 5 percent. Some, however, will contribute as much as 10 percent of your purchase total to your account. For more details or to sign up, visit www.Upromise.com. The Web site also links to a selection of no-load funds into which your account balance can be transferred automatically each quarter.

An Essential Expense

The time has come. You just can't put it off any longer. Is your living room sofa sprouting springs faster than your flower beds? Or does the wobbly leg annoy you every time you place something on the table? Regardless of what has put a damper on your replacing the piece—either the time to browse for one you like or the money to purchase it—these tips will help you to get what you want at a price that won't break you.

- Visit the clearance rooms of larger retailers. They're usually tucked in a remote corner of the showroom, but they house a most interesting mix of merchandise. The pieces are on sale for a number of reasons. Someone might have bought a sofa but not the matching love seat. Or another customer might have chosen the entire bedroom suite minus the vanity or mirror. The clearance room will be full of reduced leftovers or floor samples that, when properly placed, can add affordable flair to any decor. And as a bonus, if you know anyone with a truck or van, you can save even more by picking up your own merchandise and avoiding delivery fees.

- Watch for sales. It used to be that furniture only went on sale once or twice a year. Now, however, it seems there's a great offering every few weeks or so. Keep your eyes open for free financing discounts that are often advertised on television, in the newspaper, and through snail-mail flyers. That way, you can enjoy your new china cabinet while you save the money to pay for it. Be sure to meet the payment deadline, however, as hefty interest charges will zap you on the deadline date and beyond.

- Research furniture made in North Carolina. Because a large percentage of the nation's fine furniture is manufactured there, the state has earned its title as the Furniture Capital of the World. And because the markup on these expertly crafted items is high by the time it reaches the hands of retailers, you can save a significant amount of money by skipping the local distributors and ordering directly from the North Carolina–based stores.

Consumer Nancy Bartholomew added a stop in High Point, North Carolina, to the end of her family's East Coast beach vacation. "We budgeted one and a half days for furniture shopping," Nancy says, "but it was nowhere near enough time." The experience was almost overwhelming, at first, taking in the size of each store, the broad selection, the unbeatable prices, and the exceptional quality of the furniture.

Nancy compiled this list of tips and information for those of us who are interested in saving money when buying top-quality furniture.

- The stores are not outlets, nor do they carry "seconds"-grade furniture. All products featured are manufactured with excellence and are guaranteed by top-of-the-line furniture producers.
- Because the showrooms are not individual manufacturers' warehouses, each store carries a vast array of pieces from various producers and designers—far more than most local retailers in your area could likely carry.
- Upon your arrival, a designer greets you and becomes your sales associate.
- Using price comparisons made via the Internet or with brands and styles seen in your local stores, you can recognize unbeatable discounted savings—especially if you do your pricing homework before you go.
- Credit cards are not accepted, so be sure to have your checkbook in hand.
- The stores close their doors early on Saturdays and, for now, are not open on Sundays. Plan for weekday shopping to get the most out of your visit.
- By taking with you a notebook and pen, a wish list, accurate room measurements, room color samples, and fabric swatches, you will be well prepared.

"High Point is a very exciting place to visit," Nancy concludes, "especially if you're serious about buying high-quality furniture."

Another avid furniture consumer, Patty Steinle, furnished nearly her entire home with pieces purchased through North Carolina. "You don't need to visit the actual stores," Patty says. "I handled everything right from my hometown." It used to be that you could visit your local showroom, obtain style numbers, and order over the phone. "That's not the case anymore," Patty tells us. "Retailers are now changing reference numbers, making that more difficult." The designers at stores in North Carolina, however, are very efficient. If you befriend a good one, he or she can often identify a piece for you based solely on your description, as long as you know the manufacturer. Usually, they'll e-mail or fax you photographs for confirmation. "Best of all," Patty says, "most often, you only need to pay the shipping fees once—even if you reject an item and return it three times."

To give long-distance shopping a try, check out this handful of North Carolina furniture companies: Rose Furniture Company (www.rosefurniture.com, phone: 336-886-6050); Rose Clearance Center (www.roseclearance.com, phone: 336-886-8525); and FLS Furnitureland South (www.furniturelandsouth.com, phone: 336-841-4328). Go ahead and make those designer dreams come true.

Joinery and Grain

Custom woodwork expert and adventure racer Gordon Giffin says there are two primary elements in furniture construction that determine the quality of the manufacturing. They are the joinery and the grain. Gordon offers the following information and guidelines.

- The joinery, of course, is how the connection is formed where two pieces of wood come together. Most consumers know to look for dovetail joinery in drawers, for example, which employs male/female–type bonding. But in the absence of dovetail joinery, lots of prefab pieces are glued. At points where constant strain is a factor, such as drawer fronts, this glue can let go. Other manufacturers use screws in such applications. Though screwed joints are somewhat stronger, they can still be stripped with repeated use and release. It's essential, then, to the piece's structure that both glue and screws be used to ensure the most stable, reliable construction.
- The second primary element in assessing furniture quality is the wood grain. Check the grain of the wood—see that it runs in the proper direction for the application. In a credenza, for example, the

grain should run the width of the piece (from left to right), not the depth (from front to back). This is true for both cabinetry and fine furniture. Better-quality furniture features grains that enhance the appearance of the piece and add to its beauty.

- Chairs generally receive constant wear and tear and should be exceptionally well constructed. Use close scrutiny when purchasing. Look for cross rungs that are glued and screwed as opposed to those that are just glued. Ready-to-assemble chairs don't ordinarily feature such a distinction.

- Direct sunlight can affect the look of wood over time. When purchasing furniture, take care to note the application. In other words, take into consideration where the piece will be placed. Cherry wood, for example, when positioned in direct sunlight will turn dark over time. So if you cover a cherry dining room table with a tablecloth for an extended period, the top will remain lighter in shade while the exposed legs will turn to a deep red color.

- Furniture finishes are excellent nowadays, so general care has become quite easy. The only factor you still want to limit is furniture's worst enemy—you guessed it—water.

Gordon summarizes by telling us that looking for quality joinery (using both glue and screws) can be compared to rock climbing. "You wouldn't want to trust your life to one safety device," Gordon says. "So don't compromise the quality of the furniture you buy, either." By paying close attention to such simple details, you'll purchase well-crafted pieces that can be passed in your family from one generation to the next.

SNIPPET: Did you wonder about how ladies of yesteryear squeezed their humongous hoop skirts into itty-bitty chairs? Well, they didn't. That's why the so-called courting seat was designed. Later, it was made with two sections and eventually morphed into what's known today as the love seat.

> **HIDDEN GEM:** The American Furniture Manufacturers Association hosts a Web site to help consumers learn about furniture and how to buy it. The site, www.FindYourFurniture.com, features room-by-room checklists and general shopping tips in addition to posting current information about furniture styles. Links to hundreds of manufacturers' Web sites are listed. Visitors can search by product, style, room, and price.

Buy Now, Pay Later

Some companies offer free financing to coincide with the arrival of tax refunds. Therefore, it's a good time of year to buy such big-ticket items as pianos, cars, and furniture. With the buy-now, pay-later option, why not use the company's money over the next twelve, eighteen, or thirty-six months? But you might have heard horror stories about exorbitant back-interest charges if you don't pay off the loan before the end of the promotional period. How can you keep this from happening to you?

- Mark the due date. After you've purchased your dining room suite, computer upgrade, or that much-needed Jacuzzi, ensure that you're not socked with a fee and back interest accumulated at an astronomically high rate. To steer clear of this expensive mistake, mark the deadline on your Post-It and Pay-It Planner. Include the telephone number of the finance company so you can call for the correct payoff amount when ready. Track the amount of money you've paid throughout the year because sometimes the company may quote you an incorrect balance.
- Divide the total amount of the sale by the number of finance-free months offered minus two—to obtain the monthly fee you should pay. Why minus two? While this will increase your payment by a small amount, you'll have paid off the balance long before the due date comes around.

Why go for the free-financing option, then, if there are vital precautions to take? Because you can enjoy great prices with a cushion of time to pay the bill, free of penalty charges. By simply tallying your payments, you will become a smart buyer and a happy camper.

Pet Report

Do you have a four-legged member of the family? If so, professional dog groomer Sharon Fitzgerald reminds us it's time to begin administering your pet's heartworm medication, if you don't already do so on a round-the-calendar basis. The drug can be purchased from your veterinarian or online. Of course, you'll need to check with your vet before administering any dosage (which is calculated by weight). Those pesky disease-carrying mosquitoes will soon be hatching and making their way through your furry friend's coat, so grab that medicine and prevent the problem, now.

DARLING LITTLE ANGELS (AND THE WHOLE BLISSFUL BUNCH)

Holiday Happenings: Mom's Day

If Mom is local, make Mother's Day plans including brunch or dinner either out or at home. If your mother lives long distance, be sure to buy cards and gifts and get them in the mail on time. If she is no longer living, do something in remembrance of her, such as planting her favorite flower or vegetable, or baking her special recipe and sharing stories about her with your children or spouse.

Ever feel like wiping Mother's Day off the calendar because you still have to make beds, settle disputes, and clean up spills? Why not develop, design, and execute a new way—your way—to celebrate this special occasion and make it an annual activity?

How about a few suggestions to warm up your thinking cap?

- Enjoy a "moms only" lunch or tea with other women you know. Make reservations at a Victorian tearoom, an inn, or an upscale restaurant. Make a pact to talk about something other than the kids.
- Similarly, plan a "chick flick" night. Rent romantic comedies or girl-power films you know everyone will love. Order take-out Asian food or have a pig-out potluck supper. Who cares about the calories? You'll probably laugh them off anyway.
- Enjoy the thrill of roller coasters and the taste of cotton candy once again. Utilize this more family-oriented option by visiting an amusement park for the day. Not only will you enjoy a fun celebration, but you'll miss the heat wave of summer and also the hordes of people that come with it. Invite parents, siblings, aunts, uncles, and cousins. If the park supplies a picnic pavilion, take refreshments and go early to reserve your spot. This outing provides a designated meeting place for everyone and saves money on refreshments, too.
- For the nature lover, go to the zoo, aviary, or conservatory. Pack a gourmet lunch and stop by your favorite scenic spot on the way home. Don't forget the hand wipes for use after feeding and petting the animals.
- Partake in an event such as the Komen Pittsburgh Race for the Cure held every year on Mother's Day. Although this is a way to donate to a worthy cause, for some the race has become an annual tradition with three and four generations participating.

SNIPPET: The Susan G. Komen Breast Cancer Foundation, established by Nancy Brinker to honor the memory of her sister who died of breast cancer at the age of thirty-six, is one of the nation's largest private funders of research dedicated solely to breast cancer. The Komen Race for the Cure, the grandest series of its kind, is presented in 116 cities in the United States and five cities in other parts of the world. In 2002, more than one million walkers and runners had participated.

Whatever you choose to do, consider making it a yearly affair. And remember, if your Sunday is usually booked, you have the option of scheduling this event the weekend before, the day before, or the weekend after Mother's Day.

Second Chance: Summer Child Care Options

This is your second chance to make summer child care arrangements. If you merely skimmed the information provided in our February chapter, we're dishing it up again. How will you direct the care of your little ones during their hiatus? Especially if you work outside the home, don't put off making day care decisions any longer.

- Inquire about flextime. Might you be able to go to work an hour earlier or shorten your lunch period to get home to the family sooner? Examine your schedule and work to free up some time to be with the kids.
- Ask friends and family whether they know of any college students in their religious community or neighborhood who would be willing to come to your home to watch your children for the summer months. If the student has a car, she can drive to your house in the morning, allowing your kids to sleep in. This also gives her the freedom to take the children on day trips to the park or zoo, or to scheduled activities. Be prepared to pay the student what she would make elsewhere, or more. Aren't your kids worth it? And, as always, be sure the student comes with a solid recommendation from someone you know well.
- If you can't find a reputable college student, consider a senior citizen family member or a friend who might welcome the extra income, the excitement, and the affection kids bring. In return, the children will come to relish the individualized time spent with older family members and the tighter bonds that will form.
- If you have older children, once they're out of school and home

alone, try setting up a phoning system in which the kids call you, or you call them, at a certain time during the day to keep them safe and the relationship strong.

- If you don't have access to a phone at work and cannot carry a cell phone, think about obtaining a pager that receives messages. This is a good, nonintrusive way for kids to check in with important notes—or even less critical ones like "pick up more snacks." Then, you'll know what they want or need well before you reach your vehicle.

Over and above the usual information you provide to caregivers, Jill Burnett, a part-time in-home nanny and college student, offers the following tips regarding child care courtesies from a provider's point of view.

- *Supply a schedule*. Not only do caregivers need to know the times of activities and appointments, but it's great to know when children ordinarily awaken or are to be awakened, when they like to eat (and what), and which TV programs they are permitted to watch (including channels, please). Allow the sitter some flexibility, however, as schedule surprises never fail to crop up when dealing with children.

- *Always provide contact information*. This should include your office and cell phone numbers, and where you'll be and when. If you have an appointment out of the office, for example, let your caregiver know. Not only will she be able to reach you in the event of an emergency, but she can also prevent the kids from calling to talk with you when you're in the middle of a presentation.

- *Don't hide sicknesses*. If your child is ill with a contagious disease (even if it is as ordinary as the common cold), call the provider to let her know. She will appreciate your honesty and, at least, can take precautions to prevent contracting the illness. It goes without saying that you must inform the caregiver about all chronic diseases such as epilepsy and asthma. Offer warning signs and emergency procedures. Don't overlook food or drug allergies, and show her where you keep antidotes and how to administer them.

- *Be on time*. Believe it or not, your caregiver has a life outside of her work. And because she might have plans, you should make it a point to be on time to relieve the sitter of her duties. Attempt to be home at a regular time each day and offer a small monetary bonus should you get waylaid.
- *Pay on time*. It's as easy as it sounds. Your child care provider expects to be paid as promptly and fully as you are. So be sure to abide.

"I love being with the kids," Jill says. "And when they have responsible, informative, courteous parents, the work is that much more enjoyable."

Summer Camp

Here's your second chance to finalize summer camp reservations now, or else you'll be giving yourself a good swift kick the week before camp starts, wishing you had registered your children. Mark the drop-off and pickup dates on your home and office calendars. Before you know it, you'll be packing the kids' bags and kissing them good-bye.

Summer Programs

Check into ethnic community centers, religious-affiliated groups, and school district–sponsored recreation programs that offer lessons and classes, such as weight training, diving, cartooning, and vacation Bible school. Inquire at a nearby state park for any nature events offered. These are usually less expensive or free-of-charge and are equally rewarding for the children. Are you hesitant to crash the community activities of a different race or religion? Fear not. Most associations don't require participants to be formally affiliated with the group. So forge ahead and join in.

Gifts Galore

This month, it's a good possibility that your mail carrier will be delivering invitation upon invitation. Get a head start by purchasing gifts for such upcoming events as graduations, weddings, possible bar mitzvahs and bat mitzvahs, communions, or confirmations. Remember to mark your calendar and R.S.V.P. immediately.

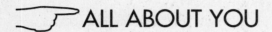 # ALL ABOUT YOU

Interoffice Memo: Time Off

Put in for summer vacation, upcoming weddings, getaways, or other time off you plan to take over the next few months. Don't forget to hop on this as soon as your little athlete or performer comes home with the travel team or competition schedule. Notifying work early is especially important when only a limited number of employees can be away from the office at one time or when the policy at work is "first come/first served" for assigning weeks off.

Making the World a Better Place

April is recognized on the calendar as Volunteer Appreciation Month. Do you want to offer your services to a charitable organization or cause but just can't seem to find the time? With the crazy lives we lead, there aren't nearly as many volunteers today as there were twenty or thirty years ago. So, how can you offer your helping hand, yet keep yourself from becoming burned out?

Here are ways to volunteer without adding to the franticness of your everyday life.

- If attending association meetings strains your schedule, work out other means of support. What can you do from home or the office? Record stats, update mailing lists, or balance financial accounts if you're computer savvy. Offer to make phone calls, design brochures, photocopy, or fold and stuff envelopes for mailings. You can collect funds or store and dispense fund-raising products from home. Will you be the one to research the best bargain or solicit donations online or over the phone?

- If you enjoy baking at home, whip up a batch of cookies, brownies, or muffins for the next bake sale. Make hand-crafted gifts to be sold or auctioned off. Or how about asking your company to donate logo merchandise for door prizes?
- If your group needs a designated shopper to buy supplies for upcoming events or is looking for someone to pick up and deliver orders, work these errands into your schedule, without taking time away from your own responsibilities.
- If you have little ones, provide baby-sitting services at the next meeting. Then, take turns, allowing everyone to stay involved.

A Family Affair

Don't forget to involve your children in your volunteering efforts. By making it a family affair, you're teaching kids about compassion and virtue. Encourage the gift of giving at an early age by showing children how to donate toys, clothes, and their own money. Taking them to soup kitchens and personal care facilities offers kids the chance to see the ups and downs of real life. Just think, they'll be learning valuable lessons without receiving a lecture from you. Even preschoolers can contribute by helping you bake or package cookies for programs like Meals on Wheels, create greeting cards to be donated to a nursing home, or collect nonperishables for church or charity.

When Plum Paradise Park, a playground built by community volunteers in western Pennsylvania, was under construction, kids under the age of ten were registered in a child care program provided by the coordinators. These children soaped nails and screws, sanded wood, and washed tires to contribute their share. And they had a blast doing so.

For one final family affair, solve this riddle: What volunteering act provides gratification in a short period of time and involves everyone from granny to teens and tots? Walks for charities. In one brief weekend morning, the whole family can walk, talk, laugh, and have a good time while contributing funds to a worthy cause. What a satisfying way to share a good time, exercise, and give on the go.

An Extra Perk

Aside from touching others' lives and boosting your own inner spirit, you never know how else the act of volunteering might help you down the road. The efforts you put into a nonprofit organization or school might enable you to qualify for a future job or promotion. And the networking you've cultivated could put you in touch with someone who might help to further or jump-start your career.

Lorraine Aland, wife and mother of two, is a perfect example. Lorraine volunteered her way into a permanent position as an after-school-care program coordinator. She demonstrated her enthusiasm by dedicating her time to the classroom, lunchroom, and for fund-raising projects at her sons' school. So when a new position was created to support an after-school-care program for the students, Lorraine was the perfect candidate to coordinate and head up the project. Several years later, she is still enjoying the benefit of her unexpected and fulfilling job-op that came her way due to her spirit of volunteerism.

Take Five: For the Love of It

What does the football coach with four daughters have in common with the empty nester who runs a story-time program for tots? Both volunteers are giving to children purely because they love what they're doing. Many times adults will coach, teach, or mentor, not in their business fields, but rather in an area of interest to them. Or they might center on a hobby or a sport they once played, allowing them to stay in the game. When you see an adult coaching, teaching, or mentoring who does not have a child in the program, you know he or she is volunteering for no other reason than *for the love of it*.

Look at Mary Ann DeSimone. She has made time in her busy life to pursue her interest—a love for animals. Even though Mary Ann spends many hours working in the administration of the family business, she still finds the time to volunteer at a local wildlife preserve where she is able to swim with the manatees, nurse an ill snake, or feed an abandoned owlet. The satisfaction Mary Ann receives from those few hours a week spent doing what she loves makes her a more focused person on the job. In plain words, to Mary Ann the giving of herself and the reward that flows from it are priceless.

Is there something you would love to do that would give you the opportunity to welcome the pleasure and, at the same time, to extend your knowledge to others who can benefit from it? Take a moment to jot several possibilities in your Frantic Journal.

ONE-STEP-AT-A-TIME CHECKLIST

Date
completed
Or N/A   Task

_____   Have air conditioning system checked.

_____   File tax return immediately.

_____   Pay quarterly taxes.

_____   Track expenses for a week or longer.

_____   Fill out college or private school financial aid forms.

_____   Buy an essential household item.

_____   Mark your big-ticket purchase on your Post-It and Pay-It Planner.

_____   Buy and administer your pet's heartworm medication.

_____   Make Mother's Day plans. Buy cards and gifts.

_____   Finalize summer child care arrangements.

_____   Register kids for summer camp.

_____   Research local summer program options.

_____   Purchase gifts for spring parties.

_____   Request any vacation days you'll need for summer.

_____   Volunteer within your community.

_____   Make assisting others a family affair.

_____   Evaluate whether your community efforts can benefit you.

_____   Volunteer in a field related to an interest or hobby of yours.

Healthy Life

May. Ahh, the sweet fragrance of blossoms grabs your attention every time you walk out your front door. And that nagging little voice reminds you on a daily basis to stop and smell the roses. But flowers aren't the only living, breathing things that should be blooming during the month of May. You should be too—both inside and out. So for the next thirty-one days, you're going to concentrate on health-related issues by scheduling those much-needed medical appointments, coaxing the family to handle a bit of the housework, and showering some deserved pampering upon yourself.

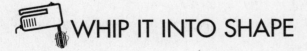 WHIP IT INTO SHAPE

Applied Science

Remember the concept you learned in school that warm air rises? Did you ever think it would actually apply to your home's central cooling system? Some houses have multiple built-in vents in each room, a few at floor height and others at seven feet or so off the floor. If you can control the opening and closing of these, you'll want the ones near the floor to be closed and the upper vents to be opened before you turn on the air conditioner. Why? Because in opposition to warm air rising, cold air falls. Therefore, as the chilled air moves from top to bottom, you'll cool the room much more efficiently.

It goes without saying that the converse is true with your central heating system. You'll want to push that warmed air through the lower vents and allow it to rise and heat everything in its path. (We'll remind you of this later in the year.)

We Must, We Must

May is the month to spruce up the outside of the house for summer. Clean gutters, edge sidewalks and landscaping beds, and do other maintenance work. Does the mailbox post need to be painted or replaced? Paint doors and windows; treat concrete, asphalt, decks, wooden swing sets, and cedar shingles; and power-wash aluminum siding. Paint the exterior of the house before the weather turns hot and humid. Otherwise, the paint won't adhere properly. The same is true for interior painting jobs, too—especially if you don't have central air conditioning.

Now that the unglamorous work is done, add plants and flowers, and expand the landscaping in areas that are in need of perking up. If you don't have extra funds to pump into the landscaping beds around your house, ask friends, neighbors, and relatives what shrubbery they have to share. Often plants like pampas grass, hostas, and even some perennial flowers can be easily thinned out and transplanted, giving your lawn a new look while helping to prune your neighbor's yard, as well. All you need to do is cut off a portion of the plant's root ball, replant in topsoil, fertilize, and enjoy.

If the phrase "yard work" isn't in your family's vocabulary, consider replacing yearly mulch with river rocks or crushed brick to cut down on maintenance. Make sure lawn fabric or plastic is put down first so weeds don't sprout up through the rocks.

Doctors and More

Keeping your family's health appointments on schedule is enough to give any woman a headache. And for the frantic woman, just the thought of it brings on an intense migraine. To ease the burden, take it one appointment at a time.

Throughout the month, schedule summer doctor appointments including annual physicals, mammograms, cholesterol checks, dentist, orthodontic, optometry, and other specialist checkups—especially ones for the kids so you don't have to pull them out of school.

Take with you any school, sports-related, or camp-required medical forms that must be filled out by the doctor in order for your child to participate. A second trip to the office for a signature might cost you an additional fee.

Work out a doctor-visit system that fits your lifestyle. For example, you might choose to schedule kids' annual physical appointments all on the same day. While this is a killer afternoon for you, it's over and done with in just a few hours. And it saves you from having to hire a sitter for the other children while taking them one at a time to the doctor.

Likewise, schedule the family's dental appointments two at a time. With two hygienists, you and your daughter can have the same time slot on one day while your husband and son have theirs on another.

You might be able to find similar ways to handle your own appointments. Administrative assistant Linda Bellini found a medical facility she was comfortable with to handle two of her yearly appointments. By doubling up, Linda has her annual physical and gynecological exams in the same building on the same day.

Too Much of a Good Thing

Speaking of health issues, have you ever wondered whether it's more harmful to consume too little of a vitamin or too much? The most important thing to remember is that vitamins are intended to supplement a good diet, not replace the natural sources of the vitamins we gain through healthy eating. When supplements are taken, they are in a larger concentration than would naturally be found in foods, so they are absorbed more quickly and thoroughly, especially on an empty stomach.

Even though vitamin pills are available over the counter, you must read the label and take only as directed. Registered nurse Elizabeth Joos cautions to keep all vitamins out of children's reach. "Because chewable vitamins taste good," Elizabeth says, "they're tempting for kids." But you must never give them more than one per day. And take care to store them in a locked cabinet or drawer with your other medications.

Registered dietitian Judy Dodd compiled the following data about the effects of consuming more than the daily upper limits of certain vitamins.

- Daily intakes of more than 100 milligrams of vitamin B_6 over a period of time can result in nerve damage to the arms and legs.
- Excess vitamin C in long-term use has been known to cause nausea, diarrhea, cramps, and kidney stones. The upper limit for males and females over thirty is 2,000 milligrams per day.

Similarly, the overuse of herbs and other natural substances like St. John's wort have been shown to cause medical complications in some people. Because these are available over the counter, many people forget to give these substances the respect they deserve. Dangerous chemical interactions can occur within the body when someone is using herbs and taking prescription medications, for example.

Our expert herbalist and author of *Herbs for All Seasons*, Karen Patterson, has a few words of caution. "Hundreds of years ago, Native Americans believed that herbs could heal most anything. Once thought to be just an old wives' tale, the use of herbal products and herbal remedies has become a multi-billion-dollar business in the United States and an essential part of our culture."

"Though they are a natural product, do your homework before taking any herbs to avoid possible interactions with prescription medicines or other herbal compounds," Karen suggests. "Make a list of what you are taking and ask your doctor or pharmacist if there is any possibility of adverse interactions."

Here are a few of Karen's practical rules to follow.

- Always report the herbal supplements you are taking to your doctor.
- Follow the dosage recommendations on the label, starting with the lowest dose and gradually increasing once you've observed the effect on your unique biological system.
- Never take more than is recommended.
- Buy the standardized extract of U.S. and European herbs; this is usually the best quality.
- Always check the label for the name and address of the manufacturer, the amount of the active ingredient, plant parts used, and expiration date.
- Always buy single herbs, not combinations or blends, so you know exactly what you are taking.

To read more about herbal remedies and supplements, visit the following Internet sites.

- Click on the "People's Pharmacy" page of the HealthCentral.com site (www.healthcentral.com) to read about interactions between herbs and drugs.
- Type the word "herbs" into the search block on the Look Smart Web site (www.looksmart.com) for general information about herbs.
- Research the American Botanical Council site, which offers information about the safe use of herbs (www.herbalgram.org).

Medical Tidbits

Where, oh where, are those medical numbers, notes, files, and folders? Follow this advice to order and organize them.

- Use a separate address book for doctors' names. This allows you to keep the emergency numbers readily accessible. Ask the receptionist whether there is a direct phone number for scheduling rather than being connected to the main line, then waiting to be transferred to the appointment secretary.

- Use self-stick notes hung by the telephone for writing down questions—whether you will be phoning the doctor or waiting for his call. Do the same when visiting the doctor. How many times have you left the office having forgotten to ask about one or two of the concerns you wanted to address? A sticky note attached to your insurance card and copayment will help avoid the frustration of forgetting these important issues—and save you from having to call about them later. Registered nurse Elizabeth Joos recommends starting a separate medical journal for each child. This doesn't have to be anything official—just an informal record of aches and pains, illnesses (both serious and minor), medications administered, and sleep habits. The journal comes in handy when tracking a recurring ailment. If your athlete complains of a sore knee off and on, for instance, you can look in your journal to see how long it's been bothering her. "Sometimes busy parents can't remember exactly when a particular problem started," Elizabeth says. "But with the journal, you can find what you need to report to the physician with just the flip of a page." Elizabeth reminds us to write questions for the doctor in the journal, too. And try not to forget to take it with you to the kids' appointments.

- As we suggested in part one, use one file folder for each family member, thereby placing medical data at your fingertips. Each year, update with a new folder to avoid sifting through years of records. By having all the medical receipts in one place, you're also able to total and document your out-of-pocket medical expenses with ease. Be sure to insert all prescription sales slips to complete the file. (See the January chapter for tax information regarding this file.)

- Ask the pediatrician or a staff member to give you a medical chart for each child, verifying immunizations and the dates received. When the kids are little, trying to keep tabs on their shots is difficult. Often, you'll need a copy of your child's immunization records for school, sports, or camp registrations. Once you have the form in hand, make ten copies to be distributed as needed and file the original for safekeeping.

- Follow Katie Coyle's example. Katie stashes a small envelope with a copy of health insurance cards, medical records, and birth certificates in the glove compartment of her car. "When you have kids, you never know when you'll need it," she says. Once when registering for a work permit for her child, Katie's friend had to make two trips to the school, having forgotten the required birth certificate. In the same situation, Katie walked out to her car to fetch all the materials she needed. This envelope of information comes in handy in case of an emergency, too. But it is hoped that you'll never have to use it.

- If you have someone in the household taking a number of medications, follow this tip from paramedic Pat Douglas. "Keep a list of medications updated and hang it on the outside of the refrigerator or in a prescription bottle inside the top front shelf of the refrigerator," Pat says. If an emergency arises and 9-1-1 is called, the paramedics will know to look on or in the refrigerator for what medications the person is taking. Many senior citizen care facilities use this safety method in their buildings.

Benefits to You

Because May is National Health Awareness Month, not only do we encourage you to schedule all summer doctor appointments, but we have another job for you. Dig into your health benefits binder to be sure you're taking advantage of all that is offered. Does your company or your spouse's pay for coverage for only the employee or for your entire family? Reevaluate whose allowances better meet your family's needs, since companies are so often changing their medical, dental, and eye coverages. It's especially important for divorced parents to take the time to reassess whose insurance plan is best for all involved.

In addition to neglecting to weigh their health benefits, employees sometimes overlook the tuition reimbursement option. While you might ask, "How can I possibly go back to school?—I'm too busy," give it some thought. Some companies will pay for noncredit and lifelong learning classes, in addition to conferences, seminars, and continuing education credits.

Sometimes educational allowances extend to other family members. Mother of four Barb Burnett was compelled to take a closer look at her benefits and those of her husband when their oldest daughter, Kassie, was attending a private college that was costing them plenty of dough. Upon digging into the employee benefits file, Barb found that Kassie could attend an excellent state-supported university, affiliated with her husband's place of employment, and would be required to pay only half of the state college fees. As a result, Kassie transferred schools and her tuition dropped a whopping 70 percent. Armed with this new information, Barb can happily afford to educate her three younger daughters, as well.

Similarly, Linda Tempalski had started working a few months after her company had issued an education reimbursement plan. Because she was a new employee, Linda assumed her daughter's tuition would not be covered. In conversation, a coworker mentioned to her that this perk didn't have a time-served requirement, and thus went into effect the first day she started. That tidbit of knowledge saved Linda many thousands of dollars in college tuition costs.

Don't forget to ask at the office about reimbursement for any membership fees you must pay when joining a professional organization that is work related. Not only do you benefit as a member of a professional organization like the American Association of University Women (AAUW), American Nurses Association (ANA), and Women in Technology International (WITI), but your company does, too. How? Most organizations publish an annual membership directory with members' names and company affiliations. (Psst! That's a form of free advertising.)

Make an effort to take a closer look at all the benefits you might be missing out on. You'll be glad you did.

Nest Egg

Take a minute to consider whether or not you're able to extract a portion of your paycheck, no matter how small, and deposit it into a savings or vacation fund, a college account, or a retirement plan. As a convenience, some companies will withhold a fixed amount of your earnings and purchase savings bonds for you or deposit it directly into your savings account.

As an aside, if you haven't joined your credit union yet, this might be a good time to compare their lending rates, investment returns, and other banking fees with your current institution. You'll never know how much you can save in monthly fees until you weigh all your options.

DARLING LITTLE ANGELS (AND THE WHOLE BLISSFUL BUNCH)

Holiday Happenings: Parents' Days and Memorial Day

If you haven't yet crossed this off your list, confirm plans for how you will spend Mother's Day. Flip back to the April chapter for memorable possibilities. Now is your last chance to pick up cards and gifts.

> **SNIPPET:** Even though mothering has been around since Eve had Cain, official Mother's Day celebrations can be traced back to the 1600s. It all started when England named the fourth Sunday of Lent "Mothering Sunday" honoring England's mothers.

Arrange your Memorial Day activities. Will you attend opening day at the pool, picnic with friends, or celebrate with a small family outing? Consider honoring deceased family members by decorating and grooming grave sites. Take the family along to show them your example of respect and honor.

Because Mary Jo's husband, Stu, had lost his mother when he was barely a teenager, many of his family's Jewish traditions and customs were not passed along to him. For many years while he was paying his respects at the cemetery, he found blades of grass or small stones on his mother's grave site. Somewhat annoyed, Stu would clear away the debris. Recently at a family gathering, he had mentioned the mysterious rubble and how he felt it was an act of disrespect for his mother. His cousin Andrea overheard his comment and boomed, "That was me. It's one of our traditions to leave a stone or blade of grass at the grave showing someone was there." On his next trip to the cemetery, Stu left behind a small stone and a blade of grass.

Buy Father's Day cards and gifts and plan a visit or a dinner out. If your father is no longer living, do something in his memory. (See the Mother's Day section in our April chapter for some unique ideas.)

If you're married with children, encourage the kids to make a card or to pick out a small present for their dad. Stay away from neckties, socks, and hankies. Dads have been receiving them for centuries. Instead, why not wrap a *TV Guide*, the remote, his favorite snack, and a coupon for a night of interference-free channel changing? Or put together a package containing microwave popcorn, a baseball hat, and tickets to a game. Come up with an idea that is customized just for him. If funds are free-flowing, plan a trip to one of the sports halls of fame. Or give him a permit for a fishing getaway with friends. Keep his interests in mind when you come up with your gift idea and watch how appreciated your efforts will be.

Summer Wardrobe

With your closets clutter-free, or almost (we hope), sorting through summer things shouldn't be difficult at all. And summer clothes are so much fun. Assess what you and the kids can wear from last year. Do the basics still fit? What can you mix and match? What stylish items can you mesh with the things already hanging in your closet for a less expensive wardrobe update?

It's time to buy all summer supplies including sandals, clothes, swimming gear, and toys. If you wait until June or July, the style and size selections for your family will be slim pickin's.

> **HIDDEN GEM:** If you don't own a little black dress, then put it on your shopping list. What can you do with this one article of clothing? We're so glad you asked.

By including a black dress in your wardrobe you can . . .

- wear the dress in its basic form with sandals for a day of shopping.
- add heels, black hose, jewelry, and a belt for a quiet dinner date.
- top with a blazer and pearls for the executive look.
- slip a cotton sweater over the dress and you are ready for a day at the office.
- pull on a sheer blouse and some trendy jewelry for a night on the town.

What new combinations can you come up with for that little black dress that's been hanging in your closet?

Kids' Activities

We know it comes at a time when you want to shout, "Enough!" But you must look into tryouts and sign-ups for next fall's sports and commitments now. Many school-affiliated and township teams have spring registrations so coaches can organize practices over the summer. This usually involves such activities as cheerleading, volleyball, football, and baseball, to name a few.

Keeping Them Focused

Right about now, the kids have had it with school. They're looking forward to summer fun and lots of free time. But they still have homework, exams, and projects due. And you don't want them to blow their end-of-the-year grading period. So what can you do? Teacher, tutor, and mother of four Lynn Schneider advises you change the *where*, *when*, and *how* of homework to keep kids focused.

- *Where:* If your child ordinarily completes homework at the kitchen table, change the setting by letting him work on the back porch with a fun snack. Allow him to read an assigned chapter while swaying on the porch swing or huddling in his tree house.

- *When:* If you put your child to work the minute she walks in the door, give her a break, for a change. Allow her to play outdoors for a while; then call her in a little early for dinner. Have her complete some of the homework before you eat and some after. Encourage your child to finish so she can continue to play outside until dark. You might have to push bedtime back by half an hour or so, but that's okay—school's almost over. Besides, she'll sleep extra soundly after her outdoor adventures.

- *How:* Purchase items that will make homework more appealing. You can buy theme notepads for sports and music at teaching and office-supply stores. Buy colored poster board and stamping markers for projects to help fill in white space. If you have a say in deciding on a project, choose an active one—one that involves finding treasures outside or interviewing neighbors or family members in person, for instance—rather than something that requires a lot of book research. If a visit to the library is necessary, go to a different branch. Add lunch and a stop at the playground—turning it into a field trip. For reading assignments, take turns—you read one page, he reads another. Glue flash cards or review math problems on fun notepads. To go over test material, write or type questions on colored index cards (adding stickers, if you'd like) and invite him to draw from the pile. Allow him to quiz you, too, for hearing the information is as good a practice as reciting it.

"Whatever you do," Lynn says, "remain positive about homework and show enthusiasm. Your child won't benefit from hearing you gripe about all the work that's been assigned."

Summer Chores for All

Summer chores for the kids should be discussed, mapped out, and adopted since the kids will soon be home during the day. Make it a new practice, for example, to have everyone in the family rinse or soak their own plates. That way, even though you might still come home to a sink full of dishes, at least what remains of the food won't be congealed and stuck. In addition, you won't have cups and plates decorating the table and every countertop.

If one of your pet peeves is that no one seems to load the dishwasher the way you do, make it a rule that you load, but the family unloads. After all, now that they're home they'll be using more dishes than you will. Hang a two-sided magnetic sign on the outside of the dishwasher that reads "Clean" or "Dirty" to avoid mix-ups that require the whole load to be rewashed and dried.

Kids in Biz

Is your young teen costing you mucho money for his movies, pizza, and CD purchases? Cultivate an interest of his so he can earn extra money and reduce a bit of the drain on you. Other than the traditional jobs of cutting grass and baby-sitting, suitable occupations for kids include disc jockeying, painting fences and wooden swing sets, and making crafts to sell. Enterprising, computer-savvy kids can market just about anything on auction Web sites like eBay with your help.

Resist the urge to leave your ten- or eleven-year-old alone. According to experts, they're just not ready to handle the job. Keep in mind,

---

◇ **HIDDEN GEM:** Pediatrician Mary Goessler believes that despite our rush to have young ones help out, children should be twelve to fourteen years old before they are given baby-sitting duties or left alone in the house—of course depending upon the child's level of maturity and willingness to accept responsibility.

baby-sitting classes are offered in some pediatricians' offices, local hospitals, YMCAs, community colleges, and recreation centers.

No matter how much income your child earns, accountant and financial adviser John K. Burnett recommends opening a savings account in his or her name (with you or your spouse co-signing as the custodial party). Decide on a fixed amount each pay period (anywhere from 30 to 50 percent of earnings) to be deposited into the new savings account. "By saving with every paycheck," John says, "you're not only encouraging responsible saving, you're instilling good spending habits, as well." This way, blowing an entire paycheck won't be an option.

John also recommends that kids, when able, purchase a few shares of a blue-chip stock, allowing them to be a part of the purchasing process. "Children become excited to own stock in their favorite companies like Disney, Nike, or a clothing company," John says. As they learn to check stock standings and begin to receive proxies in the mail, they'll view earning and spending as a financial system, rather than just a means of purchasing CDs and trendy clothes.

Second Chance: The Big "Vay-Cay"

We're giving you a second chance to finalize your big vacation plans. If you haven't booked a vacation home, condo, or hotel yet, ask an agent for late-reservation discounts. Often, if the rental property you've chosen hasn't been reserved, you can receive a discount since the owner's chances of renting the property now are growing slim. If you can, vacation during what they call the shoulder season (before Memorial Day and after Labor Day)—when prices are usually lower than they are in mid-summer. Find out what is available by searching online and then contacting the individual real estate agencies mentioned. Most agencies have 800-numbers listed on regional Internet sites and some will have their own Web pages. Be honest with the agent you contact, letting her know what you expect in decor, service, and location. She'll do what she can to offer you the best rental properties available to keep you coming back year after year.

For those without Internet access or who'd prefer not to use it, contact your destination's Chamber of Commerce. Most times, the chamber will mail you a compilation of accommodations, attractions, and dining brochures.

Mini-Getaways

Aside from your big family vacation, more than likely you'll be packing your bags in the next few months and heading for somewhere—though it might not be your over-the-rainbow destination. You might be traveling to a different state for your child's sports tournament or performance of some kind. Or you might have a high school junior who's exploring possible universities. Before you hit the road, here are some suggestions for tucking in a few short getaways this summer. Make the most of your excursions, whether they originated by choice or by obligation.

- If you're headed to a certain area, look through the Sunday paper for advertised specials. Take a family vote on a different type of trip such as a farm vacation, historical tour, or frontier festival. Plenty of books are available on day trips, too. In fact, there are probably several focusing on getaways from your area. Check the Internet or reserve your copies through the library to help plan what's within driving distance of your hometown.

- Plan college visits. Check with the schools your child is interested in attending to schedule a tour. Or better yet, if you have time, plan to visit while school is in session, either now or next fall. It's often easier for kids to get a feel for the school's environment when the students are bustling about, heading to class, and hanging out. Feeling comfortable in a college setting for kids is just like buying a wedding dress. You can't decide which dress you like when they're on the hangers, but once you try a few on, you can tell immediately which one is right for you.

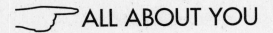 # ALL ABOUT YOU

Interoffice Memo:
A Professional Helping Hand

Although we had you volunteering to your heart's content in April, this month we're asking you to go one step further. Don't necessarily limit volunteering to your personal life, but allow it to filter into your workplace, as well. Are you qualified to offer a class in-house to your coworkers or to the community, whether the topic be business related or recreational? Would such a feat make both you and your company "look" better? Might it bring in more business and help others at the same time? Think about the things you do well and discuss the possibility of sharing these talents with those around you. You can do so anywhere from the company conference room, to the public library, to your local community college classroom.

By the way, did you know that community colleges are always looking for local professionals to teach a class and are open to considering new course options, especially in their continuing education divisions? Extending your help might fulfill a dream or even put you on a new career path.

Personal Garden

Grow a personal garden including your favorite herbs, berries, and flowers. If you don't have enough space, container gardens are popular and easily handled. You don't need to be a seasoned green thumb to give this a try. Just purchase the preplanted pots and read the directions, and you'll be snipping live herbs in no "thyme."

Take Five: Fresh Look

Even though you're too busy to think about yourself and how you look, every now and then you must peek in the mirror and evaluate. Prepare yourself for summer with fresh nail and makeup colors. Find out what's in by asking at your salon or by taking advantage of the free makeovers at your local department store. Keep in mind, these makeovers take time and the cosmetic representative will want to sell her products. Before you park in her chair, therefore, have a limit in mind for yourself of what products you really need and how much you'll spend. By staying within your predetermined budget, the experience will be a positive one, rather than a joyous-turned-regretful occasion.

While you're in the self-evaluation mode, set a hair goal. Have you styled your tresses the same way for the past three years? Is there a new style or color you'd love to have? Let your stylist know you're ready to take the plunge and update your look. He might have an idea he's been anxious to try on you. You'll be amazed at how refreshing and uplifting a simple hair or makeup change can be.

Even after you've adopted a new look from the neck up, are you dreading the onset of shorts-wearing season? Whether you're genetically stuck with ostrich or elephant legs, all types will look better with a warm, healthy glow. However, you've been good about protecting your skin from the sun and the uncertain risks involved with spray booths and tanning beds. So what can you do? Self-tan, that's what. You've heard those bronzing horror stories, and maybe even have a few to tell yourself, about orange-striped legs and stains on your clothes. But artificial tanning need not be so disastrous.

HIDDEN GEM: Nancy Dorn, mother of two and administrator of the family business, tans with ease right in her own bathroom. Nancy suggests purchasing a tanning product either from a department store or drugstore, whatever your budget will allow. "All you have to do is put a drop the size of a nickel in your palm and rub your hands together," Nancy says. "Then lightly massage the lotion into the smooth skin on your arms, legs, chest, and shoulders. Avoid wrinkle-prone areas like elbows, wrists, knees, and ankles." She recommends applying every day after showering, just as you would a moisturizer. You don't need to pay too much attention to panty lines and so forth. When applying lightly, as Nancy recommends, you'll enrich your overall skin color without a drastic, ta-da look that will have all your friends questioning the nature of its origin.

ONE-STEP-AT-A-TIME CHECKLIST

Date
completed
Or N/A   Task

_____ Change register vents for more efficient air conditioning.

_____ Groom the outside of the house.

_____ Make all doctor appointments for the family including specialists.

_____ Be certain you're following directions for over-the-counter herbs and vitamins.

_____ Create a health folder for each family member, if you haven't already done so.

_____ Reevaluate the benefits available to you, your spouse, and your children.

_____ Start building your nest egg.

_____ Confirm Mother's Day celebrations and make Memorial Day and Father's Day plans.

_____ Purchase summer wardrobe for all and buy summer supplies.

_____ Register kids for fall activities.

_____ Utilize tips to keep kids focused on schoolwork.

_____ Assign summer chores to everyone.

_____ Discuss summer money-making opportunities with the kids.

_____ Confirm family vacation reservations.

_____ Map out mini-getaways.

_____ Volunteer within your workplace or field of expertise.

_____ Plant a personal garden.

_____ Update your overall look and style.

Summer Kickoff

June joggles memories of adventurous anticipation, happy times, and carefree days. Remember as a kid, racing home on the last day of school, full of ideas, expectations, and plans for summer fun? June kicks off the lazy days, allowing your pace to slow while giving you the chance to act like a kid again—without anyone questioning your performance. When else can you toss someone into the pool, put the pedal to the metal in a high-speed go-kart, or run around in shorts and bare feet? Make the most of summertime by developing a new interest, introducing the kid in you to your own gang, and reuniting the branches of the family tree. Get ready to entertain, relax, and have fun.

 WHIP IT INTO SHAPE

Summer Giveaway

Throw out the summer things you know you won't use, such as the splintered picnic table, bent beach umbrella, tattered lawn chair, rusty sprinkler, leaky garden hose, and needs-to-be patched raft. If you've already replaced appliances, toys, or gadgets, chances are slim that you'll ever get around to fixing up the old ones. So take a deep breath and pitch, pitch, pitch.

HIDDEN GEM: As an alternative, consider what Chris Sartori's parents did. Before Chris's father, a music teacher, tossed anything—whether it was a small appliance, lamp, or piece of furniture—he considered how much time and money it would take to repair it. Then he'd roll up his sleeves and get right on it. He became so adept at putting things back together again that the neighbors began giving him their throwaways, too. After fixing the discards, he stashed the just-like-new pieces in a designated spot. Then, when he had collected enough, he and Chris's mom would sell them at garage sales and flea markets.

One day, Chris watched her father carry a lamp into the garage and asked, "What do you see in that ugly thing?" He replied with a cheery smile, "Ireland."

The money he and his wife earned from the sale of each item was placed in a special savings account. And when they accumulated enough, they'd take the family on an out-of-the-ordinary vacation. Even though the kids have grown and gone, Chris's parents are still hard at it. In fact, the two of them recently returned from a junk-funded trip to the Emerald Isle.

Second Chance:
Doctor Appointments

This is your second chance to schedule health appointments for you and the family. Make doctor, dentist, orthodontist, ophthalmologist, and other specialist appointments. If it's easier for you, scatter scheduled dates throughout the summer. Or cram them all into one week to get the obligation over with. It might be a good time, too, to purchase, review, or upgrade your eye and dental insurance coverage. Certain health plans allow changes or additions to be made only at specific times of year. Research the details in your benefits folder and mark the dates to make coverage changes in your Post-It and Pay-It Planner accordingly.

Repair or Replace Book Bags

Although the school doors have barely closed, we recommend that you rescue book bags before they hit the bottom of the closet or, worse yet, the trash bin. Many backpack manufacturers, such as Jansport and Eastpak, offer a lifetime warranty on their products, so check each bag for any needed repairs. Then, if yours is covered under a warranty, send the pack back to the company before summer is in full swing. Don't delay or the mended bag might not arrive before the first day of school.

Alternatively, if it's time for a new backpack, beat the rush and order now. You might even find a few styles on sale.

Quarterly Taxes

If required of you, the time is here again to pay your federal and state income taxes—due by the 15th of the month—for your second-quarter earnings.

Reminder Alert

This is an instant reminder for you: Remember to flip the bed mattresses this month.

JOTS & THOUGHTS QUIZ
Summer Cooking Interrupted

Does it seem that during the summer months you barely have time to breeze through the kitchen, let alone cook a full-fledged family meal? How much time or thought have you devoted to cooking for your family these days?

Take this quiz to pinpoint some of the problem areas. Check "Once in a blue moon" if you succumb to these no-nos occasionally. But if you find yourself doing so more than you'd like, check "Caught red-handed." Now, don't cheat, hem and haw, or make excuses. Bite the bagel, by all means, and be honest.

1. Are you constantly searching the freezer for what can be zapped and served?

    ___Once in a blue moon   ___Caught red-handed

2. Do you wish you had the guts, time, and energy to experiment more with that patio grill?

    ___Once in a blue moon   ___Caught red-handed

3. Do you find you're "driving through" for that semi-nutritious dinner on the way home, so you can rush back out the door again?

    ___Once in a blue moon   ___Caught red-handed

4. Have unbalanced and hurried meals caused your family to grab for unhealthy snacks more often than they should?

    ___Once in a blue moon   ___Caught red-handed

5. Would "Jeannie" popping out of her bottle—ready to blink a gourmet meal in front of your hungry family—be a wish come true?

    ___Once in a blue moon   ___Caught red-handed

6. Do you long to find thirty minutes of uninterrupted time to sit down with a cup of coffee to plan the week's menu?

    ___Once in a blue moon   ___Caught red-handed

7. Are you eating out more than ever because you can't stir the energy to cook when the sun is shining, knowing your limited time would be more enjoyed outdoors, poolside, on the court, on the course, or with friends?

    ___Once in a blue moon   ___Caught red-handed

If you checked more "Once in a blue moon" answers: Bravo! You're adept at not allowing the summer schedule to interfere with your home-cooked meals. You probably aced your food pyramid test in the fourth grade, too. And best of all, you aren't blowing the family budget at fast-food cafés.

If you marked more "Caught red-handed" answers: Dump the "I have nothing for dinner" attitude. Yes, we know, your hectic schedule lacks spare time, forcing you into last-minute planning and on-the-spot decisions. Thus, once again, you find those burger joints beckoning. No wonder you're on a first-name basis with the drive-through cashier. But stay tuned. Because coming right up is our weekly special, "Chef's Corner."

Chef's Corner

As you stand and stir at the kitchen counter, you fight the temptation to go out and play. Although you might feel shackled to the stove, summer cooking needn't place such demands on you. Think of it as a big buffet. Some people approach an all-you-can-eat salad bar as what we call *Nibblers*. If you're a Nibbler, you trek to the buffet so many times that you wear a path in the carpeting—sampling a little of this and that with each trip. Other people are *Pilers*. The Piler's plate resembles a pyramid and her soup bowl is filled to the brim. While the Nibbler is jumping like a jack-in-the-box, the Piler is relishing the taste of hot soup and salad in one fell swoop.

Similarly, the frantic-woman Nibbler faces the pains of summer cooking on a nightly basis. For the dog days of summer, therefore, try to become a Piler who takes on cooking for the week all at once. If you love the taste and convenience of grilling, do so every Sunday for the whole week ahead. Grill half chickens or breasts, dogs, burgers, steaks, chops, ribs, smoked sausage, and whatever else you can pull from the freezer. Set aside dinners for the next three days; then freeze the rest for later. When you rush in from work, the pool, or a game, just whip up a few side dishes, heat the main course, and serve.

For a no-pot meal, cook vegetables on the grill too. Try any variety of fresh peppers, unpeeled halved potatoes, halved onions, zucchini, or squash for a colorful char-grilled burst of flavor.

Do you savor the taste of the gourmet mushrooms you order for beaucoup bucks in la-di-da restaurants? Well, now you can prepare the tasty delights at home. The most popular gourmet mushrooms are the portobello, shitake, cremini, enoki, morel, oyster, and white. And while they might be somewhat difficult to pronounce, they're as easy as pie to prepare.

For mushrooms or any type of grilled veggies, do our foil-oil treatment. Form a rectangle of foil into a canoe shape. Place cubed vegetables in the boat and sprinkle with your favorite oil, salt, pepper, and choice of seasonings. Fold the foil to seal the mix. Heat on medium, avoiding the direct line of fire. Check periodically as grilling times vary with vegetable size, volume, and type of grill.

> **HIDDEN GEM:** Ever tried cob corn on the grill? Here's how to do it. Remove the husks and silk, and cut off any damaged portions of the corn. Soak in water, milk, or buttermilk for an hour or longer. Remove from liquid, pat dry, wrap in foil, and roast over medium heat on the grill until desired tenderness is achieved. Add butter and salt if desired.

With the heat of summer, big meals aren't always necessary or even appreciated. Salads of all kinds including chef, fruit, tuna, chicken, and pasta are great ways to cool off and ease your crunch time in the kitchen. Toss in unusual toppings like mandarin oranges, almonds, trail mix, and pitted cherries. Add muffins or bread and an easy dessert to round out the menu. Other light meal options loaded with nutritious flavor include shish kebabs, tacos, fajitas, pita wraps, sandwiches, and subs (or hoagies, as we call them in this region). Serve with fruit or potato salad to balance the meal.

Buy fresh vegetables when they're in season—like green and red peppers, Vidalia onions, and scallions. Chop and freeze them in small zippered plastic bags in half-cup portions. When preparing stir-fry, stews, soups, and other dinners, unzip the desired amount and add the flavors of summer to your meals all fall. As a word of caution, frozen veggies must be cooked before eating or you'll have a mushy mess on your hands.

HIDDEN GEM: Make up a chart for the times it takes to reheat or prepare favorite foods in your microwave. Tape the chart on the inside of a kitchen cabinet so the kids or your spouse can refer to it and make their own grab-and-go meals, especially when a sit-down dinner isn't on the agenda.

Mary Jo mixes up large batches of pancakes and French toast. Once they are made, she places single servings in small freezer bags. Her teenaged son, who is ever munching, pops the breakfast wonders into the microwave or toaster whenever his stomach growls. Be sure to down these within a few weeks, though, because they become soggy, floppy Frisbees after a month or so in the freezer.

Along these lines, experiment with freezing other home-cooked foods in single-sized portions so kids can take them out, one at a time, and heat in the microwave for snacks or quick meals on the run. This is a great way to make your own prepared food, which is cheaper and healthier than the frozen supermarket and warehouse club stuff. Some kids will zap hamburgers, grilled chicken breasts, even single servings of their favorite spaghetti sauce or lasagna. Open your pantry and refrigerator to see what frantic fun-meal you can pre-prepare. Check out "A Wee Bit More," part three, for a list of ingredients that should be lining your pantry shelves.

SNIPPET: Since we're discussing the art of snacking, ever wonder who came up with the idea to put meat and cheese on bread? In 1762, John Montagu, the Earl of Sandwich in England, created the first sandwich. He was playing a card game and didn't want to take a break. Instead of stopping, he asked for a lunch to go, consisting of two slabs of beef between two slices of bread. Wouldn't it have been strange if they had decided to call it a montagu?

DARLING LITTLE ANGELS (AND THE WHOLE BLISSFUL BUNCH)

Holiday Happenings: The Fourth

Make Fourth of July plans. Schedule parties or R.S.V.P. to invitations. If you're hosting the bash, map out the menu, grocery list, and activities for the day. Investigate local fireworks or carnivals being held for the occasion.

Do you want to entertain but are feeling too frantic to put it together? Often local swimming pools and parks sponsor holiday parties with games and hurly-burly for the kids. Invite guests and relax. What better way to reciprocate invitations?

SNIPPET: Navy Captain William Driver gave the American flag its most famous nickname. In 1837, when he retired from a life at sea, he brought home his trusty flag and called it "Old Glory."

Let Us Entertain

Summer entertaining both at home and out (at clubs or restaurants) can be gratifying, even when you're the hostess.

- Get together with friends at free outdoor concerts, parades, and baseball games.
- Join at least one other family for a flashback night, taking all to a drive-in movie. Pack lawn chairs, sleeping bags, fun snacks, soft drinks for the kids and drivers, and a little choice wine for the other adults. This is an inexpensive way to delight in the company of friends while keeping the kids happy, too.
- Celebrate summer by having a snack party get-together. This

works for a quiet evening with your immediate family or a bash inviting everyone you can think of. Ask guests to bring their favorite snack foods, either packaged or homemade. That means anything from Oreo cookies to baked Brie. Give prizes for the healthiest, the most fat-laden, and the most unique snacks. Be sure to take presentation into account, as well. For a quick picnic, add veggie burgers, chicken dogs, and a little croquet. This snack party idea makes a splash for teen gatherings, too.

SNIPPET: Creamy dreams. The total amount of cream filling used in Oreo cookies in one year is enough to ice all the wedding cakes served in the United States for two years. That's 4.7 million three-tiered cakes. And wouldn't an Oreo-cream wedding cake be a tasty alternative? It'd be like eating the middle first with every bite. Mmm.

Summer Pastimes

Need some quick ideas for summer family fun? Try one or all of the following suggestions.

- Visit your local branch of the public library and join their summer reading program. Libraries usually sponsor great kids' programs to entice children of all ages to read, regardless of their abilities. Crafts, contests, and challenges add to the fun. Prizes, free fast-food coupons, gift certificates, ball game tickets, and more can be earned. In some locations, adults are able to join in the fun and receive prizes, too.

- While visiting your public library, read the monthly calendar to find out about book discussion groups and other class offerings open to the public. If any of these pique your interest, don't hesitate to participate. Take a friend along, or hire a sitter for a low-budget evening out with your spouse. Remember, it's healthy to stir the intellect and challenge the mind. So sign up today.

- Everyone loves a good old-fashioned chalkboard, but try this new-fangled twist. Some manufacturers produce a paint that can be written on with chalk and erased like the surface of a chalkboard. You can use this product to turn the backside of your basement or laundry room door or an accessible wall into an interactive message board. Add colored chalk and some festive erasers in a doorknob basket. You'll be surprised how this project encourages a new form of communication among family members—and besides, it's oodles of fun!

- As an alternative, make your door half chalkboard and half magnetic surface. Yes, there is a magnetic paint you can apply in the same manner as traditional paint. Imagine what a blast the kids will have leaving messages with colorful magnetic letters.

- For outdoors, purchase white marking paint—sold at hardware, home improvement, and paint stores—and turn the driveway into a basketball or tennis court. You can also add the outline for hopscotch, four-square, or shuffleboard to revive old favorites from days gone by.

> **SNIPPET:** Did you know the game of hopscotch actually began as a military exercise? The original hopscotch courts were over one hundred feet long during the early Roman Empire. Roman children copied the soldiers' courts but made them smaller and added a scoring system. Make your own hopscotch court and hop, hop, hop with your kids today.

- Plan day trips to a zoo, lake, historical site, museum, waterslide park, driving range, or nature center, or to a working farm to pick berries. Look for weekday discounts and plan accordingly. Or grab a few friends and their families and ask for a group rate.

- Take sailing, water aerobics, line dancing, or horseback riding lessons. Yes, that means you. We women always find the time and money to enroll kids in such beneficial programs. This year, we're encouraging you to sign yourself up, as well. (Remember, a frantic woman who is physically active makes for a much more energetic spouse, mother, and all-around companion.)

Vacation Groundwork

Begin to gather all vacation materials in an out-of-the-way place, such as a corner of the dining or living room. That way, you can assess how much baggage you're accumulating before you pack the flight bag or car.

- Involve kids in planning and packing for your summer vacation. Ask children to retrieve the snorkel, fins, inner tubes, and beach toys from storage while you round up beach towels, sunscreen, and insect repellent.
- Have kids collect toiletries and other such necessities as adhesive bandages, cotton swabs, and first aid cream. Use zippered plastic bags to house each family member's medications, both prescription and over the counter, and label with a black permanent marker. Remember to take vitamins, pain reliever, decongestant, motion sickness medicine, and remedies for an upset stomach. Pack all medical provisions in one small carry-on or duffel and stow at arm's length. Make it a distinct or brightly colored one—so you're able to spot it during those mini-emergencies that arise on the road or in the air.

HIDDEN GEM: Pack feminine protection products, just in case, especially if you're traveling out of the country. Why? Because Mother Nature seems to do her own thing. Even if you don't foresee the need, traveling—particularly by air—can bring on your period rather unexpectedly. Although that's not grounded in scientific fact, you don't want to be stuck en route or in a strange town without the feminine products you prefer. And you better believe your teenaged daughters will count on you to pack their favorite essentials, as well. Whether you're flying, driving, or taking the train, there are more packing tips in "A Wee Bit More," part three.

HIDDEN GEM: If you have an infant or toddler who'll be getting in the water with you, chances are good that you'll be purchasing and packing some disposable swimming diapers. But when you're swimming every day, doesn't the cost of this convenience just kill you—especially when some babies are only in the water for such a short period of time? And isn't it a shame that they come so few in a package? Not really! While these pants are labeled "disposable," you can actually wash them in the washer using hot water and your usual laundry detergent, dry them in the dryer, and reuse them several times—provided the child *only* urinates in them. When the material on the sides of the pants begins to show signs of thinning (usually after three to five washings), discard and start another pair. Now, you can confidently change these disposable swimming pants on your toddler several times a day and not have to break your budget to do it.

- Prepare a chart of bonus chores kids can do to earn vacation spending money while helping you. Add a column stating how much each chore is worth. Give them a dime or quarter for each trip they make toting things upstairs or down for you. Pay them to run the vacuum cleaner, dust baseboards, or pick up after younger ones. Kids can be compensated for everything from mowing the grass and trimming the hedges to sweeping the driveway or weeding the garden. If you can't seem to motivate your teens, entice them with thoughts of wave runners, parasailing, or trips to the boardwalk shops. And stick to your guns here—if kids don't work now, don't let them play later. Sitting out for an activity while everyone else is participating will get the message across for next year. Be sure the chores assigned are ones that actually help you. And even though your wallet will feel a slight pinch, you'll likely be spending the money anyway. Only now, you won't be as bogged down with the light-duty housework that gobbles up your time. Start tipping for tasks weeks or even months before your departure date.

For a list of resources available to make your vacation memorable—whether your kids are toddlers, teens, or in between—see "A Wee Bit More," part three.

HIDDEN GEM: While planning your vacation escape, keep a file or large envelope containing all reservation information. Include maps and brochures gathered from tourist Web sites or via snail mail. Pack this file in an accessible carry-on bag, to be kept with you in flight or in the front seat of the car. That way, you'll have all guides and other essentials right at your fingertips. As you travel to your destination, read the brochures and tentatively plan out the family's activities for the week—if you're not the designated driver, of course. Throughout your stay, insert receipts into this file for bike and boat rentals, restaurants, and other activities. Jot notes on the sales slips indicating whether it was a thumbs-up or thumbs-down, especially if you plan on vacationing there again. Hoard hot-spot receipts, magnets, or matches that usually list addresses and phone numbers, enabling you to easily relocate your favorites next time.

Off to Camp

Preparing your child mentally for her first camping trip without Mom or Dad is just as important as determining what to pack in her bag. Susan Orr of Girl Scouts of Southwestern Pennsylvania offers the following eleven helpful tips for parents to keep in mind while getting their kids ready for camp.

1. Read camp information the day it arrives in your mailbox. Parents sometimes wait until the night before their children leave to read camp material. At that point, it might be too late to take care of some of the essentials.
2. Make a check-off list for mandatory information, such as health and medicine forms, camp fees, parental information, and approval sheets.

3. Make sure your child has had a physical exam within two years of his or her camping date, and that your physician has signed the health form. Also, make a copy of the paper so that you can use it again the following year.

4. Have your child pack for camp with your help. This teaches her responsibility, and also lets her know what she will have on hand. Follow an equipment check-off list.

5. Don't promise your child something unless you've spoken with the camp director. (Example: Don't tell your child that she can call home any time. Camp procedures often state that no calls are to be made unless there is an emergency or prior arrangements have been made.)

6. Send mail. Leave a letter with the camp office when dropping off your child. Ask for the address to send more. Follow camp rules about mailing care packages. (Some camps do not allow this, because not all campers will receive packages from their families.)

7. Have campers write their names on all clothing and equipment. Use name tags or a laundry marker.

8. Encourage campers to stay for the full length of their camp session. It's natural for kids to experience homesickness while away from their regular routine. Staff members are trained to work with homesick campers. Note that kids are not immediately dismissed if they are homesick.

9. Make a list of the names and addresses of people to whom your child will send cards or letters (or even make mailing labels). Address and stamp envelopes for younger children.

10. If your child plans to take pictures, give pointers on loading and unloading film. (Or consider sending a disposable, waterproof camera. Be sure to remove it from the package and write your camper's name on it using a permanent marker.)

11. If you're going out of town while your child is at camp, make sure the camp knows where to find you.

What does your child need when going off to camp? See "A Wee Bit More" in part three for packing know-how.

Serious Family Fun

Summer is an ideal time to schedule a family reunion. But who wants to take on the responsibility? Although it might seem like a tedious job, if no one plans the family gathering, valuable boughs of the family tree might bend and break. If you're not willing to let that happen, you have but one choice: Roll up your sleeves and dive in. You can plan a quick reunion for the upcoming summer months or a more whoop-dee-do gathering for sometime next year.

- First, create an e-mail, snail-mail, or phone questionnaire. Find out when vacations have been scheduled, who will likely come, what they'd like to do, and how much each family is willing to spend. Offer options as simple as a picnic in a park or as elaborate as a family cruise or a resort/spa getaway. To save yourself a few headaches, propose several dates and locations and have people rank their top three choices. You might want to include a self-addressed stamped envelope to collect a small advance to help defray some of the initial costs.

- Once you've gathered and tabulated the data, remember that you can't please everyone. It's important, though, to accommodate older relatives—as they are usually the foundation of the family and might have travel constraints. Also, be sure the location you choose is accessible to family members with disabilities.

- After choosing a date and place, stick to it. If people truly want to be there, remember the old adage *If there's a will, there's a way.* Word will get around about how wonderful the event was, compelling even more to come next time.

- As a bonus, type up the contact information of all extended family. List addresses and include home, work, cell, fax, and beeper numbers, e-mail addys, and even birthdays and anniversaries. Print out or photocopy this data for everyone invited. Scroll it and tie with a ribbon for a practical party favor. Or why not compile a cookbook containing all family members' choice recipes featuring those lost-and-forgotten ethnic favorites? Col-

lect them by e-mail or snail mail and print out or copy and spiral bind. At the party, let the family cookbook double as an auto-
graph book, having everyone sign their recipes with a
personalized note.

Janice Lane Palko recently organized her husband's family
reunion, inviting more than four hundred people. To handle the food,
each family head (the parent of every tree branch) was responsible for
a meat dish. Their offspring (the children, now grown) brought
desserts and side dishes. During each year's celebration, the host snaps
family photos and places them in a continuous album that is passed
on to the following year's host or hostess. How do they decide who's
turn it is? They start with the oldest parent sibling and work their way
to the youngest. So each one knows, well in advance, when his or her
turn is coming.

- If a "land" gathering is out of the question, try a cyber reunion
  as a feasible alternative. Set up a chat room for the gang. E-mail
  notification of the date, time, and Web address. Then, whoever
  signs on can :>) and LOL for as long as they'd like. Create a chat
  log for those who missed. If all goes well, you can make the event
  a semiannual or even a monthly occurrence.
- Arrange a party for no reason—hosting a barbeque or potluck
  dinner with relatives (no friends, please, as they'll tend to disrupt the family dynamics). This works well in the summer when
  people are in the mood to get together without the pressures of
  a holiday season. Propose more regular shindigs, varying the person who hosts the party.
- If thoughts of entertaining that many people at home make you
  squirm, plan a family outing. Mary Jo's mom held her grandchildren's family birthday parties at bowling alleys and kids' party
  places where even the adults enjoyed good, wholesome fun. For
  a less lengthy meeting, you might decide to assemble at a fifties'
  diner, an old-fashioned candy store, or an ice cream parlor.

> **SNIPPET:** What is the main ingredient in ice cream? If you answered, "milk," "cream," "sugar," or "vanilla," you were wrong. The main ingredient in ice cream is air. Yes, air is what makes ice cream so fluffy and smooth.

If planned parties aren't for you, do something spontaneous by calling family members to see if they can join you. Don't cancel if everyone can't come—just go and enjoy. Here are a few suggestions.

- Your spur-of-the-moment function might involve a quick trip to the mall, a stop for coffee, or a dinner out. You might choose ladies only, if that helps with the baby-sitting problem—as Judith, her two sisters, and two sisters-in-law do. Having nineteen children combined, the "girls" are more likely to be able to get together if the husbands or older siblings are around to watch the younger ones.

- Another option is to allow all the kids to gather at one house for baby-sitting, while the parents run out for an appetizer and some good conversation. Make sure the chosen house is well equipped with a basketball hoop, video games, or the latest movies to keep kids busy. By doing this often, kids will look forward to (and treasure) the time they spend with their cousins.

- You might explore a few more enticing alternatives like booking an evening boat ride, reserving concert tickets, or renting a swimming pool for some adult family merrymaking. If everyone chips in, the costs won't be prohibitive and Bics will be flicked for an encore performance.

Let your imagination soar when coming up with ideas for family outings. Judith's parents approached the local historical society and arranged to give the family a guided bus tour of their city. The blend of facts, sites, and humorous familial outpourings made for a delightfully memorable experience for all.

Of course, if you don't have any family members in your area, you can always embark on these appealing possibilities with neighbors, coworkers, and friends.

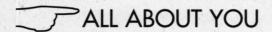 ALL ABOUT YOU

One More Time

Squeeze in one last just-for-fun outing with friends in the first few days of June, before school lets out for good. Whether you visit a traveling art exhibit or pull together a girls-only jam session, be sure to relish the adult conversation that will soon be replaced with discussions of summer job opportunities, tree-shack designs, and how earthworms have babies.

Hometown Happenings

Does it seem that newcomers to your area are more versed at recommending local places to go than you are? Have you longed to explore various museums, restaurants, and other attractions but never seem to get around to doing so? Vow to take in some of the local sites this summer. View your town or city as a visitor would. Discover arts-and-crafts festivals, free concerts, polo matches, outdoor theater events, and other special attractions in your area. Check newspapers for weekly listings. Local cable channels also announce such upcoming events. Take advantage of these proposed jaunts early in the season, so you don't find yourself at the end of August having allowed another summer to slip by without further touring your hometown.

Exploring B&Bs

Even though you've probably planned a vacation getaway for the family, take into consideration this advice about arranging an escape for yourself. Doris Larson, travel writer and author of *Bed & Breakfast Getaways from Cleveland*, describes a hand-rubbed cherry banister on a winding stairway, fresh daisies in an earthenware pitcher, a pot of English tea by the fire—it sounds like the perfect setting for a romantic weekend for two at a bed and breakfast (B&B). It's also an idyllic place for you to get off life's busy merry-go-round.

Doris says women traveling solo or with friends are discovering B&Bs. Some stay as business travelers during the week. Others gather friends and take over an accommodation to attend festivals or to shop for antiques. One of the best reasons to seek a B&B is to treat yourself to a getaway with no work schedule or family demands.

Doris recommends that you find an inn and savor the quiet countryside. Or visit a Victorian B&B in a small town where you can explore the quaint shops and cafés lining Main Street. If you plan a city stay, you can finally spend time at that museum you always wanted to visit. Or you might simply decide to sleep late under a puffy duvet, read to your heart's content, and take the longest bubble bath of your life. "Relax," Doris says. "Someone else is making breakfast for a change."

On Your Own

Have you been wanting to visit faraway lands but can't seem to interest anyone in joining you? Or will you be away on business and know you should take advantage of the sights and scenes but hesitate to do so because you're traveling alone? Well, fear no longer.

When Lois Dabney-Smith retired from her private psychotherapy practice, she wanted to explore new lands, hike vast terrains, and meet the people of cultures near and far. And she wanted to experience this fresh taste of the world alone. So Lois said good-bye to her husband and children, packed her bags, and traveled around the world.

"After years of encouraging my patients to do what made their hearts sing," Lois says, "I was determined to follow my own advice. With the ink of retirement barely dry, a forty-pound pack on my back, a song in my heart, and a map of adventure in my pocket, I trekked through China, Nepal, India, Thailand, Burma, Africa, and France. I returned home, my world expanded, my spirit renewed, more bounce to my step, and a new song in my heart."

Want a bit more advice on how to ensure your safety, find new friends in foreign places, and assess true dangers as they arise in your travels? We recommend reading *Safety and Security for Women Who Travel* by Sheila Swan and Peter Laufer. This guide helps you determine when a threat is real and lets you know how to still enjoy yourself when travel snafus crop up to jeopardize the fun. For additional advice on driving alone, click on the American Commerce Insurance Company's Web site (www.acilink.com) or visit your local AAA office to pick up the brochure.

Are You Covered?

If you're traveling out of the country, it's likely that your medical insurance will not cover you while you're away. Even if you're cruising the Caribbean or the South Pacific, often once you're ten miles offshore, your medical coverage fades to nil. Talk to your insurance agent about purchasing options to protect you and your family as you travel. You can do so for the limited amount of time you'll be away. AAA, other travel agencies, and cruise lines can help with information on medical coverage, as well. And the fee is well worth the security it provides. Whatever you do, don't leave home without it.

Take Five: Just for You

Ah, you've laid the groundwork and you're on your way to your vacation destination. But once again in the rush, you find yourself sitting on a plane, train, or as a passenger in the car thinking, "I wish I had something good to read." The same thought might cross your mind later, too, when you are stretched out on the beach. But this year, you won't be caught empty-handed.

Plan now what you'll do with the precious free time that is coming your way. Buy a few books by your favorite author, stock up on magazines and catalogs, or buy a new CD and borrow your child's personal CD player. Save yourself money by shopping at a warehouse club or used-book store rather than paying full price at newsstands on the road or in airport shops.

If none of these ideas appeals to you, take along your Frantic Journal and update your holiday gift list or expand your wish list for renovating or redecorating the house.

ONE-STEP-AT-A-TIME CHECKLIST

Date
completed
Or N/A | Task

_____ Toss tattered summer items and replace.

_____ Make any doctor appointments you skipped in May.

_____ Send backpacks under warranty to be repaired.

_____ Pay quarterly taxes.

_____ Flip bed mattresses.

_____ Adapt cooking methods to fit your summer schedule.

_____ Make plans for Fourth of July celebrations.

_____ Plan summertime parties and get-togethers.

_____ Sample a few summer pastimes with the family.

_____ Lay the groundwork for vacation packing. Encourage kids to pitch in.

_____ Prepare children for camp.

_____ Propose a new way to gather extended family for fun.

_____ Squeeze in one last outing with friends before school lets out.

_____ Discover local treasures by visiting your area's hot spots.

_____ Explore a B&B by yourself or with friends.

_____ Arrange to take a coveted trip just for you.

_____ Before you depart, inquire about insurance coverage while away from home.

_____ Purchase books, CDs, and magazines for some simple personal fulfillment.

Cruising

By the time July rolls around, we've finally adapted to the change in our schedules and we're settling into the swing of summer. While the longer, sun-filled days are probably still jam packed with responsibilities, our pace, mood, and attitude have slowly shifted to a more relaxed gear. Scented air, summer breezes, and sizzling barbeques appeal to our playful side, giving us the chance to unwind and have a good time. So put up your feet, grab your favorite refreshment, and cruise on to happy days.

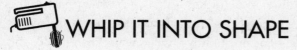

WHIP IT INTO SHAPE

Double Duty

How can you wisely use those countless moments spent at the pool or the ball field this summer? How about crossing something off your to-do list or asking others for references? Here's what we mean.

- Talk with others and obtain information. For example, if you're looking to change doctors, visit a specialist, or hire a tutor for your children, ask others about their likes and dislikes. Enlist such help when changing or entering a new school, seeking computer-related recommendations, or when job hunting. Are you in the market for camera equipment or a new appliance? Ask what brands others have relied upon. If you're hosting a party soon, ask for decor tips, party theme ideas, or preferred recipes. Seek recommendations for handymen, landscapers, house painters, cleaning services, and interior designers. It's more risky to let your fingers do the walking than to let friends do the talking.

- Accomplish menial tasks, such as stuffing envelopes or cutting supplies for a volunteer craft project, by taking them along to games, practices, and other summer events. And just maybe others will pitch in—facilitating your progress while enjoying it, too.
- Pull out an old hobby or unfinished project and dive back into it while playing lifeguard at the pool or perched in the bleachers. Wouldn't it be great to finish the needlepoint stockings, cross-stitched bibs, or quilt squares you worked on many moons ago? In fact, does the thought of crossing names off your gift list compel you to make some small holiday presents?

When setting your project goals, however, remember to stay within reasonable limits. Once Judith and her then-toddler children visited a book boutique in the Midwest. The owner of the store had placed a basket of cloth fruit on the floor for the kids to play with while Mom browsed. The girls loved the faux fruit so much that Judith decided to take on stuffing some of her own. Later, when buying the pattern and material, she purchased enough to make her three nieces fruit sets, too. As time went on, Judith's list grew and eventually she found herself stuffing ninety-six cloth carrots! Up to her eyes in fiberfill and felt, she never did stitch her way to the string beans.

Photo Fun

Summer moments seem to bring out the photographer in all of us. While it's easy to be snap happy with the camera, having film developed and placing photos in albums is a never-ending task. With the slower pace of July days, this is your chance to organize your pictures. What better way to escape the household duties than by reliving fond memories? This round, though, you can skip the guilt trip, because you're actually getting something done.

- First, sort photographs by approximate date. If your picture-perfect memories are from long ago, focus on several telltale signs. Look at hairstyles and clothes. Do you remember the outfits, the toys, or the friends? Next, examine the background to tell when and where. Don't dwell too much on pinpointing the specific time frame for each shot. Lump it into a general season or year; then, mark the dates on the back in colored pencil.

HIDDEN GEM: When writing on the backs of photographs, avoid using a ballpoint pen because the ink will eventually bleed through and ruin the front of your photo.

- Assemble dated photo packets in large manila envelopes or shoe boxes by year. Mark the outside with permanent marker and order them chronologically. Or if your prefer, arrange them in categories for "Summer Vacation," "Holidays," "Sporting Events," "Back to School," and "Daily Life" albums.
- When placing photos into albums, start with the earliest time frame and work toward the present. If this approach seems monumental to you, begin with the present and vow to keep up from here on, so as not to fall any further behind. Collect the leftover pictures in a waterproof bin. Once they have been archived, you'll feel freed of the overwhelming stacks that have relentlessly haunted you.
- When you have a few moments while waiting at the doctor's office or chatting on the phone, arrange photos into albums. By working for fifteen minutes several times a day, you'll put this task behind you in no time.

> **HIDDEN GEM:** Create a "Snapshot Satchel" full of essential supplies for updating albums on the run. Pack a season's worth of prints in an envelope and place in a zippered plastic bag for safe-keeping. Gather scissors for cropping, a set of colored permanent markers, pastel-colored index cards, and an album. Tuck into a canvas tote or nylon backpack and stow in the car for use during those unexpected waiting periods. For moms of involved teens, this is a great time-filler for those practice pickups when kids are dismissed long after they're supposed to be.

- Be sure to label the spine of each album with a paint pen for easy retrieving. If you have children, consider creating an album for each of them using duplicate or look-alike prints. Add some artwork and even a quick blurb on your reflections. Then when kids fly the nest, share the albums as a simple gift from your heart.
- Try scrapbooking, a productive way for preteens and teens to spend their rainy-day downtime. Let the kids flip through your photo stash to select their own favorites. Make it a rule that they choose only doubles or look-alikes, leaving you with at least one original. Or you might want to buy disposable cameras for the kids to snap their hearts out with friends or on vacation. Scrapbooking supplies and kits can be bought or made with what you have around the house. Gather stickers, stencils, fun foam cutouts, construction paper, wrapping paper, vacation brochures, and ticket stubs. Especially for the younger ones, try not to force your influence on them. The more the child's creativity shines through, regardless of talent, the more cherished the finished product will be. To make it even easier for kids, purchase tablets of printed scrapbook pages in 8½-by-11-inch sheets. Then encourage children to tear out the sheets and work on them separately, one at a time. When a page has been completed, insert it into a standard clear plastic sheet protector and add it to a reg-

ular three-ringed binder, rather than using a traditional scrap-book. This allows the kids to discard mistakes and, if they have a big enough binder, to add to the book for years to come.

For serious scrapbookers, Denise Dahl, a scrapbook consultant, suggests these tips.

- Use acid-free, lignin-free, buffered scrapbook pages and photo mounting paper. You don't want to have to re-do your scrapbook because the pages are yellowing or deteriorating and turning your photos yellow.
- Invest in acid-free, fade-proof, waterproof pens as well so that your treasured stories won't fade or disappear. Little sweaty hands and accidental spills won't blur or erase the only page with Great Grandpa's letter to them about the first time he saw them.
- Make sure your adhesive is acid-free and photo-safe as well. Nothing is worse than opening up your book and having all the photos fall off the pages.
- Keep things simple by balancing basic pages with more elaborate ones.
- Remember, your words are your most important decorations. Add a caption or two expressing your thoughts. Twenty years from now, your loved ones would rather have your story than the cutest stickers and fancy-print paper.

And now, we move to the digital option. Amateur photographer and retirement village manager Jan Capasso suggests these tips on how to get organized with a digital camera.

"If you like to take pictures, you probably have countless albums and shoe boxes full of old prints lying around the house," Jan says. "And do you ever know what to do with all those old negatives? More than likely, you can't find the right one when you need it anyway." If this sounds familiar, then Jan believes a digital camera might be the answer for you. A digital can help you organize your photographs, as well as different areas of your home. Here's what to do.

- *Organize your snapshots.* If you have access to a computer and know how to create directories, you can easily organize your favorite photographs. First, create a directory on your computer. "I named mine 'Photos,'" says Jan. Then add subdirectories, such as "Nelson Wedding," "Orlando Vacation," and "Christmas." Next, copy your pictures onto your computer (through the cable or card reader that came with your camera) and save them in the appropriate directories. Using your camera's photo-editing software, you can even fix such problems as "red eye." You can also reuse your camera's memory card, stick, or disk to take even more pictures—over and over again. And you will no longer have to wait for your prints to be developed or face the disappointment of some of them not turning out.

- *Create a digital photo album.* Various software packages on the market as well as a number of Web sites allow you to design computerized photo albums to share online or e-mail to friends and relatives. You can even insert annotations on each picture, including names, dates, and places. Several programs enable you to download your albums onto a CD. "The FlipAlbum software allowed me to create realistic 3-D page-flipping digital albums from the wedding pictures I took," Jan says. "And then I downloaded them onto CDs for the newly married couples to enjoy for years to come." This type of software has the tools to crop pictures, add special effects, and download background music onto the CDs. Most color printers will allow you to print out your favorite pictures on photo paper for sharing with those who don't have computer access.

- *Document your home inventory.* Insurance companies have recommended taking photographs of personal possessions and storing them in a safe place, such as a safety deposit box. With a digital camera, you can record various rooms in your home, your major appliances, electronics, vehicles, etc., and copy them onto your computer. You can create a digital photo album, as described in the previous tip, and add important annotations such as purchase price, year of purchase, and serial number. If you choose, for added security, you can take the memory card, stick, or disk on which your pictures were initially stored and keep it in your home safe or safety deposit box.

- *Record your collectibles.* You can do the same with any collectible items, adding annotations such as the name of the person who gave it to you, whether it was a gift, and the occasion on which it was given. Some collectors like to record the location of the sale and the purchase price, too.

These are just a few of the many ways that a digital camera can be used to help you become better organized. Thanks, Jan!

HIDDEN GEM: Do rolls of undeveloped vacation film sit in your closet months or years after they've been snapped? Next time while you're still away, take the film to a one-hour or one-day developing service as soon as you've emptied the camera. That way, you'll be bringing home prints or CDs rather than rolls (and another job to do). If you're really organized, take your Snapshot Satchel on your trip and you'll be further ahead in the game.

Just Do It

With the longer days and stronger rays beaming in your windows, do you find yourself still staring at a blank wall? Why? Because you haven't yet hung the paintings and framed photos that you slid under the sofa or tucked in a closet all year. Without homework hassles and the regimen of school, take the initiative this month to display your magnificent framings. Don't worry about choosing the perfect spot for each. Go with your hunch, pound the nail, and hook it up.

If you don't have what you need to get started—and Bob Vila you're not—flag down the experts at your local home improvement store. But before you wave and waggle, take the following information with you: approximate weight of each object; exact size, shape, and orientation (meaning, are you going to hang it horizontally or vertically?); whether mounting brackets are in place and, if so, how many; and the type of wall construction (drywall, plaster, brick and mortar, etc.). With that, the sales associate will help fill your basket with the right nails, screws, wires, and hooks.

Back home, find a wall stud to secure the fixture. Use a stud finder, if you have one, or employ the sophisticated system we use. When no one is looking, tap the section with your knuckles, proceeding to the right or left as you go. When the sound changes, mark the spot with a pencil. And voilà! You've found your stud.

(Hint: All electrical outlets are anchored on a stud, so you can use them as a guide. As a general rule, in many newer homes studs are sixteen inches apart, compared with the twelve-inch spacing in older ones.)

Bear in mind, the position you choose for each painting is not a permanent addition to your home. You can have second thoughts, take it down, and putty over the hole in a flash with spackle.

Interior decorator Christine A. Singer lets us in on a few wall-hanging basics.

- Visually anchor any wall hanging to the floor. A console table, large plant, chair, or sofa placed beneath it will accomplish this.
- Group together small photographs, prints, and paintings to create a strong visual impact. These can be arranged on the floor and mapped out before they are hung on the wall.
- Choose prints and paintings that will coordinate or complement your decorating scheme. An overly ornate frame, for instance, might not complement your kitchen decor as well as a simple painted one in a harmonizing color would.
- Try to avoid using too many different styles of frames for your photographs, as well.
- Position your hangings at eye level for ease of enjoyment.

Now, let loose your creative side and savor the feeling of having transformed that blank wall into an eye-catching conversation piece.

Renovation Projects

Take on any renovation projects that might ordinarily get pushed off until fall. Why? According to home restoration and renovation specialist Alexandra Sabina, author of *A Woman's Guide to Hiring a Contractor*, the weather can have an impact on how well exterior work is performed, as well as how well you and your family survive the home improvement process. "When electing to implement projects in the spring and summer months," Alexandra says, "unlike the winter months, you can take advantage of partially living outdoors while work progresses inside your home." She suggests that cooking on the grill and relaxing on the patio after a hard day's work can make living through home improvements much more comfortable.

What type of renovation endeavors should you consider this time of year?

- Architectural flooring.
- Architectural woodworking and moldings.
- Room enhancements, redefining or expanding living space.
- Kitchen renovation.
- Bathroom upgrades.
- Window installation.
- Door installation.

Alexandra believes that in most regions large home improvements should not be performed around the house between November 1st and February 28th (with the exception of winterizing your home and an annual furnace check). Many of you are wondering, "But what about the holiday renovation?" A home owner should never take on last-minute projects. This means that you should be planning home renovation at least one season before the work is to be performed. "The holidays are for entertaining and celebrating with friends," Alexandra says, "not being frantic while wondering if the project will be completed by Thanksgiving Day."

Don't hesitate. Mark your plans and make your calls to obtain contractor estimates today.

Re-Thinking, Re-Doing

The two areas in the home that are most often in need of updating are the kitchen and baths. Susan George, a kitchen and bath specialist, shares these essential questions to ask yourself before tearing out showers and replacing cabinets. (Write concrete answers and explore possibilities on the pages of your Frantic Journal.)

- As a part of the planning process, reflect upon what has and has not worked for you in the past and communicate those discoveries to a problem-solving expert in the field. For instance, if you struggle daily with that pile of pots to get to your favorite, would a pot rack fit your decor? Or would a spacious cabinet with slide-out shelves be a better option?
- When updating the kitchen, consider the following:

  1. *Appliance requirements:* Ask yourself specific questions regarding each kitchen appliance. For example, do you prefer the flame control that gas affords, or do you like the predictability of an electric burner with fixed settings? Are you a serious entertainer in need of a double oven? Do you want a flat cooktop because you dread scrubbing the grills, knobs, and insert pans after every meal? These answers will affect the size, style, and quality of the appliances you choose.
  2. *Storage needs:* Do you own a slew of stockpots and oversized colanders that you use with regularity? A peninsula or center island might help to alleviate your storage problem. Is your collection of dishware bulky and weighty? If so, you'll want to choose cabinets with extra-sturdy shelving.
  3. *Seating:* Are you barely able to fit the family around your tiny kitchen table? A built-in bench or counter seating might provide the extra chair space you need.
  4. *A well-laid-out lighting scheme:* Do you like a soft light over the table, but a bright one above the island and countertops? Or do you favor indirect illumination? The entire ambiance of

the kitchen can be altered to your liking with a lighting scheme designed just for you.

- Ask the same questions when renovating a bathroom. Do you want a heated fan above the exit to your shower? And what type of showerhead do you prefer? Do bulky bath towels and lots of toiletries fill your cabinets and linen closet? Do you want faucets and fixtures that are ornate, or easy to clean? Will you be putting on makeup requiring vanity lighting?

Answering these questions before you consult with a professional will ease the process. "If you don't feel you want to replace your kitchen or bath completely," Susan says, "these rooms can be refreshed dramatically with changes to countertops, faucets, hardware, wallpaper or paint, and window treatments."

Decorating with Annuals

Most people plant annuals and perennials in May; however, high summer is a great time to purchase them—including hanging baskets and decorative planters—at lower prices. Sowing in July still leaves a few warm months in most regions to enjoy the added color and flair. After a dose or two of plant fertilizer and with regular waterings thereafter, the plants and flowers will thrive. Decorate for a picnic or party with blossoms bought at an affordable price.

Holiday Happenings:
Christmas in July

Even though you're busy packing for vacations and camps, shuffling kids from lessons to events, and even shopping those irresistible sales, this really is a relaxing time of year. (We can picture it now: You're lounging on a hammock, in the shade of an oak, nibbling chocolate truffles while some gorgeous hunk is doing your laundry and whipping up a soufflé.) This month *should* be more restful, especially in

---

✂ **SNIPPET:** Sandy Feather, of the Pennsylvania State University Cooperative Extension, clarifies some confusion about the link between dog urine and damaged lawns. Sandy says that the nitrogen present in the urine of meat-eaters, including dogs, cats, and humans, causes the brown spots to appear. Sandy dispels the myth that female dogs have more acidic urine than males do. In fact, she says, they don't have more nitrogen in their urine either. Females tend to expel more at one time, while male dogs spray here and there to mark their territories. Sandy also says no evidence exists that adding tomato juice, baking soda, or other dietary supplements to your dog's diet reduces nitrogen content. In fact, doing so might negatively impact your dog's health. So what can you do about this annoying problem? Take the garden hose and water the area after your dog urinates or train your pet to "go" in a designated spot—preferably one that is covered in mulch or dirt rather than grass.

---

contrast to the winter holiday stresses that will reenter your life come November and December.

Although you probably don't want to think about it, the hustle-and-bustle season is just around the corner. If you use the same approach for jingle-bell preparations as you did when planning your summer vacation, you'll be in the right frame of mind for our Christmas in July. For instance, you'd never enjoy your week at the beach without first surfing the Internet months prior to your departure, then dieting and exercising, buying new clothes, cleaning, and packing. And that's exactly how you must approach the Christmas season—in a somewhat methodical, step-by-step manner.

No, you can't really decorate the house or tree this early (at least, not without your neighbors whispering that you've really lost your mind), but here are two things you can do starting today. First, pull out your Frantic Journal and make a new Christmas list. Yes, while the kids are playing outside or when dinner is on the grill, jot at random every person you'll need to remember with a gift this holiday season, including family, friends, neighbors, and service people. Add teachers, bus drivers, car pool moms, office administrators, the mail carrier, your hairstylist, and even your dog groomer. Don't forget to note children's friends, coaches, instrument instructors, tutors, and anyone else who has offered a helping hand to you or the kids throughout the year.

Next, examine your list and categorize the recipients into gift groupings. For example, group together teenaged nieces, neighborhood sitters, and kids' friends in the same age range. Your sisters and sisters-in-law can be lumped into another set. If service people and coaches are all males, combine them. The same tactic applies to everyone on your list. When finished, tally how many names are in each group. At a glance, you can look at that list and say, "I need four toddler gifts, five for men, three elderly, and two for young moms."

Why engage in such a seemingly time-consuming exercise? Classifying people into gift categories simplifies your shopping efforts and helps to minimize any ill feelings that might surface when different gifts are given to same-aged recipients. A couple of teenagers, for example, will definitely analyze whether their gifts were on par with those of their cousins. And preschoolers measure a present's value by size.

On to the second way to jump-start your holidays while the sun is high in the July sky—shopping.

> ✂ SNIPPET: If you view shopping as child's play, allow these numbers to sit in your Santa sack. The National Retail Federation reported that total December sales in 2001 were $309 billion. How many frantic women do you think it takes to ring up that astronomical total during the holly-jolly season?

When hitting the stores between now and Christmas, take a copy of your list with you. To get into the swing of shopping, start with those easy-to-buy-for people on your list like young kids and casual friends. Or those traditional repeaters like elderly relatives for whom you buy gift certificates year after year. Purchase the same item (in varying colors, if you wish) for all the people in each grouping—such as cartoon-figure pajamas for the toddlers or name-brand sweatshirts for the older kids. Scan the stores for gift sets discounted from Father's Day such as valets, mugs, and bathroom books for the men on your list. If a friend has an Americana or seashell decor, pick up accent items at ridiculously low prices. Crystal, wooden, and painted frames make great presents for service people and kids' friends and are always on the summer clearance tables.

Don't overlook outlets, factories, and specialty shops when you're going to and from activities—especially ones that are a distance from home. For example, one sunny Saturday in July when Mary Jo's son was playing in a baseball tournament, the moms decided to take off during the four-hour break between games. Leaving the dads behind to watch over the kids, the ladies headed for a china outlet and a hand-blown glass factory about thirty minutes from the field. Due to the slow shopping season, both retailers had radically slashed their prices. Three hours later, weighed down by hand-crafted vases, discounted ornaments, china clocks, and crystal lamps, the moms returned not only invigorated, but having crossed several names off their lists.

No excuses. Here's your assignment: Get shopping.

Quarterly Taxes

Pay your local wage tax for the second quarter. Depending upon your municipality, it's probably due by the 31st of this month.

DARLING LITTLE ANGELS (AND THE WHOLE BLISSFUL BUNCH)

School Clothes

Who wants to think about school clothes in the middle of summer? Well, we're not giving you a choice. By the time mid-August rolls around, many sizes and prime selections will have vanished from the racks and crowds will have thickened. Invest in jeans, pants, skirts, tops, belts, and shoes now. While you're at it, snoop the sale stuff for lightweight items to start off the school year, including shorts and gym clothes. When prices are this low, it's either now or never.

This advice also applies to students who wear uniforms to school. To complement the plaid from the uniform company, kids are often allowed to wear general styles in blue, khaki, white, and other colors. The trendier attire and desired hues are gone long before the first day of school. So don't wait for a rainy afternoon. Hit the mall today.

Bargains Galore

Far more than just clothing is on sale this month.

- Take advantage of summer deals to snatch up supplies for your college student. Not sure what to buy? Check out our "Back to Campus" list in "A Wee Bit More," part three.
- Let your child spruce up her bedroom decor by having her select from sale or clearance lines. Every kid loves a room makeover, so make it an incentive: If she keeps her room in good order or helps you weed through what's cluttering her closets and drawers, she can pick out a new comforter, a decorative pillow, a new-fangled lamp, or a funky chair.
- Don't forget to pick up reduced supplies like paper products of all kinds to be used for easy cleanup anytime. Don't turn your nose up at holiday, movie-linked, or picnic-look styles. Solid reds can be used for Christmas, while blues accent any Hanukkah and winter parties.
- Stock up on fall birthday gifts at summer-discount prices, too.

Kids and Friends

Help your kids develop positive friendships. Try to encourage your young child not to have only one "best" friend—you might be fooled by the false sense of security it provides. Though this seems vitally important, tant to kids, such friendships can cause a dependency upon one another and an exclusion of others. If you let children know from an early age that friends will move, come and go, and so forth, they will be better able to handle these changes. Here are a few suggestions to help.

- When inviting a friend along, vary the playmate you choose to expand and develop potential friendships.
- If your children aren't in a neighborhood school, keep in contact with the students they enjoyed being with during the previous year.
- Occasionally select a friend—from the neighborhood, scouts, or an activity—who does not go to school with your child. In light of all the competition that surfaces in the classroom, it's a break for kids to be with others on a purely social basis.
- Keep the "friend thing" in check. If you have buddies over all the time, little ones will come to expect it—and won't see it as a privilege anymore. They might even become bored with siblings and parents if they're too accustomed to the excitement of friends. Invite companions sparingly so as not to disrupt the delicate, all-important family dynamics.

Boredom-Free Summer

Despite a busy season of vacationing and outdoor play, your kids are probably ready for a change. No doubt they're beginning to feel restless as the start of a new school year looms in the wake of the passing midpoint of summer. If you hear "I'm bored" or "There's nothing to do" complaints, here are twenty-four ways to keep them busy, twenty-four hours a day.

1. *Host an olympics day.* Organize 100-yard dashes, relay races, and Frisbee throws. Mix in neighbors and a little lemonade. Award ribbons.
2. *Create an obstacle course.* Use old tires as a crawl through, a

piece of wood or a line of bricks for a balance beam, and a skateboard for scooting sitting down. Add bicycle serpentines and tricks on a swing set if one is available. Give freezer treats or lollipops as prizes.

3. *Plan a neighborhood dog show.* Invite owners and hounds to parade and perform tricks. Supply treats and ribbons for all participants.

4. *Plan a progressive lunch.* Divide the menu among several neighborhood homes. Start at your house for salad. Once completed, walk to the next house for the entrée. Let the lunch-goers finish at the third house for dessert. It helps if the progression ends at a house with a pool, playset, or sandbox.

5. *Make a family idea jar.* Write several preferred ideas that everyone would like to do over the next few weeks. Whenever you have a chance, pick one idea from the jar. Make it a rule that no pouting is allowed if your suggestion didn't get picked. That goes for you, too, Mom.

6. *Plan a kid's backyard BBQ.* Have kids plan a menu, invite a limited number of guests, organize the setup, and help with cleaning up.

7. *Take in area craft shows.* Visit a craft show featuring demonstrations in candle dipping, whittling, weaving, or ironworking— using today's technology or that from colonial times.

8. *Take a nature scavenger hunt.* List ten specific items to find on your walk: a miniature pinecone, a yellow leaf, a smooth rock, etc.

9. *Plan a "no-TV" rainy day.* Play cards, play charades, read, or take a walk with flip-flops and umbies.

10. *Play balloon hockey.* Use water-filled balloons instead of a ball or puck. See how many goals can be scored before the balloon breaks.

11. *Start a collection.* Spur your child's imagination by helping him start a collection of rocks, pressed leaves, shells, coins, stamps, key chains, thimbles, postcards, fossils, autographs, or buttons.

12. *Play old-fashioned games.* Kick the can, monkey in the middle, flashlight tag, freeze tag, green light, and dodgeball are favorites, day or night.

13. *Build a backyard miniature golf course.* Set up boards, bricks, plastic pipes, empty cans, or buckets. Make flags from paper towels and wooden dowel rods. Use toy clubs or baseball bats and balls.

14. *Start a neighborhood book or toy swap.* Have each person donate three items. Draw names lottery style. The first child picks her choice of one item, and so on. Toss the names back in the hat and repeat two more times.

15. *Head up a service project.* Perform a good deed such as supporting a clothing drive for the needy, pulling weeds for a church or senior neighbor, or collecting canned goods for a soup kitchen.

16. *Create a chalk town.* Draw roads, stop signs, gas stations, buildings, and parking lots on the driveway, sidewalk, or street (provided it's not busy with traffic, of course). Add small cars and trucks or even scooters and bikes.

17. *Embark on a garage sale hunt.* If it's your bag, teach children to shop for treasures at flea markets and garage sales—including the art of dickering for prices. This is a great place to find pieces to add to the new collection they started in number eleven.

18. *Enjoy a backward lunch.* Allow children to plan the meal, starting with dessert and ending up with yogurt or sandwiches.

19. *Invite friends to a cookie-and-ice cream bash.* Make a batch or two of slice-and-bake cookies. Serve with scoops of ice cream. Allow kids to add their own toppings like sauces, sprinkles, chocolate morsels, candies, and maraschino cherries.

20. *Design edible necklaces.* With licorice as the thread, string cereal or candy. Knot, wear, and eat.

21. *Make a school supply list.* Have children read advertisements to find the best buys for notebooks, pens, and book covers. Then, venture out to purchase.

22. *Go soda can bowling.* Rinse ten empty soda cans, line up in V formation, and use rubber balls to knock 'em down. For a variation, save ten two-liter bottles and do the same.

23. *Plan a rainy-day game-a-thon.* Everyone picks his or her favorite board game to play. Draw game pieces out of a hat to see which one to play first.

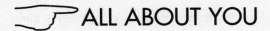

24. *Create a summer collage.* Find photos, brochures, postcards, newspapers, and magazine clippings to capture summer memories. Cut and glue to poster board. Hang the finished products in the kids' rooms or present them to Grandma and Grandpa.

See "A Wee Bit More" in part three for a description of a summer survival kit.

☞ ALL ABOUT YOU

Wardrobe Rut

Are you in a wardrobe rut? With Independence Day behind us, summer wear will be hitting the clearance racks to make way for fall merchandise. For deals that can't be beat, check mailed flyers and newspaper ads for department and specialty shop sales. In July crowds are light, leaving plenty of elbowroom to dig for good buys. At this time of year, you can acquire higher quality clothing for less than off-brand prices, enabling you to inexpensively update your look. Take a fashion risk by trying on knit tops and blouses in colors you never dared to don before. Add a trendy accessory such as a belt, hat, purse, or costume jewelry that puts a swing into your step. The stylish results will be worth the effort.

💎 **HIDDEN GEM:** According to image consultant Happy Barber, "Summer is a time when we women like to go more natural with our makeup." And the bottom line, Happy says, is that means wearing less. But because your accents are less obvious, the shades are more important. Be certain you're wearing colors that make you look your healthiest and most vibrant. Happy recommends cutting down on the time you spend in front of the mirror and still look polished by sweeping on a powder foundation to even out your skin tone. Or for a sun-kissed look, use a bronzer. Add eyeliner in a smoke or dark brown, and a soft pink lipstick. For a variation, use lip gloss. Ahh, won't we feel refreshed sporting our new look?

Take Five: Adults Only

Arrange an adults-only day trip or night out with your spouse, coworkers, or friends. There are plenty of one-day tours provided by luxury bus transportation companies or travel agencies. For the latest offerings, check the weekend insert in your area newspaper, local freebie magazines found in grocery and bookstores, and the cable television FYI channel. Keep in mind, too, that many local religious-affiliated groups, senior citizen centers, and women's clubs open their outings to nonmembers to fill their minimum reservation quotas.

If you can, put together your own overnight or weekend getaway to a nearby town focusing on anything from a cultural interest of yours to just plain shopping satisfaction. Now that school's out, you ought to be able to land a college-aged baby-sitter to cover for you while you rejuvenate.

ONE-STEP-AT-A-TIME CHECKLIST

Date completed Or N/A   **Task**

_____ Use downtime at the pool or ball games to gather references, decor and party tips, or to finish projects.

_____ Organize family photos into albums or scrapbooks.

_____ Hang framed pictures and prints.

_____ Start or finish home improvement endeavors.

_____ Customize kitchen and baths to meet your needs.

_____ Buy discounted annuals and perennials to accent landscaping.

_____ Jump-start Christmas preparations by writing up a gift-giving list. Get shopping.

_____ Pay quarterly taxes.

_____ Purchase school clothes for everyone.

_____ Take advantage of summer deals to buy supplies for your college-bound child or to update kids' bedrooms.

_____ Vary the friends you choose to invite to play with your kids.

_____ Pick one boredom-free activity a day or week to do before the end of summer.

_____ Add pizzazz to your wardrobe and jewelry collection by selecting a fresh style or color.

_____ Plan an adults-only trip for you and your spouse or friends.

Back to Reality

As the jaunty days of summer wind down, we find ourselves frantically trying to cram in *all* that we wanted to do, but never actually pulled off. As you know, once the school bells ring, reality will set in—leaving behind the excitement and freedom of going with the flow. While excursions might be penciled into our calendars, so are last-minute trips to the mall for back-to-school supplies and clothes. Our emotions are split between what we want to do and what we must do before the carefree moments are just a memory behind us. But even though there's work to be done, there's still enough time for a touch of fun.

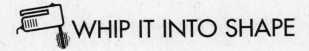 WHIP IT INTO SHAPE

To the Dungeon

After a busy yet gratifying intermission, the day has finally come to clean out the garage. Ugh. Are you uncertain what lies within the guts of your garage—beneath the workbench, behind the overturned

bins, and beside that tangled bunch of bikes? Does the place scare you
a little, reminding you of a castle's dungeon? Realistically, though, you
know you haven't touched two-thirds of that stuff in this millennium.
So follow these tips to gain control.

- Just as we recommended when cleaning your closets, you'll need
  to empty all items from within those four garage walls. Yes, that
  means dragging out absolutely everything including half-used
  paint cans, mismatched nuts and bolts, and all handled tools.
  Pull out bikes, car motors, blow-up swimming pools, the broken
  lawn mower, and weed-cutting devices in various sizes. When
  you place your hands on an item, make a decision about it immediately—preferably choosing to toss or give away, if you haven't
  used it in a while. Think about how, each time you begin a home
  improvement project, you love to purchase fresh supplies to work
  with. So why save the old? Let the kids finish off the spray paint
  on their skateboards and helmets during their next burst of creativity. Or if you can't handle the mess of such a project, simply
  turn your head and toss.
- As you're hauling and sorting, you'll probably come upon lots of
  construction materials that have accumulated over the years—
  including half-used bags of dry cement mix, pieces of drywall,
  plywood, wood trimmings, and extra bricks and tiles from inside
  the house and out. How do you decide what to keep? That's easy.
  Hang on to the items that would be difficult to replace like
  bricks and floor tiles, but pitch the plywood, drywall, or the
  wood scraps (unless you or a friend has a log-burning fireplace
  and can use them for kindling). By the time you reach for them,
  they'll probably be splattered, stained, and warped anyway. Once
  again, donate supplies to the kids' treehouse, bike ramps, and
  other projects.
- Many times in the garage, we ignore our wall-potential. Take a
  look at what's on the floor. What else can you move upward
  besides a rake, broom, and hoe? Pound concrete cut nails (special nails that are made to penetrate concrete as opposed to reg-

ular nails that are made to go through wood) into cement block walls to hold bicycles, sleds, and ladders that swallow up so much valuable floor space.

- Do you need to affix some additional shelving? Several types can be purchased at home improvement stores, from metal to wood. Be sure to anchor shelving to the foundation to avoid injuries and prevent tilting or toppling. If you have young children or pets, think about purchasing a locked steel cabinet to store paint cans, fertilizers, and other items you must keep out of their reach.
- Do you have holiday wreaths, signs, or light displays lying about? If so, drive cut nails into the concrete block. Cover the wreath in a plastic bag, then hang from the hook.

Now that you've turned your castle's dungeon into a place where you can actually park the car, you can sport a shameless smile each time the garage door is raised.

Outdoor Deals

Watch for reduced prices on landscaping needs including plants and trees, mulch, and other such outdoor supplies as patio furniture, barbeque grills, sports equipment (like volleyball nets, badminton sets, croquet), and swimming pool cleaning tools and chemicals. Is there a patio set, swing set, or hammock you've eyed and wanted but never got around to purchasing? Were you waiting for it to go on sale? Stores need to move these bulky space gobblers rather than store them in the warehouse for another year. If the asking dollar amount still lies outside your budget, ask the store manager if and when the price will be pruned again. If you're lucky, he'll take your telephone number and tip you off on the clearance sale date. If not, call every day to inquire.

On the Road

Give some attention to the car. Is it time for a tune-up, oil and filter change, overhaul, wash, wax, or vacuum? Keep a rag or a container of dashboard wipes inside your glove compartment for quick dusting while waiting in traffic, at the drive through, or in the parking lot at school.

Prepare for daily car trips by keeping a supply of hand wipes or waterless sanitizer on hand, quarters for the toll road or vending machines, non-aspirin products, a first aid kit, tissues, hair brush and scrunchies, a blanket, umbrellas, a detailed map of the vicinity, music, travel games, decks of cards, small toys, crayons, and paper. Store bulkier supplies in a plastic container with a snap-on lid in the trunk or in the back of the van or SUV. See our complete list, "Everything You'll Ever Need on the Go," in part three, "A Wee Bit More."

SNIPPET: Feel like you're forever chauffeuring the family? The first taxicabs appeared in 1907 with meters and gasoline-powered engines. Wouldn't we eat up the kids' allowances pretty quickly if we kept our own car meters running?

Veggie Patch Surplus

Here we are near the end of the growing season and your garden is abounding with tomatoes, peppers, and succulent cucumbers. You've got more zucchini and squash than any one family can consume, even with the hungriest pack of teenaged boys. (Of course, if you were growing pepperoni pizzas, it would be a completely different story.) With the surplus from your fresh vegetable patch, you can prepare a chunky garden salsa, some tasty pasta sauce, or moist and delicious zucchini breads. Freeze the excess finished products (except the salsa) in order to enjoy the veggies of your labor for months to come.

While you're at it, make batches of breads or salsa for your child's school or organization to sell. Or if putting on a chef's hat isn't your idea of a party, donate the extra produce to a homeless shelter whose staff will welcome the fresh additions to their menus.

If you neglected to sow and reap this season but know someone

> 💎 **HIDDEN GEM:** As a bonus, you can take your food donation as a tax deduction. Just be sure to document with receipts the purchase of plants, fertilizer, and other needs. Then, you'll have to accurately estimate what percentage of your garden was used for charity. Lastly, be sure the institution you're donating to is registered with the IRS as a charitable organization. Ask for receipts from the soup kitchen as proof of your giving. It sounds complicated, but it's not. That's called creative tax planning.

who did, don't hesitate to mention how you'd love any leftovers from the backyards of friends and neighbors. Many times, gardeners are searching for outlets to give away their extras that will soon be on the rotting road.

> 💎 **HIDDEN GEM:** After you've concocted your homemade spaghetti sauce, use it as a base for a great in-between or after-school snack for the kids. What's the snack? Pizza bagels. Spread homemade sauce over one-half of a sliced bagel. Top with shredded cheese and toppings. Repeat for desired quantity. Lay prepared singles on a cookie sheet and place the tray in the freezer until frozen. Deposit several frozen snacks into individual freezer bags. Microwave on defrost for 1 minute, then zap at medium power for 60 seconds. (Due to the varying rate of cooking in microwave ovens, times are approximate.) What? You have no bagels in the bread drawer? Reach for a canister of ready-to-bake dinner rolls. Flatten rolls on a cookie sheet and spread the sauce. Add cheese and toppings and bake for six to eight minutes at 350 degrees F. Then flash-freeze and zap as directed above. You can probably think of many more variations of this delightful snack—English muffins, thick slices of French bread—the list goes on and on!

DARLING LITTLE ANGELS (AND THE WHOLE BLISSFUL BUNCH)

Holiday Happenings: Labor Day

Make Labor Day plans. Will you have a picnic at your place or will you be a guest elsewhere? Haven't received an invitation? Take the family on one last great adventure either in town to a favorite destination or on a special getaway weekend. At the very least, participate in closing-day celebrations at your local swimming pool.

Child Care

Plan before- and after-school care if you work later than school dismissal times. Ponder these questions before making your decisions.

- Are you able to send your school-aged kids to the same caregiver as your toddler?
- Does your school district offer in-school/after-hours supervision?
- Do nearby churches, community centers, or day care facilities have affordable options?
- Have you considered hiring a teenager to come to your home instead?
- Will the provider prompt the kids to start on their homework?
- Is there an after-school recreation program, such as those sponsored by certain establishments like bowling centers, that will pick up the students at school one day a week? A responsible party will bus them to the center, where parents can claim their little ones later. Opportunities like this give kids a fun break from the mundane routine of everyday child care.

Kids' Activities

Finalize the kids' extracurricular activities for fall. Look into school team tryouts, intramurals, local leagues, and club sports. Don't forget such extras as chess club, art classes, forensics team, and chorus. Some of these might not be offered until September, but call coaches and organizers to find out what is required in order for your child to participate. Some might already have a practice and event schedule worked out for you.

Take the following factors into account when evaluating what activities to add to your child's weekly schedule.

Of Primary Importance
- How well does your child handle the pressures of schoolwork? Remember, classes should be his number one responsibility. So if he has to study hard to keep his grades up to par, you might not want to enroll him in more than one or two activities.

The Right Motives
- *Wants:* Does your child really want to participate in the sports program you're recommending or is it something you want her to do? Are you signing him up for piano lessons because your friend's child has played? Instead, pay attention to what sparks your children's natural curiosity. By choosing a program in that field of interest, you're encouraging them to do something they want to do. And this sends out a positive signal because they are playing a role in the decision-making process.
- *Needs:* Are there certain activities your child needs to be involved in for various physical, social, or emotional reasons? For example, you might want to enroll the child who needs to refine her gross motor skills in dance class. An introverted child might benefit more from the confidence-building tae kwon do. And the independent child might blossom on a soccer or basketball team, while your socialite will learn to focus if immersed in the self-expression of art or music classes. For instance, when it became clear that karate would help Loriann Hoff Oberlin's youngest son with his slight case of cerebral palsy, she enrolled him to help refine his gross motor skills. It was a workout recommended by the doctors because it required him to use all parts of his body.

Extent of Commitment

- *Energy:* What is the energy level of training required for the team or activity? Can your son or daughter maintain the stamina needed for the commitment? For example, you don't want to enroll your still-napping toddler in an afternoon story time at the library. Or will related events, such as late-evening games, interfere with your growing teen's need to sleep? Though some children can handle going to bed an hour or two later than usual, others cannot. Know your child's energy level and sign him up fittingly.
- *Time:* How much time does each commitment require? Some teams call for kids to be at practice four or five days a week. Others like the science club or junior soccer might meet once or twice a week, at most.
- *Duration:* What is the duration of the undertaking? Some activities offer seasons that last eight weeks and others that run from September through April. Consider your child's stamina and only register her for what she can fulfill to completion.

Hidden Drawbacks

- *Money:* The money question is plain and simple—can you afford this activity? No one will benefit from an enrichment program if you have to stretch the family budget to enroll. Ask about hidden costs that crop up as the season rolls on—tournament fees, special equipment, and extra uniform purchases. Some programs offer ways to ease the financial burden. Just ask.
- *Fund-raisers:* Will you be expected to donate time and to support fund-raisers along the way? Find out if these are optional or mandatory.

Based on the information gathered, decide what responsibilities your child can manage and register accordingly.

You might want to follow the advice of single parent and mother of four Mary Lee Gannon. As a public relations consultant, Mary Lee found that simplifying children's activities works best for everyone, especially single parents. "One trip to a sport or activity turns into two. Multiply that by four children and I could be spending most of my day in the car." Mary Lee's children participate in one sport in the winter and they all swim on the same team in the summer. "Swim teams are great because they are co-ed and, most of the time, all the children practice in the same place at the same time, minimizing my driving duties."

In addition, playing musical instruments and singing in the chorus are part of the school activities in Mary Lee's district. Her kids take advantage of this opportunity because instruction is given during the school day. As an added bonus, the lessons are usually free and the only thing left is the cost to rent or purchase the instrument. Mary Lee feels that keeping all her children in the same ventures has brought the kids closer. "We are more of a family now, and tend to pull together for each other."

One last word of advice. Dr. Tim Murphy, coauthor of *The Angry Child*, suggests that parents take a careful look at the number of activities their children participate in. Too many activities can overwhelm a child. Dr. Murphy says he's never met a child whose emotional problem resulted from not being allowed to partake in multiple after-school activities, but the converse is definitely true. Ask your child to pick one or two activities, and don't be surprised if she has a tough time prioritizing. This is symptomatic of individuals in a frantic family. Dr. Murphy assures parents that they aren't punishing a child by requiring him to read a book or by finding something else to occupy his time that doesn't involve a scheduling commitment and many dollars' worth of equipment.

Second Chance: School Wear

As a second chance, sort through the closets for summer items the kids can wear at the beginning of the school year. What shorts, shirts, and dresses are still in good shape? Check for stains, tears, or missing buttons. Decide which ones you have the energy to repair and which should go to the donation box. Do their jackets and favorite sweatshirts still pass inspection? If your son grew like the Jolly Green Giant, you might have to buy a pair or two of shorts or lightweight pants to get him through the first few weeks of school—before diving into his new fall wardrobe.

School Preparations

Obtain school supplies during the back-to-school sales. Because prices are so low, stock up on extra glue bottles and sticks, tape, notebooks, pencils, erasers, markers, pens, crayons, chalk, loose-leaf paper, index cards, and folders that will undoubtedly need to be replenished throughout the school year.

HIDDEN GEM: With bargain-basement discounts on schoolroom basics, buy enough crayons, markers, and colored pencils to give out as usable favors for upcoming birthday parties, classroom handouts for Halloween celebrations, or practical stuffers for Christmas stockings.

College Bound

The clock is ticking and, while your college-aged kids have been concentrating on the all-important collegiate wardrobe expansion, most parents are more concerned with the necessities. The list of supplies needed for one university-bound student is mind-boggling. To complicate matters, an average dorm room is about the size of a walk-in closet. So, how can you manage to stuff everything into that small space and still make your son or daughter's life away from home comfortable?

When your child collaborates with her future roommate, aside from discussing who will bring the essentials (TV, DVD, VCR), remind them of overlooked items like a coffeemaker, toaster oven, and a George Foreman grill (if allowed). First, read the information packet sent by the school to find out the regulations regarding in-room appliances. Some schools only permit students to use the minifridge/microwave combo that can be rented through the institution.

Even if your student has a weekly menu plan, a fridge and coffeemaker will come in handy for those early-morning classes when he can't make it to the cafeteria beforehand or for those late-night cravings when cramming for a test. Coffeemakers are especially important if microwaves and toasters are not allowed. By adding water to packaged soups and noodles, he'll be able to prepare a hot snack on a cold winter day.

With the big items out of the way, you can focus on the little things like favorite pens, printer paper, and phone cards. To save money, acquire whatever merchandise you can, taking advantage of the loss leaders featured in store ads during August. If time is a factor, order supplies through an office supply store via the Internet and have them shipped directly to your child's dorm room.

Don't forget the munchies. Buy cereal, breakfast bars, dried fruits, trail mix, dried noodles, and soups along with his preferred junk food—which will save him from buying snacks at elevated school store prices.

As a tip, note that whatever your daughter indicates she doesn't want to take with her, she probably won't use anyway. And since space is so precious in most college dorms, you might as well save yourself the hassles of trying to fit in unwanted objects, then having to lug them all back home again. If she vetoes the umbrella and snow boots this round, you can always send them up next time. Kids tend to become more practical about keeping warm and dry once they've had to hike out in the cold and wet. It seems that after they trudge all over the campus for a while, they experience a change of heart. Suddenly, Mom has gotten smarter—well, just a little anyway.

HIDDEN GEM: Before you ring up school supply purchases, see if the office supply retailer is a Upromise supporter. (If you haven't registered for Upromise, see our February chapter.) As you stock up on all those back-to-school needs, your child's college savings account could be going ka-ching.

Depending upon the dorm setup, moving day can run smoothly or become a ripple of glitches. To make the transition easier for all, follow these tips.

- Take a broom and mop, and a bucket filled with cleaning supplies and rags. The room might have been cleaned to your liking. Then again, it might not.
- Borrow a dolly. Sometimes the wait for the dormitory elevator can take forty-five minutes or more. By loading up a dolly, not only will you make fewer trips, you'll have less frustration, too.
- Pack items in under-the-bed containers. This saves space stashing extra clothes, health and beauty supplies, or food.
- Take extra regular and heavy-duty extension cords, masking and duct tape, small hand tools—hammer, nails, screwdrivers, and batteries—drinks, and snacks.
- While moving in and setting up the room, list items you've forgotten or that come up unexpectedly. This will save you from making several trips to the nearest store.
- Take a breather and go out for lunch or dinner to calm fraying nerves. Don't bother rushing this time-consuming process. Plan on spending the day.

Aim to make the college transition as good as it can be—for you and your fledgling.

HIDDEN GEM: Don't forget to send proof of your student's full-time enrollment to your health insurance company. A copy of his schedule, tuition bill, or a letter from the school will do. This act might help reduce your monthly payments as some students are covered under umbrella policies carried by some universities. Check with the individual institution to confirm what coverage they offer. Inquire about college allowances with your auto insurance policies, as well. Sometimes, full-time, car-less students qualify for a lower rate while matriculated.

Hair Care for All

Schedule the kids' haircuts now so they don't look scraggly on the first day of school. To save time, make all appointments on the same day. Or better still, schedule cuts at the same time with different stylists. Then, rather than taking an hour and a half for three haircuts, for instance, the kids will be washed, snipped, and groomed in just 30 minutes.

Preserving the Color of Summer

Take advantage of the last blooms of summer by making dried flower notecards as an alternative to store-bought ones. Pluck flowers and their leaves, such as violets, Johnny-jump-ups, Queen Anne's lace, and impatiens, from the stems. Place between several sheets of paper towels or blotting paper available in craft stores and press under a stack of books. After two weeks or so, add a drop of glue to the back of the flower and arrange it on folded card stock or blank notecards. Cover with clear contact paper and trim the edges for cards with a colorful, natural flair.

Fun for All

Before you know it, the kids will be back in school. So squeeze in a little more fun. Take a moment to reflect upon the last two months. What did you want to do this summer but haven't gotten around to scheduling yet? Have you visited the water parks, hit the bike trails, or tried roller blading? Or why not set up backyard activities such as a miniature golf tournament or mini-pie-eating contest? Possibly your crew would rather make sand art pictures or their own frozen juice bars.

✂ **SNIPPET:** The next time your kids are slopping in the kitchen, don't shout. They could become the next Fran Epperson. In 1905 at eleven years of age, he invented the Popsicle in his mother's kitchen.

The Family Dinner

Before you find yourself rushing around with the demands of fall, make the time for some sit-down family dinners. At least once a week this month, prepare a good meal, set the table (with tablecloth and fine china, if you'd like), dine together, and let the conversation flow. Discuss the summer that's nearly passed and the upcoming school year. Talk about everything from disappointments and challenges to expectations and dreams.

☞ ALL ABOUT YOU

Interoffice Memo: Moving Ahead

If you work outside the home, examine your position thoroughly, including salary, hours, benefits, and opportunities for promotion. Evaluate employee morale and overall comfort of the work environment. Would attending classes, conferences, or continuing education courses help to improve any aspect of your employment situation? Sometimes working toward a degree in a more relevant field or obtaining an advanced degree in your area of expertise can enhance your potential on the company flowchart. If you can't commit to the structure of traditional schooling, look into credit courses offered via the Internet or on video. Confirm that the classwork is university affiliated so as not to waste your time and money.

Barb and Joanne offer two examples of improving your career situation.

Administrative assistant Barb Ralston was nudged by her inner urge to get ahead, so she decided to register for classes. In order for her to advance within her company hierarchy, she felt she needed to obtain an accounting degree. She was already handling a portion of the job, without receiving the salary to go with it, so this motivated Barb to reach her goal. Not only did the additional education enable her to apply for a better position but, as we discussed in the May chapter, the company paid for her coursework. So for Barb, it was nothing but a win-win situation.

Similarly, Joanne Emrick, a technical writer for an advertising agency, looked closely at her position at work. While she loved the job because it was within walking distance of her home and allowed her to continue to cultivate her creative side, Joanne admitted to herself that she could probably increase her salary by applying elsewhere. In a few weeks, Joanne had interviewed and accepted a job in a nearby town. With the start of college tuition payments for three kids looming, Joanne celebrated the fact that she more than doubled her salary. "I gave it a shot," Joanne says. "With a little effort and a lot of guts, I took a chance and ended up winning."

Evaluating your situation at work and considering all possibilities can be an effective, worthwhile approach for you, too.

Neighborhood Night Out

As kids are getting ready to go back to school, many of the neighborhood women are preparing for the first round of social gatherings. Reach out by joining or forming a Bunco (a dice game) group, a bridge club, or other regular activity that will ensure you a night out at least once a month. Even if you don't know many of the players, become a member. It'll give you a chance to spread beyond your usual societal boundaries. This form of connecting can take place among friends, coworkers, or family, as well.

(P.S. Don't know how to play Bunco? Check "A Wee Bit More" in part three for rules and variations of play.)

If playing games just isn't your thing, coordinate a monthly hobby night. On a regularly scheduled night (say the second Wednesday of the month), have friends or family tote to your house projects they're currently working on—whether it involves placing photos in albums, candy-making endeavors, or creating the early Christmas crafts we prompted you to start in March. If they don't have a hobby, encourage guests to bring anything at all, including birthday invitations to be filled out, papers to be sorted and filed, or even a heap of unmated socks. Work together over light refreshments for a few hours after the kids have gone to bed. Adopt this as your one evening a month to set aside all else but friends, food, and plenty of fun.

As a more educational alternative, Helen Hill and twenty-two of her female colleagues belong to a Women's Investment Network. Members allocate $20 per month each and take turns doing the research for stock investments. All transactions are handled through a broker and the taxes are figured by a professional accountant. You must be twenty-one or older to join. To form such a group, ask your broker for assistance.

Take Five: Express Yourself

If you aren't currently working full-time outside the home, evaluate the upcoming available time that will surface once the kids are back in school. What will you do? (Not that there aren't walls to be scrubbed and closets to be straightened.) Look into special events just for you like traveling exhibits, trade shows, or women-related expos. Or delve into a new venue like genealogy, feng shui, or outlining that book you always wanted to write.

Does increasing the family cash flow pique your interest? If so, it might be time to pursue the first steps in starting a home-based business. Draw up a business plan for one that utilizes your talents and know-how. You can develop a resume-writing service, start a hand-painted T-shirt business, or decide to sell wares from a party-plan company such as Pampered Chef or Longaberger.

Jump into that exercise class or "boot up" your nerve to enroll in the computer course you've put on the back burner. Or raise your hand to volunteer at the library, church, or within the community. (See our volunteering section in the April chapter.) Maybe you'd rather introduce a new fund-raising event for your child's school or team that will boost the bottom line of their bank account. Join a personal interest club for fall such as Mothers & More (www.mothersandmore.org), a book discussion group, or a prayer circle.

If you can't find anything at all that's of interest to you, start up a group of your own inviting three or four colleagues, friends, or neighbors who have a common interest. Plan a weekly or semimonthly gathering at a local coffee shop or by rotating home hosts. As an example, fashion consultant Denise Stewart and a dozen other women formed the Friday Morning Breakfast Club that meets monthly. The coffee klatch solves world problems, over-easy.

Well, if some of your kids are in school but there's still a tyke or two at home, you might consider looking into a Mother's Day Out or drop-off day care program usually run by community religious groups (though you don't have to be affiliated to participate). Most of the time, you can call a week or even a day ahead for your child to attend as long as there is a vacancy for him. So, if you need a break or have a doctor's appointment one week, off your son goes. Conversely, if you're short of cash the following week, home he stays.

If you live in a more remote area and can't get to a nearby town for events, join a newsgroup or discussion board online. There's a plethora of Web sites for busy women—including our own www.franticwoman.com!

Are you looking for something to take you away, without opening your front door? Consider debuting your own Web site, like Mia Cronan did. After she gave birth to her second child, Mia waved good-bye to the corporate world and welcomed full-time motherhood. Once home, she lunged into a project she had always wanted to try, but never seemed to have the time. Through trial and error, Mia taught herself Web designing. Three years after she created the Web site MainStreetMom.com, the site receives a million hits a month. Not bad, taking into account that she now has four children.

ONE-STEP-AT-A-TIME CHECKLIST

Date
completed
Or N/A

Task

_____ Clean and organize garage.
_____ Purchase outdoor needs and summer supplies at clearance prices.

_____ Provide maintenance care to car.

_____ Prepare sauces, salsas, and breads with garden surplus or donate what you will not use.

_____ Plan Labor Day celebrations.

_____ Confirm child care arrangements for after school.

_____ Decide which extracurricular activities will benefit the kids.

_____ Make use of this second chance to gather school clothes.

_____ Buy school supplies at bargain prices. Purchase extras for birthday and holiday party favors.

_____ Prepare college-bound student for moving day.

_____ Schedule back-to-school haircut appointments.

_____ Make pressed flower notecards.

_____ Enjoy a last round of fun before summer slips away.

_____ Host several sit-down family dinners just for your crew.

_____ Evaluate your work position and make plans to move ahead.

_____ Plan a regular neighborhood night out for the girls.

_____ Decide what you will do with available free time once kids are in school.

Adjusting

T hough the transition from spring to summer is smooth sailing for the typical frantic woman, the onset of fall seems to tow her into dangerous currents. She's swept up in a whirlwind of duties—stowing summer items and preparing the yard for fall, on top of filling out emergency forms and scrambling to school commitments and extracurricular activities. Despite the realization that learning to balance family, school, work, and outside responsibilities isn't easy, somehow in the midst of it all she needs to grab hold of her sanity and maybe even take a step back to her roots.

Looking at September as a chance for a fresh new start, this month we'll show you how to conquer the morning rush, homework hassles, and Halloween preparations.

REMEMBERING SEPTEMBER 11TH

We will never forget the tragedy and loss that changed us as a nation on September 11, 2001; therefore, we should carry on the tradition of *giving* that so many people displayed that day and for months thereafter.

- Send a thank-you to our troops for being the backbone of our nation. Involve schools, organizations, and communities in the project. Contact your local American Red Cross branch to inquire about locating troop address information.
- Spend a few hours a month on a community project within your neighborhood like joining your state's Adopt-a-Highway Litter Control program, which helps keep America beautiful. And if the kids are old enough, by all means, take the family with you.
- Give a donation to a related fund, such as the Todd M. Beamer Foundation (www.beamerfoundation.org), that focuses on the children who lost a parent in the tragedy on September 11, 2001. For most charities like this one, you can donate via snail mail or online.
- Pay tribute to your police force, fire department, and emergency medical staff whose fraternity so willingly gave everything they had. Visit, send a thank-you, and support their fund-raisers and contribution drives.
- Instill in your children the greatness of freedom, unity, and pride in being an American. For younger ones, read books on our heritage, build puzzle maps, or color patriotic printouts from relevant Web sites. For teens, rent or buy videos relating to our country's history or founding fathers. Such films as *Patton*, *The Blue and The Gray*, and *North and South* depict the reality of war and the benefits of democracy. Check public television and radio Web sites for purchasing historical documentaries. Visit American history museums, battlegrounds, forts, and other authentic sites.

Janet Fromlak, whose reservist husband was placed on active duty on the morning of September 11th, reminds us that we can help in simple ways. All you need to do is lend a hand to those families whose loved ones are serving in the armed forces and reserves. "I had to learn

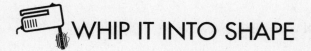

how to accept assistance from others," Janet says. "I used to be so self-sufficient." But as a nurse and mother of two, many times Janet had to be in two places at once and could no longer rely on her husband. "Friends and family offered to drive my children to games and practices," Janet says. "It was minor to them, yet their simple gestures of kindness made such a difference to me." She describes how Sharon Johnson, her sister-in-law, prepared the family's dinner at least four times a week, despite having her own work-related and familial commitments. "She'd even restock my refrigerator and pantry," Janet says.

"Although I know how fortunate I am," the thankful wife and mother concludes, "September 11th has changed my life—as it has for all of us. And on top of everything else, I am grateful for the little things people did and are still doing for me."

This is a simple way to give in honor of your country and the people who serve. Cook a meal or arrange a car pool to join the "helping" forces, today.

WHIP IT INTO SHAPE

Planning Ahead

In August, we asked you to evaluate the kids' activities as you added them to the weekly schedule. Now, we're going to test how you did. Write up a tentative weekly schedule for the entire family in your Frantic Journal. Who will you need to transport where and how often? List each day of the week, marking departure deadlines and the time you will return from the gang's mix of activities.

Now that it's in black and white, does it seem like too much for one woman to handle? Reevaluate to see what can be eliminated or changed. What car pools can you form to save time along the way? Is the schedule so jam-packed that the kids will miss life's simple pleasures, such as riding bikes, jumping rope, or playing kickball, because they're in structured activities every day of the week?

Include Mom and Dad's commitments, too. Then, post a copy of the schedule on the refrigerator, bulletin board, or some other central location. At a glance, all family members can determine who will be where and when. This written "proof" is especially helpful in preventing your daughter, for example, from volunteering you to drive the crew to the mall on a day when you're already scheduled to be here, there, and everywhere.

Single mother of two Mary Ramsey says that the most difficult transition she had to make as a newly divorced parent involved scheduling. She found that she no longer was at liberty to leave her children—even for short periods—without planning for such trips well ahead of time. "My days are so much more organized now," Mary says. "I have to plan most of the things I took for granted, like shopping for groceries, running errands, and getting to work and my classes on time." Her advice to other single moms is to diagram every hour on paper. "I include specific times for everything from buying lunch supplies at noon to blocking ten to midnight for my college coursework." While it sounds rather rigid, by planning ahead, you'll save yourself from the many headaches that result when, as a frazzled woman, you've neglected to have all your bases covered.

As you move deeper into the school year, you and yours might not require so many reminders to be published on the weekly calendar. You don't seem to check anymore, for example, to find out when violin lessons start or when soccer practice ends. So gradually drop from the printed schedule such regular commitments—those that rarely change and are almost never forgotten (notice, we said "almost never"). This action de-clutters your agenda, actually adding white space—making it easier for you to read the new additions and adaptations each week. This might be an especially appealing option for you Towelers out there, who like to look for the light at the end of the tunnel.

Getting Started

For the first week or two of September, refrain from adding extra commitments that can be put off until later in the month, like having friends over, family jaunts for entertainment purposes, and impromptu visits to Grandma's house. Why? Because you need to allow adjustment time for the hecticism of switching everyone to the new school schedule. Kids will be overly tired, so set aside downtime for them to come home from school, settle in, watch a movie, or play outside. By devoting these early days of September to helping your children adjust, not only will everyone have a chance to be comfortable as a family again, but you can plan for an earlier bedtime routine, too. As the kids begin to adapt, you can slowly add in those "luxury" engagements when everyone will be better able to handle them.

Morning Rush

Doesn't it seem that no matter how much preparing you do, the morning rush unfailingly escalates from a slight breeze to a twirling twister? So how can you stay on top of things? Phase these adaptations into your morning routine to help with everything from backpacks to outfits to breakfast cereal.

- On Sunday evenings, select the week's work and school clothes—including accessories—to eliminate morning indecision. If you can't manage to do this for the five-day period, at least attempt to pick out ensembles each evening to ready yourself for the day to come.
- When deciding on clothes to wear for the week, single out a spare outfit, too, for those mornings when you just don't want to wear the chosen garb due to weather, color, fit, or feel.
- If the calendar spotlights an important business meeting, luncheon, or function mid-week, plan your entire outfit from jewelry to shoes on Sunday night, as well. Your nerves will already be snarled up without worrying about what to wear and which shoes coordinate best with what belt, etc.
- Designate a more spacious spot to hang chosen clothes to prevent wrinkling, especially if your closet is packed to the gills. If you have nowhere to drape the week's choices, attach a tie rack to the back of your bedroom door for quick and easy access. Or

buy a couple of wreath hooks to suspend from everyone's bedroom door and hang the daily choices there.

- Purchase solid-colored slacks and short-sleeved tops in harmonious hues. This "uniform" becomes your wardrobe foundation and can easily be topped with a neutral sweater or a blazer and various accessories for a fresh look anytime.

- Buy basic shirts and sweaters in cream, white, blue, and black; they will coordinate with most suits, slacks, and patterned skirts—helping your predetermining process to proceed in a snap.

- Hang small zippered plastic bags containing selected jewelry right on the hanger with each outfit by poking a hole in the bag or suspending it from a wire Christmas ornament hook. This eliminates the hemming and hawing over bangles and beads in the morning when you can barely open your eyes.

- And now, on to the chow: Simplify matters by setting up a ready-to-go breakfast center. If everyone in the home enjoys a different kind of cold cereal in the morning, pre-pour into sealable plastic bowls the night before—allowing kids to choose their own cereal type. Keep the color of bowl the same for each person each day to avoid confusion, especially for the little ones.

- Designate a specific spot in the house for backpacks and briefcases. This could be a freestanding coatrack or one that's anchored to wall studs for stability, an over-the-door-top hook, a sturdy shelf, or even a wicker laundry basket or hamper situated in an empty corner of the kitchen.

- If you are a hair spray addict, avoid having to scrub the built-up gunk it leaves on the bathroom floor. After your morning shower, toss your towel on the floor in the same area where you do the sticky deed. After you've spritzed and sprayed, and the bits that haven't made it to your head have landed on the towel, pick it up and toss in the laundry. A towel a day keeps the buildup away.

- If you have just thirty seconds, toss in a load of laundry that needs to soak. Once it swishes, open the lid to stop it. Allow clothes to marinate while you're gone for the day. This sudsy method works best for soiled uniforms, smelly socks, and work-out tees.

- Gather samples of cosmetic products (mascara, shadow, lipstick, foundation, and blush) into an extra makeup bag or zippered plastic bag to stash in your car's glove compartment. The next time the morning chaos erupts and forces you to race out the door barefaced, you won't panic, knowing your spares are only an arm's length away.

On the Road Again

If you've followed our advice, you've set up a few car pools for relief. To keep them on a relatively smooth course, refer to the following suggestions. (To ready your vehicle for the car pool season, see the "On the Road" section in the August chapter.)

- Before you say "Yes" to the car pool commitment, be choosy about those you decide to buddy-up with. If the invited car pool child is generally argumentative and difficult, the hassles you'll face might not be worth the time you'll save. Remember, you don't want to compromise your own sanity or your child's well-being just to save a few hours' time.
- Rather than alternating car pools by day, follow Sharon Knobe-loch's example and interchange by weeks or months. Then, yes, you'll be stuck driving to soccer for the whole month of September, but you can smile and relax as your friend drives throughout October. "With fifteen-month-old twins toddling around," Sharon says, "the car pool for my kindergartner was a lifesaver. When it wasn't my week to drive, I'd hole up in my house, put the girls in for a nap, and get to work."

Are you involved in a car pool arrangement for which you can never reciprocate, either because you're a single parent or work full-time (or both)? If so, what can you do?

- If you can afford it, periodically buy gift certificates for the driver's favorite restaurant or store. When deciding on an amount to give, think about the aggravation you've avoided because he or she has offered to help. If buying certificates on a regular basis will cause you financial strain, at least remember this individual during the holiday season. (Don't worry. We'll remind you about her and other service people later in the year.)
- Every now and then, prepare dinner or dessert for the car pool driver with a sincere note of thanks. Because so few people put the pen to the page these days, a thank-you gesture goes a long, long way.
- Invite the car pool child (even if he isn't your little one's first choice) for a weekend afternoon to give the other mom a few hours off.
- Try bartering. To alleviate the stress of driving three children to three different places at the same time, Rita Bergstein found bartering to be a great tool. Another soccer mom mentioned that her daughter had an interest in writing. Rita tapped into her own literature background and offered to edit and guide the daughter through her first novel. Thrilled with the idea, the mom asked what she could do in return. Can you guess? If you answered carpooling to and from soccer practices, you sure were right.

Grab-and-Go Dinners

Along with the shift of season comes a change in the kitchen. And if you thought your summer was brimming with busy days, you ain't seen nothin' yet. Exactly how does a frantic woman feed a family when she's forever playing Guess Who's Coming to Dinner? To help take some of the load off your shoulders, we're passing along a few of our favorite recipes for quick-fix yet yummy, nutritious meals. We call them our grab-and-go dinners.

These meal suggestions can be prepared in large volumes, frozen, and zapped for hungry family members on the run.

❖ Mary Jo's Mini Strombolis ❖

INGREDIENTS

1 loaf frozen bread dough

½ pound deli lunchmeat (your choice—you can use two varieties for a thicker stromboli)

½ pound cheese (your choice)

your favorite toppings (mushrooms, olives, onions)

(Note: Vegetarians can replace lunchmeat with additional veggies—broccoli works well).

Step one: Allow bread dough to thaw and rise according to package instructions. Divide into quarters. On a floured surface, roll each section into a rectangular shape approximately 8 by 5 inches. Layer meat, cheese, and toppings. Add another layer of meat, if desired. Starting at one end, roll as if you were making a jelly roll and place on a lightly greased cookie sheet. Tuck the ends under. Use an egg white wash to paste the edges together, or seal by moistening the edges with water.

Step two: Bake at 350 degrees F for 20 to 25 minutes or until light brown.

Tips: Place cheese in the center of the rectangle to prevent oozing. You can also line the cookie sheet with foil for easy cleanup. Vary the stuffings according to your family's preferences. For example, layer pepperoni and cheese for a flavorful after-school or party snack. Make larger strombolis by dividing the frozen loaf into two parts, rather than four. Prepare in batches of 12 or 24 and freeze.

➤ Mom B.'s Foil Sandwiches ◆

INGREDIENTS

1 stick butter
1 clove garlic (minced)
1 small onion (finely chopped)
One (8-count) package of sandwich buns
1 pound shaved ham (or your favorite variety of lunchmeat)
8 slices cheese (your choice)
dill pickles, chopped (optional)

(Note: Dairy-eating vegetarians can replace meat with another type of cheese.)

Step one: Melt butter. Remove from heat and stir in garlic and onion. Spread butter mixture on inside top and bottom of buns. Place desired amount of ham on sandwich. Add one slice of cheese and pickles, if desired. Close sandwich and wrap in foil. Freeze or heat as instructed below.

Step two: When ready to eat, warm sandwiches in a 350-degree-F oven until heated through or cheese melts. (This can take 30 minutes or so, if frozen.) Or remove from foil and microwave on medium. (Much better from oven.)

Tips: Use shredded cheese for faster melting. Make several dozen and freeze. Can store frozen for 1 to 2 months.

✦ Mom S.'s Potato Boats ✦

INGREDIENTS

5 pounds potatoes (cooked and mashed)
2 3-ounce packages cream cheese
1 cup sour cream
2 tablespoons butter or margarine
2 teaspoons onion salt
salt and pepper (to taste)
cooking spray
toppings of your choice (shredded cheese, crumbled bacon, chives, etc.)
individual-sized aluminum oval boat pans approximately 5-by-2½-by-
   1-inch deep (found in larger grocery stores)

Step One: Add cream cheese, sour cream, butter, onion salt, and salt and pepper to cooked mashed potatoes. Beat wth an electric mixer until smooth. Spray aluminum boats with cooking spray to coat. Spoon in mashed potatoes. Add toppings if desired. Freeze boats on a cookie sheet until firm (approximately 1 hour), then place in individual freezer bags and freeze. Heat as instructed below.

Step Two: Warm potato boats in a 350-degree-F oven for 30 minutes or until heated through. Top with butter and sour cream, if desired.

Tips: Add the toppings before you freeze the boats or when heating them up. If you can't find the mini-aluminum tins, use ceramic custard cups. Potato boats make a great side dish to complement the mini-strombolis or foil sandwiches.

For more grab-and-go dinners, use a slow cooker—the frantic woman's best friend. Oh, what a life preserver that small appliance can be. Figure this. You fill it up, plug it in, walk away, and a few hours later you're scooping and serving a home-cooked meal. What more could you ask for? So, dust off the device and get cookin'.

The *Fix-It and Forget-It Cookbook: Feasting with Your Slow Cooker* by Dawn J. Ranck and Phyllis Pellman Good and their *Fix-It and Forget-It Recipes for Entertaining: Slow Cooker Favorites for All the Year Round* have a roundup of recipes that will satisfy everyone's taste buds. A couple of other good ones are Better Homes and Gardens' *Biggest Book of Slow Cooker Recipes*, *30-Minute Meals* by Rachael Ray and Dan Dinicola, and for you vegetarians, there's Joanna White's *The Vegetarian Slow Cooker*. (See "A Wee Bit More," part three, for a list of cookbooks that will satisfy everyone's hunger pangs.)

Despite the fact that on most nights you all won't be able to convene for dinner, continue to plan your family meal at a specified time. Accept the fact that whoever's missing just misses. Sometimes this is the only tactic that works for preserving any semblance of the family meal, especially at this time of year when so many obligations make all-inclusive sit-downs an impossible dream.

A good hour for regularly scheduled meals is immediately after school (if you're home then), before anyone has a chance to rush out the door. And as you've heard before, it's healthier to eat your biggest meal earlier in the day—a lesson we should have learned from our European friends. Then, set out a communal snack nearer to bedtime when the whole family might actually be home together.

Summer Stow Away

Get rid of all the summer clothes the family didn't wear this past warm season. Why use up the energy and space necessary to store them? Toss faded, worn clothing into your car-rag bin and stuff your donation box with all the rest. While you're in the de-cluttering mode, stow away swimming supplies and toys, extra beach towels, sand umbrellas, and other belongings that won't be of use until spring. But don't get carried away squirreling everything in sight, because there'll still be plenty of temperate days to play outdoor games like badminton, volleyball, and croquet.

If you're planning a trip during the winter months to a tropical destination, keep aside several beach towels, sand toys, and inflatable rafts. Bundle these items in a satchel or travel bag and place in the attic or closet for later. If space limitations dictate that you stow away seasonal clothes, pick out the ones you'll want to take with you and pack in a suitcase, as well. Even though they might need to be laundered or ironed before you leave, you won't have to dig out, sort, and decide. In the meantime, you might want to hit the summer clearance sales for inflatable inner tubes, buckets, and plastic trucks to take with you. At rock-bottom prices, you can use these toys, then leave them at the rental condo for other families to enjoy.

Flower Forethought

If you haven't received your catalogs showcasing spring flower bulbs, request them from your favorite mail-order company. When choosing your Holland bulbs, remember to purchase a mix based on plant height and time of blooming. Then, place your order right away. Or to cross this task off your list even sooner, shop online at sites like www.dutchbulb.com and www.dutchgardens.com, where specials and tip sheets are usually featured. A little planning today can bring blossoms of color in just a few months.

While you're in the mode, Mary Jo's husband, Stu, shares these suggestions on fall landscaping preparations in order to produce vibrant spring and summer flower beds: (a) Remove all annuals and vegetable plant debris; (b) cut perennials to ground level and discard; and (c) spread a winter fertilizer mixture such as potash on your beds.

Quarterly Taxes

Once again, it's time to pay your quarterly federal and state income taxes—this time for the third-quarter earnings—if you don't have them automatically deducted. These are due on the 15th of the month.

Reminder Alert

The time has come to flip the bed mattresses again. You don't want to be sleeping in a gutter, now, do you?

DARLING LITTLE ANGELS (AND THE WHOLE BLISSFUL BUNCH)

Holiday Happenings: A Ghoulish Time

A frightfully fun time is lurking just around the corner. Do you hear the chains rattling? Feel the ghosts hovering? What are you waiting for? Ignite that imagination! Oh, we get it. You need a push in the right direction. Start by checking out popular Web sites like those of Better Homes and Gardens (www.bhg.com), Halloween Magazine (www.halloweenmagazine.com), and Home & Garden Television (www.hgtv.com) for ideas on what to make, hang, and wear. Each site features a patch of "pumpkin" inspiration for everyone from preschoolers to the adult who still sports a costume.

You say you'd rather search for ideas by settling on the sofa with a book in hand? We've found a few that will stir your cauldron. *The Big Book of Halloween* by Laura Dover Doran and *101 Spooktacular Party Ideas* by Linda Sadler highlight an assortment of imaginings from edibles to illuminations and a witch's brew of things in between. Now, if adult crafts and decorations are more your poison, try *Halloween Crafts: Eerily Elegant Décor* by Kasey Rogers and Mark Wood for a ghoulishly good time.

Are you aiming to win "most original" in the costume contest this year, but you still haven't come up with anything creative? Scan the items around your house that exist naturally in pairs or groups like dice, salt and pepper shakers, or candlesticks. Consider creating life-sized versions of everyday things. For example, design an eight ball from a billiards game, stuffing a black-and-white fabric sack—easily sewn with upper and lower drawstrings—with fiberfill, tissue, or crumpled newspaper. (See "A Wee Bit More," part three, for step-by-step directions for turning one easy template into many different costumes.) If you have more than one child, transform each one into a different-numbered ball. Don't forget to make one solid and another striped. If you need more kids to pull this off, round up a few relatives or neighbors to join in. With only two more, you can add a cue stick and an oversized block of cue chalk.

Imagine seeing a group of condiments walking up your sidewalk. Ketchup, mustard, relish, and mayo would make even the Wicked Witch of the West smile. By using felt, a glue gun, and hand stitches, even non-sewers can manage. White, green, or purple grapes created by using blown-up balloons pinned to a leotard will be a hit with any child. Add an apple (from the billiard-ball template described previously) to present the Fruit of the Loom bunch. A bottle of nail polish, remover, and a puffy cotton ball beget a perfect combination for girls who've outgrown their princess costumes.

Turkey Travel and Jingle Jaunts

Although it seems a little early for "Over the river and through the woods," the Thanksgiving/Christmas/Hanukkah season will soon be upon us. We know, you're just coming off of summer and the last thing on your mind is the commotion of the jingle season, but you mustn't wait. Decide now where you'll be going for the holidays. Remember, when mapping out your itinerary, look for discounts online, through AAA, coupon books, and Sunday newspapers, and consider any club or corporate reductions you are entitled to. However, take note. On certain dates, usually the day before and after major holidays, some deals do not apply.

Settle everything from airfare to rental cars to obtaining maps and tour books now, leaving lots of time for whipping up some goodies to take with you, wrapping gifts, and packing. And what a courtesy you'll be providing your host by letting her know this far in advance when you'll be knocking on her front door.

Even with the travel plans behind you, there's one more thing to do. Prepare now for the gift-opening ceremony on Christmas morning. How?

When it comes to celebrating Christmas many miles away from home, mother-of-three Linda's first tip is to ship early. Every December from the time her kids were toddlers, Linda has made the trip from western Pennsylvania to southern Florida to spend the holidays with her husband's parents. And more than twenty years later, the annual tradition continues with one slight change—the toddlers are now Linda's grandchildren. Here are eight tips to ensure a fuss-free Santa delivery from our seasoned holiday traveler.

1. If you haven't started buying the gifts that need to be sent, do so now.

2. If you need to pick up one or two of the last-minute "got-to-have" toys that are advertised *after Thanksgiving*, buy small versions or accessories of the trendier items and tuck them into your suitcase.

3. Wrap, without bows, and pack everything into cardboard boxes. If you wait until you get to your destination to wrap the gifts (usually this is only a couple of days before Christmas), you'll add more stress to your holiday celebrations.

4. Use the United Parcel Service of America, Inc. (UPS) to ship packages. If an item is too big to send, and it is one the child truly wants, wrap a picture of it instead. Once you're back home again, he or she can unwrap the actual gift.

5. Send everything *prior* to Thanksgiving weekend because once the holiday season arrives, with the huge increase in parcels being shipped, there's a greater chance of packages being lost. And how do you explain to a child that Santa didn't make it this year?

6. Call your family member (where you'll be staying) to inform her that your boxes have been shipped and give her an approximate delivery date. This way she can let you know if they don't arrive.

7. Once you've landed at your destination, pull out the bundles, freshen up any presents that might have a tear or two in the paper, and add bows.

8. And finally, if the celebration environment is different from

home, forewarn your children that Santa might arrive by an untraditional mode of transportation—like a motorboat when the kids are expecting to see a sleigh.

Now, you can sit back, relax, and enjoy being the guest while someone else is playing hostess. Thanks, Linda!

School Adjustment

Are you overwhelmed with all the little things that are cropping up at the start of the new school year—like organizing the numerous papers being sent home from school, not to mention being pressed for time to prepare meals, pack lunches, and launder school clothes? How can you adjust to the demands placed on you with the onset of homework, fall sports, and other obligations? Follow these simple suggestions to stay ahead of the game. (And don't forget those we mentioned in our "Morning Rush" section earlier in this chapter.)

- Fill the bookbags the night before with everything from books and homework to cough drops, gym clothes, and lunch money.
- If your kids carry their lunches, pack the dry components, including the crackers and fruit snacks, in the evening. Quickly add the sandwich or yogurt and cold drink in the morning. Incorporate this into your after-dinner routine, brown-bagging while you clean up or while dishing out the bedtime snack.

SNIPPET: Tired of spreading the PB&J? Think of how the kids must feel. The average child will consume 1,500 peanut butter and jelly sandwiches by the time he graduates from high school. Kind of makes you want to switch to grilled ham and cheese, huh?

- Make a handy, easy-to-mount paper organizer by permanently attaching (with glue or nails) several heavy-duty clips to a yardstick. Mount the stick in the laundry room, by the back door, in the corner of the kitchen, or in the garage. Hang important papers that you'll need to refer to regularly—like sports schedules, student lists, phone chains, and district snow emergency procedures. You might even want to laminate these pages so they'll hold up to repeated handlings.

- Photocopy indispensable papers including school schedules, health forms for upcoming physicals, and teacher's contact numbers and policies, and file in a safe place. That way, if the copy you're using gets misplaced, you'll know exactly where a second has been stashed. If your child plays more than one sport in the same season, such as fall soccer and cross country, duplicates of the same physical form signed by your physician can be given to both coaches directly from this file.

- Use separate legal-sized accordion files to hold children's schoolwork—even for the older ones. Mark the name, year, school, and teacher's name on the outside. Transfer papers directly from the backpack to the accordion file. Then, when your child has a math chapter test, for example, you can pull out the recent math papers and homework assignments and review with ease.

- Allocate another file for announcements, keepsake cards, awards and certificates, newspaper clippings, and any other special papers that surface throughout the school year. Label accordingly.

Homework Helpers

Does the thought of solving algebraic equations and unveiling the symbolism in *Lord of the Flies* make you cringe? It seems especially difficult to concentrate on such matters when visions of so many other responsibilities are swirling around in your brain. Utilize the following homework helpers for making the daily task less of a hassle.

The first step in easing the pressure accompanying continual assignments is to create a Homework Station. You can easily design the super-duper station by purchasing a rectangular plastic bin the size of a copy-paper box (approximately 20 by 14 by 18 inches or larger). For a colorful Homework Station, stencil or paint the outside. Or to personalize it even further, glue on photos taken on the first day of school, then cover them with clear contact paper to seal.

Next, see if you can locate a compartmentalized utensil caddy to hold pencils and other supplies. (You should be able to find these on the clearance tables now, with the discontinued picnic stock.) Use wire or duct tape to secure the caddy to the inside of the bin. Store pencils and pens in one section; white correction fluid, glue sticks, and a ruler in another; and markers or colored pencils in the third. Stow index cards, sticky notes, and tape in the napkin compartment. Now load the remaining space of the bin with filler and construction paper, notebooks, and small sheets of poster board.

For a less expensive version, obtain a copy-paper box. Tape three plastic cups (ones from restaurants work well) inside the short end of the box. A small shoe or bank-check box can be tucked in to prevent supplies like paper clips and rubber bands from getting lost.

Now that you've assembled your Homework Station, you're ready for the following tips.

- Encourage kids to make use of the time teachers allot in school to get started on homework, if you feel they are not utilizing this time constructively. Remind kids that the more work they finish before they walk in the door, the more time they'll have to play outside, talk on the phone, or surf the Net. Do make sure they bring home their work, though, for you to look over and check, if need be.

- Get kids in the habit of starting on homework not long after they come in the door. Resist the temptation to turn on the tube. Just grab a quick snack and snap open the books. While you might feel your kids need a break after a long day's work, by teaching them to get the job done early, they'll learn to better budget their time and to realize that play is much more fun once the work is done.

- Decide if your child needs to take the Tackler or Toweler approach as we described in "Year Round," part one. Is his attitude better when he tackles the challenging assignments first and leaves the easy stuff for last (Tackler)? Or does he need to build up to the harder jobs, completing all the painless homework first (Toweler)?

- Have kids do homework at the kitchen table while you're preparing dinner. Being in the same room with them while they're working encourages them to stay focused. However, if your child requires a less distracting environment, ship her off to a predetermined spot like the dining room table or a desk in the study—but not to her diversion-filled room.

- Pay attention to how many minutes your child can work diligently before he loses his concentration. For older students, be sure they stretch and take a breather when working for an hour or longer. Younger ones will need to break more often.

- Make use of time in the car to go over lessons like spelling words, vocabulary definitions, and reviewing facts for exams. You can discuss the concept of metamorphosis as easily behind the wheel as you can at the kitchen table.

- Offer guidance and support during the homework process, but avoid doing assignments and projects for them. All that does is squelch their confidence and autonomy. We once heard best-selling author Dr. John Rosemond advise parents to set a time limit on when assignments should be completed. Once the clock strikes the deadline, books should be closed and put away for the night. He also suggests parents restrict the number of times offspring can ask for help to prevent them from inquiring about answers they can figure out for themselves. His advice makes sense when you think about the general rule that goes something like this: The more you do for them, the more they'll expect you to do. And then, the less independent they become.

- Despite your frustrations, don't complain about homework in front of the kids. This wears away at the respect a child should have for her teacher. And losing that will only add to your woes.

If our Homework Helpers don't solve your after-school problems, listen to what Carol Utay, Ph.D. and executive director of Total Learning Centers, has to say. "Don't let a problem go on too long. Bad study habits will be harder to break in the spring," she says. "Typically, it takes one year after a student begins having problems in school before they get professional help." Why wait? Heed the following professional advice from Dr. Utay.

- Conference with the teacher to find out what he or she expects, how long homework should take, how assignments are given (orally, written on the board, distributed as handouts), and policies toward such things as neatness, or typed versus hand-written. You want to leave better able to respond to your child's pleas: "This is good enough. This is all the teacher really wants us to do. He never looks at these anyway. Neatness doesn't count. We're supposed to only do that in class."

- If after putting the information you learned from the teacher(s) into practice homework is still a battle, call for reinforcements. Have your child professionally evaluated either inside or outside of the school system. Learning centers often have testing available and operate supervised homework stations. Make sure there is a certified teacher on staff and that studying is part of the homework time.

"If homework issues aren't new for you," Dr. Utay says, "that's all the more reason to do something now, to prepare today for success tomorrow."

If you go the learning-center route, inquire at several places before making a decision. Visit during regular sessions to get a feel for the type of programs they offer. Ask what level of progress the director feels your child will reach and within what time frame.

Simple Assistance

For some simple assistance to supplement your child's knowledge in certain subjects, look into these possibilities.

- Nonfiction books and videos can assist in the learning process, especially when larger projects are assigned. Videos give children a visual understanding of events and places in today's world and throughout history.

- The same goes for science. A hands-on experiment goes a long way in encouraging curiosity and development. (Don't use one from their schoolbook, though, or they might view that as homework. Remember, you want it to be fun.) Check the library or search the Internet for doable suggestions.

- Children can learn math concepts by using their hobbies. For example, by figuring out a baseball batting average, kids can practice addition and division. Playing a card game of math war (just like the traditional war game but players shout out the sum, difference, product, or quotient for the two cards shown) is both fun and great practice for drilling those addition, subtraction, multiplication, and division facts.

HIDDEN GEM: Are your kids overwhelmed by the volume of information Web searches generate? We say, go back to the basics. When older kids are researching a project, begin in the children's section of the library. Middle-grade biographies and historical accounts highlight important facts and are a great place to start. And picture books on the subject can provide an easy overview and a good outline to follow.

Enticing Family to Do Their Share

With all the hurrying to and from extracurricular obligations this season, an extra pair of hands at home sure would come in handy. Did we hear you say you can't afford a housekeeper? Well, that's not what we meant. The answer lies in your spin-off generation. Uh-huh, we're suggesting you happily hand the kids their new chore charts for fall.

Dr. Ruth Peters, who appears regularly on the *Today* show, outlines these chores and more in her book *Laying Down the Law: The 25 Laws of Parenting*.

Two-Year-Olds

Between twenty-four and thirty-six months of age, your child develops the ability to handle many behavioral responsibilities. Use a timer to motivate your child to clean up specific toys before the buzzer goes off.

Three-Year-Olds

Between three and four years of age, children are able to perform daily chores such as putting dirty clothes in a hamper and helping you to make the beds. Threes can fill pet bowls and brush their teeth with your guidance.

Four-Year-Olds

Four-year-olds can put their dirty dishes on the counter and pick out their clothes for the next day.

Early Grade Schoolers

Five-, six-, and seven-year-olds can help to make their own simple lunches and aid younger siblings with dressing tasks. They can help clean up after their baths, put their clean clothes in drawers, pick up their bedrooms daily, and answer the telephone.

Older Grade Schooler

Eight-, nine-, ten-, and eleven-year-olds can bring in the mail and take out the trash cans. They can help out with family chores such as dusting and setting and clearing the table.

Middle Schoolers

Twelve-, thirteen-, and fourteen-year-olds can cook, help clean, do yard work, and wash the car. They can do their own laundry and baby-sit younger siblings.

High Schoolers

Teens can be very self-sufficient and can help with family chores, not just their own.

Assign One More Task

Have you ever dashed into the house five minutes before a game to find your son digging out the smelly football jersey from his gym bag? Even so, once you're in the car, you breathe a sigh of relief knowing you'll still make it to the field before kickoff. But as the child jumps out of the car, he hits you with this one: "Ah, Mom, my spikes are in Dad's car!"

How can you avoid similar situations? Encourage kids to keep track of their own sports, instrument, and other activity-related belongings in totes or gym bags. Canvas bags can be used to store library books or sheet music for lessons. Consider keeping library cards or the check for the piano teacher in a zippered pouch in each respective tote. Have older kids put a prepaid phone card, several quarters and dollar bills, plus a house key in their bags for emergencies. It's a good idea to throw in a deck of cards, a magazine, or a *Chicken Soup for the Soul* book for good measure, too, as teens often find themselves stuck waiting for rides.

Place a freestanding coatrack or a large wicker basket in each child's room to collect all prepacked "responsibility" sacks. Just think how easy it will be to rush off to a track meet when the uniform, socks, running shoes, and water bottle (which will need to be filled, of course) are all in one place and at arm's reach.

HIDDEN GEM: If you're taking along younger ones who need to be entertained during the lesson or game, stockpile sticker books, art stuff, flash cards, and Matchbox cars or a couple of Barbie dolls in a designated bag stored on their coatracks or in wicker baskets, ready to grab at a moment's notice. In fact, youngsters should have *separate* activity bags pre-stuffed for restaurant trips, religious services, friends' houses, and long car rides— because the range of appropriate entertainment varies with each activity. You wouldn't want your child playing a handheld video game during a religious service, for instance, but it's a great pastime for lengthy rides in the car.

Comforts of Home

Through all the frustration, flusters, and fumbles, do you miss the warmth and comfort of your roots? Yes, your time is surely limited, but you *need* this connection to soothe your soul. Initiate the steps toward bringing extended family further into your life. It's time to reach beyond holiday visits.

Here's what we do.

- Mary Jo meets her mom on Saturday mornings for breakfast. Afterward, they browse the estate sales, shop for bargains, see box office hits, or take in the sights. The clincher is that they meet at a restaurant where Mary Jo's brother and niece Tabitha work—so the whole thing becomes a family affair.
- Once a year, the women in Judith's family gather for a weekend of shopping excitement. The catch is that they book a hotel only twenty minutes from home. Half the fun is just getting away together. While the women are gone, the men and children meet at a family log cabin for some untamed fun. (At other times of the year, even the guys in Judith's family get in on it by scheduling early-morning coffee jaunts before heading to the home improvement stores. Wouldn't it be amusing if the ladies showed up at the same diner some week?)
- Another trick we use is to incorporate duties with fun. Ask your mother, sister, or aunt to accompany you while you hunt for that new living room couch or a gift for the boss, or while driving your college student back to campus.
- Sometimes we take the whole extended bunch on a quick getaway to a local lodge or family campsite. In the off-season, prices are often discounted. Cart with you lots of food, board games, outdoor sports equipment, scrapbooking supplies, simple crafts, and home movies. While you're nurturing your roots, the kids will be sprouting in down-home fun.

☞ ALL ABOUT YOU

Interoffice Memo: Lend a Hand

Probably because it's the month that children head back to school, September is when women join the workforce or switch jobs the most. But even if you're not seeking a change yourself, look around your company office. Is there a new kid on the block? Remember how it felt to be the newbie? Is there a way you can help her adjust? Why not suggest a couple of work-related tips specific to your place of business? Or point out the mistakes you made when you started. Sharing them over a cup of coffee along with a few comforting chuckles will make the newcomer feel right at home.

Boot Camp

Add a formal exercise regimen for autumn—taking into consideration the upcoming change in weather and new fall schedule. Are you now able to sign up for a morning exercise class or get back in the workout groove? Meet a neighbor or friend for a brisk walk after the kids hop on the bus in the morning. Don't delay in taking a heart-healthy initiative. In other words, just get up and move.

Take Five: "Me" Nights

If you are able, isolate one evening a week as "I have nowhere to go" night. That means no errands, appointments, or car pools to lure you from the house. Even if it sounds impossible, give this tactic a try and you'll see how your scheduled home time will soon become your favorite priority.

ONE-STEP-AT-A-TIME CHECKLIST

Date
completed
Or N/A

Task

_____ Remember September 11th by paying tribute to service people and their families.

_____ Write up a weekly schedule of the family's daily activities.

_____ Keep the first two weeks of September free from added commitments and outings.

_____ Reorganize the morning routine to help it run more smoothly for all.

_____ Make the most of car pool arrangements.

_____ Prepare grab-and-go meals to lighten your cooking load.

_____ Stow summer items, remembering to toss weathered ones.

_____ Order spring flower bulbs.

_____ Pay quarterly taxes.

_____ Flip the bed mattresses.

_____ Buy or create kids' Halloween costumes and decorations.

_____ Look into holiday travel arrangements for November and December.

_____ Adopt our night-before tips to ease the school adjustment period.

_____ Incorporate homework helpers to ease the tension.

_____ Add simple ways to assist your child's learning process.

_____ Assign family members new chores for fall.

_____ Make kids responsible for their own activity-related equipment and gear.

_____ Connect with extended family members by doing something together.

_____ Lend a hand to a newcomer this month.

_____ Jump back into your exercise program.

_____ Isolate one evening a week as "I have nowhere to go" night.

Balance

As the first of October gushes in, it suddenly hits you: "What the heck happened to September?" It seems as soon as you kiss the summer good-bye, time creeps away faster than you can say "supercalifragilisticexpialidocious."

And as if battling homework and the morning rush isn't enough, starting this month, you're bombarded with one holiday after another. You're not able to catch your breath, let alone stop long enough to take a deep one. With that in mind, we're guiding you through preparing for winter, combating flu season, and gearing up for the holly holiday. So, inhale. Exhale. Now, let's get moving.

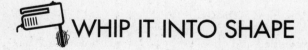 WHIP IT INTO SHAPE

We Must, We Must

If you brushed over some portion of spring-cleaning way back when, now is the time to complete the task, ridding out (as we call it) any parts of the house you might have skipped. With the holidays rolling forth, you won't have a spare minute to do these time-consuming tasks later. So roll up your sleeves, pull on those rubber gloves, and get started. Dust off that classic book collection you've been avoiding or root out the box that's been calling your name for months. With the nagging chore behind you, you won't become red-faced when your ultra-perfect neighbor rings the doorbell, white gloves in hand.

Second Chance: Re-Thinking, Re-Doing

This is your second chance to redecorate, rearrange furniture, or add pizzazz for the holidays.

Grounds Crew

Winterize the outside of the home, pruning shrubs and trees, and clearing gutters. If the weather allows, make sidewalk or step repairs and paint the front door, window frames, and mailbox. Give the outside of the house a good grooming so it looks nice and is safe for those eager trick-or-treaters.

While you're out there, cover the air conditioner, using an actual cover designed for that purpose. Or, if you don't have one, simply place a board or tarp on top and anchor with a few bricks. It's most important to keep snow from piling on top of the unit and melting down in to it. Store or cover patio furniture. Turn off the spigots before freezing temperatures set in.

Inside

Have the furnace cleaned and checked by a professional before that first cold night nips at your nose, and switch your vents again, if you have central heating. Heat should enter through the floor vents because (remember that science lesson?) warm air rises. You'll also want to switch your humidifier setting to avoid the effects of the season's dry air.

If it's been a while, hire that suction guy to rid the air ducts of contaminants that cause allergy flare-ups, sinus problems, excess dust on furniture, and musty odors when your heat or a/c is running.

If you haven't done so already, consider installing a carbon monoxide detector that can be readily purchased at home improvement or hardware stores.

Winter Driving

With Old Man Winter on the horizon, National Public Radio's "Car Talk" hosts Tom and Ray Magliozzi, a.k.a. Click & Clack, offer this very crucial winter driving suggestion from the Car Talk section of cars.com. For more tips, visit them at http://cartalk.cars.com.

- One question we get asked frequently is, "If I have a front-wheel-drive or all-wheel-drive car, do I need to have snow tires?" The answer is, if you really need to drive in the snow, yes. If you really, truly need to get around before the streets are plowed, four snow tires are the single best thing you can do. And the reason you'd still want them on a car is because they not only help get you started, they also increase your traction when you're braking and turning.
- Our best tip is still this: Move to Hawaii.

Thanks, Tom and Ray. We love ya!

Second Chance: Psst! List Reminders

Back in January, you stapled a list of holiday needs to your October calendar and now it should be staring you in the face. (If not, hurry up and scribble one while we're not looking.) Examine the list and purchase those items that you can't get through the season without. Do it now while the selection is top-notch. You wouldn't want to decorate the tree in twinkling pink and have to finish it off with multicolored strands.

In addition, we encouraged you to write up a detailed holiday gift list while you lounged poolside this summer. What's that, you say? You didn't? Well, here's your second chance to open that Frantic Journal and get cracking. See our tips for remembering one and all in the "Christmas in July" section of the July chapter.

Give a Gift

Now is the time to order any customized baskets, tins, or gift sets you'll be sending in honor of the approaching festivities. Why so early? Many companies offer a discount for orders taken in October—mainly because it helps them get a jump on the busy season. And while saving 10 percent of your total might not seem like a lot, when you're sending more than one collection of goods, that measly amount can really add up.

Many gift-oriented companies gear their products to the interests of the recipient—focusing on sports or some profession like nursing. But are you looking for something different to send? Check out merchants that promote a local specialty like www.pghbaskets.com and www.pghsnax.com. When ordering baskets containing perishables, Richard J. Cuneo, owner of Pittsburgh Snax and Nut Company, advises that you order directly from establishments that actually manufacture the product to ensure you're getting the freshest quality foods. "If the products are cooked or manufactured on the premises," Richard says, "they'll have a longer shelf life." He adds that the best part of ordering gift tins and baskets is that the company takes care of the preparation, packaging, and shipping for you. "All you have to do is wait for the thank-you card!"

Some specialty stores in your area might also offer holiday merchandise with a customized twist. Mary Alice Gorman of Mystery Lovers Bookstore (www.mysterylovers.com) says, "Folks tell us what they want to spend and one thing about the recipient—what he or she likes to do, occupation, favorite city, age—and we fashion a gift basket for them." It can encompass a bon voyage wish, a fly-fishing interest, or a celebration of menopause. "There really are so many mystery books with a wide variety of themes," Mary Alice says. She complements the basket collection with a number of niceties like tiny wine jams, clotted cream, honey straws, and small panettone cakes. "Ordering early guarantees you'll get the best selection of books and treats. And early shipping leaves plenty of time to track delivery delays should they arise."

Easy-on-the-Budget

Have you decided to hand-craft some presents this season to cut down on costs, but you're dragging your feet about getting the job done? As a variation of the hobby night we suggested in our August chapter, why not host a craft night for a couple of friends and neighbors who'd like to create for others, too?

If you seriously need to cut down your list of recipients, consider these additional options.

- Propose giving one gift for the entire family, such as a game, a movie basket, or mall gift certificates.
- Have a make-or-bake exchange.
- Suggest that only the children participate in the gift giving.
- Within a predetermined price range, have each parent buy gifts for their own children to be wrapped and given by the aunts and uncles. This cuts down on shopping and returning time because parents know what their kids want or need. And because they're receiving what you know they'll like, the kids are happy, too.
- For an inexpensive way to remember teens, 'tweens, and little ones, shop for the logo or trademarked art and school supplies such as bound journals, matching desk sets, backpacks, and fabric notebooks. Why now? These back-to-school items are now heavily reduced, but are fancy enough to pose as gifts.

Holiday Greetings

Every year you say, "This is absurd." You send out one hundred holiday greeting cards and receive one-third or less in return. But don't cross any names off your list just yet. We're about to show you ways to reduce the time and effort involved in sending out gleeful greetings.

- Create a greetings box in which you'll store everything from holiday cards and your master list to address labels, family photos, stickers, envelopes, gel pens, and stamps. All you need is a storage container. Plastic holds up better than cardboard since you'll be using it year after year. You might want to use a shoe box or, as an alternative, try a plastic 9-by-12-inch accordion file folder. With this convenient contraption, you can whittle away at your card list as time allows. Take the greetings container with you and work while waiting at doctors' offices, kids' practices, or commuting to and from the workplace if you take public transportation or carpool.

- Create a master list to eliminate time wasted searching for addresses, holiday after holiday. This should include both snailmail and e-mail addresses. Your list can be computer generated or handwritten. Card and bookstores sell pre-made journal-type versions with an annual checklist for cards sent and received. For keyboard-tapping folks, use the address book in your e-mail program like Outlook Express—or experiment with Excel or a similar spreadsheet program. Otherwise, you might log on to www.holidayorganizer.com. If you can't face locating addresses and recording them now, vow to make it one of your New Year's resolutions. Commit yourself to the deed by recording your intentions in your Frantic Journal.

- Fill out greeting cards and address the envelopes. That's right, do it now. If you miss this window of opportunity, it might remain closed for the rest of the year.

- If you dread the added step of placing photos in your cards, consider having photo cards made. Most drug stores and some grocery stores offer this service at a minimal cost. Without making an ordeal of what kids are wearing, what the background is, or how they're posed, snap photos and pick out one that captures a sense of cheer. (Outside shots make particularly appealing choices because of the crisp freshness they convey. See our suggestions in "Holiday Happenings: Outings and Treats," this chapter, for photo ops at Halloween adventures.) Within a week or so, you'll be stuffing your cards and stamping with glee—because you're so far ahead of the game. Sometimes, you'll even receive a discount for ordering early. Of course, you digital camera owners can create and print out your own personalized photo cards to send.

- If you don't have the time or desire to choose a photograph and re-order in the form of cards, just snap an entire roll or two of the family, have double prints made, and use the various poses to send with your greetings. This is a budget-friendly, one-step process you can accomplish in less than an afternoon.

- If you have considered writing a unique family newsletter, but don't like the braggadocio kind you've received from others, follow our quick and easy steps in "A Wee Bit More," part three, to write a snappy, memorable enclosure.

SNIPPET: Do you get the sense that the tradition of sending holiday greetings is passé? Well, according to American Greetings Corporation research, over one billion Christmas cards are sent each year. And women account for 89 percent of the total gift-card buyers and senders. So rest assured that the practice of remembering others in the form of snail-mailed salutations is here to stay.

Quarterly Taxes

Yes, it's time again to pay your local quarterly wage tax, due on Halloween day for your third-quarter earnings.

DARLING LITTLE ANGELS (AND THE WHOLE BLISSFUL BUNCH)

Second Chance: Spooky Time Prep

We're giving you a second chance to plan for Halloween—covering costumes, parties, and handouts. Decorate if you haven't already done so.

Are you a frantic woman who secretly feels that Halloween is one of the most stressful days of the year? If you're a mom, not only must you organize all the pieces to all the costumes, including fake blood and fangs, but you have to clean the house (in case that nosy neighbor claims she has to use the bathroom), gather the treats for giving, and worst of all, feed the kids before you go. But you don't want to cook—and they don't want to eat. Well, Ann Schneider relieves some of the pressure for her daughters-in-law by inviting the families over for dinner. Often, she and her husband will even pick up the kids from school, giving Mom more time to collect the cameras, light the jack-o'-lanterns, and pack the sacks for goodie-gathering. Ann serves a good meal, helps with the costumes, and snaps a few pictures. "It all started," Ann says, "because I wanted to see the kids in costume." Not only does Ann get to see the kids, but she helps their moms beyond measure.

Holiday Happenings: Outings and Treats

Gobs of Halloween fun await at the pumpkin patch, local farm, apple cider mill, Octoberfest celebrations, bonfires, and haunted houses for charity. Set out to participate in at least one ghoulish adventure during the first weekend of the month. That'll save you from three more weeks of the repetitive "When can we pick our pumpkins, Mom?" If the weather is iffy, go anyway. Lines will be shorter and the patch will be less picked over. After all, even in decent weather, you end up coming home sopping wet, brushing off strands of hay, and covered in specks of mud.

While everyone's together on the outing, snap a family photo that can be duplicated and enclosed in holiday cards. In addition, take advantage of items made available to you there—buying bales of hay and cornstalks for decorating, pumpkins for carving, and autumn popcorn for munching.

Or better yet, mix together a bowl of your own. Kathleen Gahagan brews up a big batch of her Baked Caramel Corn every October and bundles it in decorative cans, giving them as just-because gifts to friends and family. Here's her tasty recipe.

✦ Baked Caramel Corn ✦

INGREDIENTS
1 cup butter or margarine
2 cups packed brown sugar
½ cup light corn syrup
1 teaspoon salt
½ teaspoon baking soda
1 teaspoon vanilla
6 quarts popped corn

Step one: Melt butter in a 2-quart saucepan. Stir in sugar, corn syrup, and salt. Heat to boiling, stirring constantly. Boil for 5 additional minutes without stirring. Remove from heat. Stir in baking soda and vanilla. Pour gradually over popped corn, mixing well. Turn into two large shallow baking pans.

Step two: Bake at 250 degrees F for 1 hour, stirring every 15 minutes. Remove from oven. Cool completely. Break apart. Store in tightly covered containers.

Yields 6 quarts.

(Note: Molasses or honey or a combination of the two can be used in place of corn syrup. You can also add about a cup or more of nuts, if desired.)

And for one final suggestion, stop playing the guessing game. Record what you give out for Halloween and how many in your Frantic Journal so you can refer to it when preparing next year.

Summer Camp Preregistration

Although summer is just behind us, you might want to think about preregistering for summer camps that fill up early in larger metropolitan areas. For more tips on finding a camp that's right for your child, check "Summer Camps" in the February chapter.

The Ah-Choo Attack

The fall season brings about umpteen illnesses for young and old alike. And how many times has that first cold or fever of the season hit you unprepared? This year, arm yourself to fight against the flu by stocking up on vitamin C, cold and cough medicines, decongestants, non-aspirin pain relievers, vapor-rub creams, and tissues with lotion for those sure-to-be-sore noses. Replace the thermometer, humidifier, and vaporizer, if need be. Be certain you have heating pads and headache bags, too. Purchase extra toothbrushes across the board. After any illness, the current toothbrush and lip balm must be tossed. (See "A Wee Bit More," part three, for a list of necessities to stock in your medicine cabinet.)

Do you have an older relative or friend who needs your help when they're fighting a cold or the flu? Registered nurse Elizabeth Joos shares this precaution with us. Although you already know to keep the fluids flowing, be careful not to administer to the elderly sports drinks that are said to replace valuable electrolytes. The truth is that for the sensitive systems of older people, too much of those drinks actually disrupts the balance of electrolytes and can cause other problems. Water, of course, is best. But if your loved one has an upset stomach, that won't do. Instead, pour a soft drink like ginger ale into a glass and stir to remove the fizz. Serve at room temperature.

As a reminder, all bedding including sheets, blankets, comforters, mattress covers, and pillow protectors should be washed after an illness to kill any lingering germs.

◈ **HIDDEN GEM:** When your children are prescribed liquid antibiotic, ever wonder why you seem to run out of the medicine before the prescription is due to be finished? The reason goes back to another simple science lesson—evaporation. Even though you're storing the bottle in the refrigerator, some of the water is seeping out of the cap's seal, leaving less liquid behind. The solution is simple. Place your closed medicine bottle in a zippered plastic bag and squeeze out all the air before sealing. Then, put it in the refrigerator. That way, when you reach day 10 of the prescription, you'll still have enough medicine to administer to your ailing child.

Absentee

When there are sick kids in the house, they *will* miss school. Take care not to send kids back to school too soon. You should wait at least twenty-four hours after a child vomits or after her temperature returns to normal before placing her back in the classroom. The same is true for infirmities that require antibiotics; the drugs need to be in the child's system for a day or so before they knock out the bacteria enough to lower the contagiousness of the disease. Not only does your child's body need the time to recover, but you're also avoiding exposing other children to the germ.

It's a good practice to call the school and ask for missed class work to be sent home with a sibling or neighbor. Or let the secretary know you'll be picking up the assignments at the end of the day. Then, when your child shows a burst of energy, you can put him to work to stay ahead.

Or if he's too sick to get much done, ask the teacher to keep track of what work was done while your child was out, accumulating papers and assignments as she goes. Then, upon his return, see if he can have a week or so to complete the missed work. This way, your recovering offspring will be able to better comprehend and complete the owed assignments when he is feeling better. Even if you choose this option for the challenging subjects that require more focused concentration, you might want to keep up with the spelling words and handwriting assignments, so as not to be bombarded later.

The method you choose for making up missed assignments will depend on the school policies, the teacher, the student, and the duration of the illness. Either way, rely upon these additional ideas to keep your patient from falling behind.

- When students have more than one instructor, have each teacher provide her own makeup sheet. Many schools will even offer this information online, so be sure to obtain teachers' e-mail or Web addresses before you need them.
- Once you've gathered assignment information, make a combined to-do list of all responsibilities rather than accumulating several subject pages that can be more easily misplaced. Write your list on a distinctly colored sheet for ease of identification. Post. This way, scratching off the completed work will be a breeze (even if the calculations and comprehension questions are not).
- If you live in a warmer climate and the ill child is feeling up to it, take the schoolbooks outside to work on a patio or in a comfortable spot in the yard—rather than being cooped up inside.
- Vow to do a little work in the morning, afternoon, and evening to stay on track while not burning all your child's energy at once.
- For younger students, complete reading homework together before dozing off at bedtime.
- Teach spelling words with a small chalkboard or with flash cards. Make it a game and it won't put such wear and tear on the weakened child.

Business Travel for All

Do you or your spouse travel for business? If so, consider taking the kids. Kathleen Senay, preschool teacher and mother of four, regrets not doing so more often. "I wish I had allowed my children to miss school—for good reasons, of course. My husband traveled on business and we could have accompanied him, enjoying various cities across the United States and abroad." What's Kathleen's advice to others? Allow your children to experience the excitement of traveling safely with family. Don't make them miss out just because they're in school. And if you're worried about them missing class, follow the tips in the "Absentee" section in this chapter.

College Bound

If you have a high school senior, this is the semester to begin filling out college applications. It is hoped that by this point your college-bound offspring has visited a number of universities and has narrowed down her list. Work together on forms, getting started the day they arrive in the mail. (If applying online, print out a copy of the application to use as a draft.) Fill in the personal data first. Read the rest of the requirements, focusing on the special requests and essay questions. Spark an open discussion pinpointing distinct messages she'd like to convey in the essays. The whole process might seem like tedious work, but it can make or break your child's chances for being admitted. Of course, good presentation is important. Though a well-written essay won't guarantee acceptance, a bad one could certainly cut her chances.

Recognize that most applications require a fee—eventually amounting to quite an expense. So budget yourself by sending one or two forms each week or month.

To make the application process easier, refer to this tip list compiled by Jim Miller, dean of admissions at Bowdoin College in Maine, when writing your responses to essay questions.

- *Think small.* Focus on something specific, and don't try to cover your whole life's history or to solve the problems of the world.
- *Make it personal.* Writing about something subtle that's happened to you is perfectly acceptable. Not everyone at the age of seventeen has experienced a major character-building experience.
- *Don't be overly dramatic.* You're not going for an Emmy here. Be concise and to the point without trying to come up with a tear-jerker of a piece.

- *Don't "Roget" it.* Stay away from using too many 50-cent words. Rather, keep the flow going by keeping it conversational.
- *Let it marinate.* Put the essay away for a week or two. Then, pull it out and read it. Nine times out of ten, errors will jump out at you upon doing so.
- *Read it out loud.* More than likely, your essay will be read aloud to an admissions committee. So be sure to test how your essay "sounds."
- *Proofread.* Check spelling and grammar one final time.

Jim says you don't need to hire a professional essay coach to help you. And most of all, don't use a physical gimmick such as requiring the piece to be held up to a mirror, or writing in a circle so that the page has to be turned and turned. Jim says if you let your true colors shine, you'll be giving yourself the best shot you can.

HIDDEN GEM: After putting seven children through college and some through graduate school (paying in full for nearly thirty-five years of tuition, room, and board), John K. Burnett offers the following application strategies for high school seniors and their parents.

- Be certain to apply to at least one backup school, meaning one to which you'll more than likely be accepted (even if it's not on your list of top five)—to ensure you're not stuck next September *(all dressed up with no place to go)*.
- Be careful when applying for early admission to schools. If you're not a tip-top, cream-of-the-crop applicant, this can sometimes work against you, hurting your chances for standard admission.
- Choose a balance of schools when applying and go with those institutions that will best suit your needs academically and socially. Use common sense here. If you're not enticed by the allure of the big city, don't apply to schools in such settings. Likewise, if you don't like being isolated with a small number of people, a liberal arts school on a rural campus with only two thousand students won't be right for you.

- Apply to one or two long-shot schools, as well. This conveys a confidence on your other applications (indicated on the part of the form that asks for a list of all the schools to which you're applying). In other words, if the committee members think *you* think you can land an acceptance at a top-notch competitive school, that *means* something. Even if chances are slim that you'll receive an acceptance notification, you never know what might catch the eye of the admissions committee.

A Promised Reminder

We promised we'd remind you to have those winter coats cleaned now, because you tend to hold off in the spring awaiting that one last snowfall. Empty all pockets and drop off the jackets, coats, and sweaters at the dry cleaner today.

ASAP Wardrobe Basics

Examine the fall and winter wardrobe of everyone in the home. Decide which outdoor clothing to purchase for the cooler weather ahead. Check the fit of boots, coats, jackets, and snow pants. Are there enough mittens, gloves, and hats to make it through the season? Do thermal socks, coveralls, or steel-toed boots need to be replaced for outside work? If you're a winter sports enthusiast, find out if ski boots, ice skates, and goggles are in good condition. Inspect bindings, poles, and other equipment—or have a professional look them over—to ensure safe adventures in the months to come.

Back inside, determine what clothes must be updated. Are there enough jeans, slacks, sweatpants, sweatshirts, sweaters, turtlenecks, and long-sleeved shirts to keep everyone warm? List what is needed and purchase a little at a time as your budget allows. As advertisements come along, start crossing items off your list. Years ago, department stores had two big sales a year. Fortunately, stores today feature promotional reductions just about every week.

Secret Shopping Tips

Sure, you want to take advantage of the great deals promoted by mall retailers during these next few months. But, the CCs—crowds and coupons—have you quivering in your socks. Never fear, longtime department store sales associate Tawnya Senchur is here with a few tips for combating the double-Cs, making the sales work for you.

- Take advantage of the coupon promotion *before* the sale starts. Not only will you beat the crowds, but you'll have the clerks' attention and the best selection. Now, how does it work? Once you receive your flyer, go shopping (any day *before* the advertised date). Choose what you want, then see a clerk (unless one is already helping you). Inform her that you've received a flyer and want to "presale" the item(s). She'll ask for an imprint of your credit card, take your name and telephone number, and put the merchandise in a bag. She'll staple it closed and hold it in the back storage area until the sale begins. Then, on the first day the coupon is valid, the associate will ring up your purchase. And you can claim it anytime thereafter. (Hint: Wait until a downtime to retrieve your presale stuff.)
- If you have to shop during the promotion, go first thing in the morning or after nine at night (because stores are usually open earlier and close later for such sales).
- Inspect the coupon for percentages off in different departments. Some coupons are good for discounts on the entire purchase, whereas others might be good for "one item only." Certain designers might be excluded in one department, like Young Men's, but valid in others, like Juniors.
- Look for retailers who utilize punch cards (where you buy so many items and get one free) as part of their advertising budget; they often offer double-punch days. Once the punch card is filled, you can receive free merchandise. Note that double-punch deals are usually held on slow shopping days such as Tuesdays.
- Save another way by taking advantage of senior citizen shopping

days (AARP and Oasis, for example). On a specific day, sometimes the first Wednesday of the month, merchants give a percentage off the total purchase to qualified buyers. If Oasis-age you're not, this would be a great time to take an older aunt, mother, or grandmother with you, as we mentioned in the "Comforts of Home" section in the September chapter.

- Watch for "buy one get one free" deals on bras, panties, and hosiery. Double your savings by using your punch card, if applicable.
- Join the retailers' preferred shoppers club if they have one. By swiping the membership card, you're entitled to special promotions, rebates, or gift certificates based on accumulated sales totals.
- Take in a department store fashion show. Though there is a fee for admission, it is minimal and usually includes brunch, door prizes such as gift certificates, and a special coupon (for a certain percentage or dollar amount off your next purchase), making the ticket price more than worth the outlay.
- Get to know the sales associates in your favorite stores. Full-time associates and those with a few years of service will know when specific events happen and at what times of the year.

ALL ABOUT YOU

Interoffice Memo: A New Look

Spruce up your work space by adding decorations, wall hangings, plants, or new lighting. Wouldn't a string of white Christmas bulbs brighten a larger plant or tree? Look at the photos you have on your credenza. Are they from years gone by? Take the time now to update them. Find a silly photo that evokes a smile or warms your heart. Dot your decor with framed motivational or humorous sayings that help raise spirits while revealing a little something about you—adding a personal touch to your work environment.

And now that you're taking a closer look around the office, there are a few practical matters you should address, as well. Is your chair at the right height for your desk? Or do you feel like you're always leaning, bending, or reaching? Do you need to turn, tip, or raise your computer monitor? Is your keyboard at a comfortable level? Can you reposition it to take the pressure off of your wrists? Or do you need a wrist pad? Make an effort to set up a work area that's as therapeutically comfy as possible.

Interoffice Memo:
Outside Cooperation

Does your company send out holiday event flyers, advertisements, or mailings over the next two months? Are you involved in the folding, stuffing, and labeling? If so, we bet you could use a little help. Call a senior citizens independent living facility in your area and talk to the activities director. Most of the time, seniors are looking for ways to keep their hands and minds busy and are always willing to help. All you have to do is drop off the materials and explain how you want the task to be completed. Routinely, you'll have your stuffed envelopes back within a week or so. The most heart-warming part, in this case, is that one hand of the community is helping the other, leaving all to feel satisfied in the end.

Take Five:
Frantic Woman Extravaganza

Among the many festivities this month brings, October 13th marks the official date for the Frantic Woman Extravaganza. What does it mean? That much is simple. It's a day for you, the ultimate frantic woman, to celebrate your frazzled life—to acknowledge that life isn't perfect; that you're no Martha Stewart, but you're not Lucy Ricardo, either. You're probably a mix of the two—and that's a wonderful compromise.

As an amusing, yet informative break, let's take what we call the Car/Personality Test. Grab a blank piece of paper or your Frantic Journal and draw a car, any car. We'll give you sixty seconds. Have you finished? Now, are you ready to find out exactly what your drawing reveals about you?

1. If you have only two wheels showing, you're fairly frazzled and probably living through a period of change.
2. With four wheels showing, you are secure and stubborn, and stick to your ideals.
3. If you have drawn a road, you're on the right path, making headway toward the balanced life every frantic woman deserves.
4. Without a road, you're floating in mid-air. Tsk. Tsk. How many points have you really crossed off on your monthly checklists?
5. If your car is facing left, you believe in tradition, are friendly, and remember important dates well.
6. Facing right, you are innovative and active, but have to be reminded about dates, maybe even your own anniversary.
7. If your car faces front, you are candid, enjoy playing devil's advocate, and are ready to grab on to adventure.
8. If your car has a driver, you're taking control and moving in the right direction.
9. Without a driver, you're stuck and are in need of the direction this book provides.
10. If your car has many details, you are analytical and cautious.
11. If few details, you are emotional and a risk taker.
12. If your car is toward the top of the paper, you are positive and optimistic.
13. At the bottom, you're a realist.

Remember, this car/personality exercise is only a test. If this were a real emergency, we'd tell you where to tune in your area. (Or more likely, we'd recommend you flip back to page one of this book and pop the cap off your highlighter this time.)

Here's our list of the top five things you'll never hear a frantic woman say.

1. My house is spotless.
2. Go ahead, I'm not in a rush.
3. No thanks, I don't need a raise.
4. I had twelve hours of sleep last night.
5. I don't need to get away.

ONE-STEP-AT-A-TIME CHECKLIST

Date completed Or N/A   **Task**

_____ Scrub any parts of the house you missed during spring-cleaning.

_____ Re-think your redecorating projects to be completed before the joyous season ahead.

_____ Get the exterior of the house in shipshape.

_____ Get the humidifier, furnace, and vents winter-ready.

_____ Winterize your car.

_____ Pull out the holiday needs list you wrote in January and your gift-giving one from July.

_____ Order gift baskets and tins now before the holiday rush.

_____ Invite family and friends to create hand-crafted items. Reevaluate gift-giving practices.

_____ Create a greetings box. Fill out cards and address envelopes.

_____ Pay quarterly taxes.

_____ Decorate for Halloween. Finish up costume preps and purchase candy.

_____ Go to the pumpkin patch. Snap a family photo. Mix up a batch of caramel corn.

_____ Preregister the kids for summer camps.

_____ Stock your medicine cabinet for cold and flu season.

_____ Utilize absentee tips for missed schoolwork.

_____ When the opportunity arises, take kids with you on business trips.

_____ Prepare applications for college-bound students.

_____ Drop off winter coats at the dry cleaner.

_____ Examine and update winter wardrobe for all.

_____ Incorporate sale and coupon shopping tips this gift-buying season.

_____ Give your office a new look. Check your desk and chair height for comfort.

_____ Ask a senior citizens facility to help with workplace mailings.

_____ Click on to www.franticwoman.com to celebrate the Frantic Woman Extravaganza.

Giving Thanks

I n the midst of our mad dashing here, there, and everywhere, we sometimes forget how fortunate we are. And because we rarely stop long enough to smell the coffee, the mums, or even the Vicks VapoRub, we tend to allow many of the little things that mean so much to slip away. Giving thanks is the grandest of them. Sure, our families could always help out more than they do and, well, the list goes on and on. But, if we pause for an instant to contemplate what we should be thankful for—family and friends, food and fun—let's face it, that list goes on and on and on.

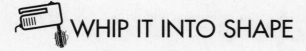 WHIP IT INTO SHAPE

De-Decorate the Orange

Start tearing down the pumpkin, witch, and goblin adornments, for the spooky season is over. Check each item to see if it will survive another year. If not, pitch. If your storage containers need replacing, consider purchasing orange rubberized bins at half price.

Second Chance:
Winterizing Vehicles

Snow is on the horizon in most parts of the country—or is already on the highways and byways—and you say you still haven't winterized your car? Well, what's stopping you? You'd best shift out of first gear and dig out the snow tires. Waiting until the first whiteout will put you in queue with many other floundering frantics, so make it a point to cross winterizing off your list today.

Check It Out

As a reminder, check your Post-It and Pay-It Planner for any special-purchase bills coming due. If you bought an item last winter that offered free financing, dig out the paperwork or call the finance company. We don't want to harp on this but, if you let this one little item slip during the Christmas chaos, you'll be paying some hefty back finance charges that have accumulated during the entire year.

Hanukkah Greetings

Take a look at the calendar to see when Hanukkah falls this year. If the celebration is early, be sure to fill out your cards and mail them on time.

Holiday Menu Prep

Whether you'll be entertaining throngs of visitors or hosting a special meal for your immediate family, now is the time to plan your guest list and menu in your Frantic Journal. Decide on the approximate number of people and what you will be serving. Then, write down all the ingredients and amounts of each you'll need. Why now? Because preplanning will save you money. Grocery stores will spotlight numerous sales over the next few weeks, so compare your ingredients list with the items in each week's advertisements, and purchase. By the time your party date rolls around, you'll have picked up all the things you need at discounted prices.

You might think, I can't be bothered worrying about saving a few pennies at this time of year. But imagine that it's the week of Christmas and you have a list of fifty items to buy. If you had picked up each one at a 50-cents savings, you would have saved a total of $25. That's 2,500 pennies down the drain.

HIDDEN GEM: If you're really on the ball, write up a list of the items you'll need in order to bake your Christmas or Hanukkah cookies next month, and purchase those supplies on sale, too. Then over the next several weeks, when a few free hours unexpectedly pop up (say on that rare occasion when the kids don't have much homework or when a snowstorm blows through, canceling all activities), you can open your cabinet and begin mixing up batches of peanut butter buckeyes without bellyaching about not having all the ingredients you need.

If you're tired of preparing the same old dishes every holiday, plan another recipe swap. Try any of these fresh ways to do so.

- *Break out the old.* Make a family member feel good by asking for her traditional family recipe.
- *Bring in the new.* Select a specific dish, such as a meat entrée, a salad, or a side dish. Then ask friends, coworkers, neighbors, and school moms if they have an irresistible recipe for that category. You'll be surprised at how excited people are to share their favorites.

One last entertaining tip: Don't feature an entire menu of dishes you've never served before. Rather, mix the old with the new. Remember, when your best friend's husband knows he's coming to your house, he's expecting to nibble on your old standbys like sauerkraut balls and mini-cheesecakes. As the saying goes, *If it ain't broke, don't fix it.*

Invitations

Open your Frantic Journal to the guest list page and write out your holiday party invitations, now. When you send them early, people will be more likely to come, blocking off time for yours before other invites come rolling in.

Company's Coming

Confirm arrival and departure dates with overnight guests. We wouldn't want you to strain yourself, only to be stood up later.

Are there any particular cleaning projects you must tackle before visitors arrive—like weeding out the space under the bathroom sink or polishing the chandelier? Or if pets reside in your castle, do you need to have the carpets cleaned and deodorized? Have you removed that spot from the living room sofa yet? Make a special-project list in your Frantic Journal and start crossing off tasks immediately.

To prepare for company, from both in town and out, scrub your house, now—including washing baseboards, window glass, and the tops of doorframes. Then, the day before your guests arrive, do a little hooey-flooey (light cleaning and refreshing), allowing you to focus more on what you're serving and how you look.

While you're flitting about the city (or community) with your out-of-towners, invite hometown kin to enjoy the events and the sightseeing, too. Involve the kids. This is a great way for everyone to interact, relax, and enjoy the local scene. Snap some pictures to take with you to the family reunion next summer. Or turn one of them into a holiday photo card if you're running behind on that October task.

Marathon Shopping

The biggest shopping day of the year surfaces this month. It's called "Black Friday," the day after Thanksgiving. And yes, some people actually love to shop on Black Friday (we do). But even if this goes against every shopping principle you've ever held, give it a try. If you're feeling adventuresome, go out at five in the morning when some of the stores open. Yes, brew your coffee, fill that thermos, grab your sale flyers, and head on out.

Here's a course of action all mapped out for you.

- Choose your method of payment for the marathon shopping experience. Set a maximum amount you'll spend in cash and credit. Stick to it to ward off the New Year's–bill blues.
- Hit the bank and the gas station on Wednesday so you'll have cash in your pocket and fuel in your tank.
- Select a small waist pouch or lightweight purse to sling over your shoulder, toting only the bare essentials, including your driver's license, chosen credit cards, cash, a copy of your gift list, and, of course, a power color of your favorite lipstick. Slip an envelope in your purse to hold receipts for safekeeping. Write "holiday purchases" across the front.
- Consider using the department store charge cards for purchases there. In the event of a return, if you misplace a receipt or two, the cashier can do a search on your account. And you'll receive what you paid for the article rather than the after-Christmas pittance price.
- Check all recipients on your gift list that you have divided into categories. (If not, go back to the "Christmas in July" section to quickly catch up.) Tally how many people you have in each group and write down several suggestions for each. Transfer the information to index cards that are the perfect size to slip in that small purse or satchel.
- On Thanksgiving Day, buy all the local papers that are stuffed plump with ads. Decide where you want to go and what items are best priced at each place, marking those as top priority. Scan the flyers for loss-leader merchandise that might be given as hostess thank-yous throughout the season or for general items that can be kept on hand for that special someone you've accidentally forgotten. Be sure to note times of store openings and early-bird specials that expire mid-morning. With gift list and sale flyers in hand, jot possible purchases and how many you'll need for each category. Map out a route based on location and

rev up your engine. If you make a day of it with friends or family, you'll enjoy yourself *and* slash items off of your list as you go.

- Pack a cooler with water, soft drinks, and snacks to hold you over as you elbow your way to bargains galore. (Caution: Stop for lunch and dinner to refuel your weary body, but dine at off-peak hours to avoid line delays.)

HIDDEN GEM: As you brainstorm gift possibilities for each category, give some thought to what we call "spin-off presents." Say your sister has been eyeing a leather jacket that would stretch your budget until it snaps. Consider a spin-off idea instead. A leather daily planner in her choice color or a handbag matching her taste and style would show your thoughts were spinning in her wish-list direction. Spin-offs can be designed from past wish lists, too. Mary Jo's mom had always wanted to see Elvis in concert, but with three growing teenagers at the height of "The King's" career, her chance never came. Mary Jo had tucked this in the back of her mind for many years. Even though she could no longer take her mom to see the real Elvis perform, Mary Jo surprised her with a trip to Graceland. One Christmas wish granted—better late than never.

Here are a few other cautionary concerns. The stores that open early are ordinarily crowded, so you might wind up waylaid and miss other early-bird specials. Solve this dilemma by engineering a system with a friend. You'll manage the mob at one store, while your shopping buddy handles another. Each of you can take the other's list, then meet at a designated time and place. Be forewarned, crowds tend to max out between mid-morning and late afternoon. If you have less patience than the average shopper, start as we suggested before the crack of dawn. Then, go home when the vast majority of people are scrambling into the stores. Grab a bite to eat and get started wrapping all those presents you bought. Then, lace up your cross trainers, sling your purse over your shoulder, and head back out the door around four o'clock.

Money Doesn't Grow on Trees

How many times have you purchased items that offer rebates, but you never send them in? With gift wrap flying and people sighing, who can remember to grab the proof-of-purchase symbol from the new CD player? Oops. There goes ten bucks out the window.

Here's how you can quit throwing money away.

- Get hold of that rebate form and fill it out now. Yes, right this minute.
- Before you give the gift having the treasured proof-of-purchase symbol, address the rebate envelope and add a stamp and your return address label. Now, put this envelope in your purse or with your unpaid bills. Then you'll know where it is when the time comes to send it in.
- If the kids are older and you won't squelch visions of Santa and reindeer, attach the receipt to the gift with tape. If the sales slip has other items on it, make a copy of it. Most stores will issue a duplicate for rebate purposes. Just ask.
- Add a note to the front of the gift's packaging stating "Do not throw box away." Then, the recipient will ask why, jogging your memory.
- (P.S. Take that extra $10 and buy yourself a treat. Or you can save all your rebate money in one piggy bank and spend it on something special.)

Deck the Halls

Decorate the house inside and out at the end of November so that you can concentrate on entertaining, shopping, and being with family in December. If Mother Nature is on your side, you'll be trimming the exterior in above-freezing temps rather than below. Brrr! Besides, the place is much more conducive to wrapping presents and baking cookies when garlanded with boughs of holly and mistletoe.

"People ask me how I can tolerate decorating for the holidays so many times over," says artist and decorator Mary Anne Peters, who ornaments country clubs, shop windows, and private homes. Rather than dread the process and rush through it, Mary Anne advises reluctant frantics to follow these steps to keep from draining the fun out of decorating.

- First, empty all your boxes, laying everything out as if it were on display at a store. Most often, we pull something from a box and put it somewhere, anywhere. But with all your bits and pieces in view, you can survey what you have to work with.
- Take your time. Many families hurry the decorating process, just to get it over with. Instead of doing it all in one day, add things at your leisure—a little at a time. This allows you to be creative, moving articles around until you find just the right spot for them.
- Place trimmings in unique spots, not where you've put them in the past out of habit. For instance, don't be afraid to change the theme of your Christmas tree or where you position it.
- If you still need ideas, leaf through popular magazines such as *Victoria* and *Mary Engelbreit's Home Companion*. Gather ideas, then make them your own. If a magazine features a centerpiece using eucalyptus, but you can pluck holly from the bushes in your yard, make the change. You'll never know how something looks until you try it.

And now, for one of Mary Anne's favorite tips. Do you relish the beauty of sidewalk luminaries, but don't like the hassle of bags blowing and burning down? Mary Anne suggests buying wide-mouth Mason jars (approximately six inches tall with a four-inch-wide opening) at a hardware or home improvement store. Insert inexpensive plumbers candles also purchased at the hardware store. Surround each candle with fresh cranberries, filling the jar about one-third full. "The combination of the candle and the red glow from the cranberries is eye-catching," Mary Anne says. "These luminaries are durable, too, so you can use them year after year." (Be sure to toss the cranberries.)

SNIPPET: Ever wonder who thought up the idea to light candles in bags on your sidewalk? It is believed that shepherds made small bonfires to light the way to the stable where Jesus was born some two thousand years ago. For centuries, the people of Mexico carried on the tradition by gathering on Christmas Eve around a bonfire to sing and celebrate. Afterward, they would go home and build small fires in front of each home to welcome the Christ Child. The tradition migrated north to New Mexico where, during the nineteenth century, people would light the path to their homes with minifires made from crossed sticks. Early in the twentieth century, one family couldn't set out the sticks because of an illness. So the youngest child placed a broken candle in a paper bag partially filled with sand in front of their home in honor of the tradition. And hence, today's luminaries were born.

Toss Away

As you're unpacking your holiday decorations, put aside any broken, worn, or outdated ones. Instead of unpacking and repacking unused items season after season, place them in a box to give away. The next time you're out and about, drop the box off at a Goodwill store, a thrift shop, or a women's shelter. Not only will this save you the hassles of dragging the unwanted decorations back into storage, but you'll also receive a tax deduction in the process.

Holiday Blooms

Although snow flurries might be covering the ground in your crook of the country, you can still grow living color inside your home using beautiful holiday blooms to balance your trimmings. Purchase an amaryllis bulb–planting kit. Though this starts out as a drab brown sphere, it quickly sprouts to approximately two feet tall and yields satiny blossoms in various colors. Remember to position the pot in a well-lit, warm place and to keep soil moist. When the stem grows to twelve inches or so, support it by tying it to a dowel rod.

DARLING LITTLE ANGELS (AND THE WHOLE BLISSFUL BUNCH)

Holiday Happenings:
Celebrations of Thanks

Plan your Thanksgiving celebration early in the month. Is there a decision to make on where you'll be spending the day? Will you be hosting the big meal or going elsewhere? Are you planning to travel out of town? If so, this is your second chance to make travel arrangements. In fact, plan your out-of-town and in-town visits and informal get-togethers now by making calls, choosing dates, and marking your calendar. You'll find it's easier to work around preselected dates than to squeeze them in later.

Are you looking for a way to show or give thanks? Many families take time during November to volunteer at a local charity as a family unit. You can participate in fund-raisers such as spaghetti dinners and breakfasts with Santa sponsored by nonprofit organizations. Or grab a snow shovel and clean your elderly neighbor's sidewalk and driveway. If Jack Frost is still in hiding, rake the neighbor's fallen debris. Don't ask your neighbor if she needs help—just do it. Get in and out as quickly as possible to remain helpful elves incognito.

As you're shopping for that all-important Thanksgiving dinner, buy an additional turkey (or turkey breast) or two and freeze. By the pound, the birds won't be priced any cheaper than they are this month. One fourteen-pounder in the oven yields many days of home-cooked dinners. Or purchase a seven- or eight-pounder as the basis for a full Sunday meal. The same goes for other Turkey Day staples including pumpkin pie mix, yams, and cranberry sauce.

For the big family day itself, try something different to involve the whole crew. Once everyone is seated and prayers have been offered, go around the table and have each guest say one line about what he or she is thankful for. If you're hosting a particularly chatty group, limit the line to twenty seconds or so.

As a variation, hand each person an index card and a pencil when she walks in the door. Ask her to write a few lines about what she's thankful for, but do so anonymously. Be sure to include the kids, too. Depending upon the group, you can collect the cards in an index card binder or small photo album so guests can flip through it as the day goes on. For the more lively bunch, read phrases of thanks aloud and have visitors guess who wrote each one.

After dinner, call out the words "role reversal" and watch as the women scramble for a spot on the couch to catch a football game on TV while the men clear the table and do the dishes.

Later, divide the gang into two groups and start a game of charades. Young and old alike will enjoy guessing the meaning of the other team's movements. Or play (girls against the boys) a game of Pictionary, Taboo, or Outburst to fit your family's style. In these games, team players shout out answers, causing chuckles and roars with some of the more outrageous exclamations.

Thanksgiving Day Assignment

With most of the family together on Thanksgiving, your assignment is to discuss and plan Christmas Eve and/or Day celebrations. Doing so now minimizes time wasted in making arrangements and playing phone tag later. Mull over what's worked in the past, what hasn't, and propose new options. Do you need to change your grab-bag strategy or make time adjustments to accommodate older family members or newborns? Take the time to work through these and other issues now.

For instance, do the family's entertaining responsibilities always fall on the same people? Well, listen to the solution Judith and her siblings came up with. They host a Christmas-in-Motion party. It used to be that everyone gathered in the late afternoon for dinner and a gift exchange. But as the family grew, there were more and more kids with more and more presents to be opened. What resulted was a mass of chatter, flying gift wrap, and all-around chaos. After all the time, effort, and money spent on preparations, the spirit of the season was lost in a garbage bag somewhere. So the family decided to spread things out a bit. Early Christmas Eve morning, say 8:30 or so, everyone gathers at one person's house for breakfast. The meal is enjoyed, a few gifts are given, and thanks are expressed. There's time for an organized game, a craft, or even for trying on new sweaters. Then, here's where the motion part comes in. The families load up their vehicles and move to another person's house for lunch (which has been conveniently pre-prepared and preheated in slow cookers, ready to serve). More exchanges are made and enjoyment had. Afterward, it's off to the church service, then over the river and through the woods. At Grandma's, a feast is spread, carols are sung, and the long-awaited arrival of Santa is satisfied. While it sounds like the day is more lengthy and tiring, it is actually much more relaxing. People take in the expressions of loved ones opening gifts, and they relish honest-to-goodness family discourse. As a plus, the breakfast and lunch duties are rotated among family members from year to year.

HIDDEN GEM: As an alternative to everyone bringing a covered dish to your house, when it's your turn to host the party, don't ask guests to bring anything. Yes, take on the full responsibility yourself. Figure, if you're in the throes of roasting a turkey anyway, you can whip up a few sides and toss a salad yourself. Then, here's the best part. When it's *not* your turn, you don't have to do one blessed thing. You simply dress your family, pack up your presents, and show up for the fun! Now that's a real bonus, isn't it? (Hint: When it's your year off, a small carefully chosen hostess gift says "thank-you" in a special way.)

Family Acceptance

Sometimes families—grudges and all—cause additional stresses in the frantic woman's life, especially around the holidays. Our most important pointer can be summarized in one word: acceptance. If you can acknowledge that some relatives will behave in certain ways, then they're less likely to grate on your nerves and add to your holiday pressures.

The next thing you can do is to take the initiative toward compromise. Go ahead—make the first move. Smooth out any past wrinkles by taking a step in the right direction. Before the holidays, ask the family member to join you for coffee and dessert. Or make it a point to talk with him at length at the next family gathering. Send him a card or e-mail that evokes a memory of when you were closer. Remember, it takes two to tango, as the saying goes, so make an effort to keep the rhythm flowing.

Holiday Wear

Your next task, if you decide to accept it, is to organize the holiday clothing you and your family will need. This includes outfits for Hanukkah celebrations, Christmas Day, special occasions, and parties. Don't forget any auxiliary articles you and your children might need like red and green sweatshirts for color day at school.

Once you have outfits ready to go, take the time to see if you have all your accessories. Assess shoes, hose, jewelry, slip, nail color, and perfume. And for the family, ask yourself if they have socks, undergarments, ties, belts, hair bows, tights, and so forth. If not, put these items on a to-buy list in your Frantic Journal.

Schedule family hair appointments for preholiday cuts or for updo styles on the day of the celebration. (For tips on scheduling, see the "Hair Care for All" section in the August chapter.)

After you've gathered, purchased, and scheduled all you need, you can breathe a sigh of relief. And maybe this year, you'll even be on time for the party.

Get Well Wishes

Along with the chaos of the holidays, wintertime seems to bring about a surge of illnesses. Whether you have friends and family recovering from the flu, minor mishaps, or major surgery, send a token treat to lift up their spirits.

A copy of a popular magazine and a jar of homemade chicken soup can heal body and soul. Send a hot-off-the-press book, a pop celebrity calendar, or a prepaid phone card to the niece who just had her wisdom teeth pulled or the nephew who broke his wrist. A package of stationery and stamps or a new journal and pen is a thoughtful surprise to any ailing recipient. And believe us, they'll remember that you remembered them—for years to come.

Elizabeth Joos, R.N., says visiting the sick and elderly is the best thing you can do for them. Throughout her twenty-four years as an R.N. supervisor in a nursing home, she says, "Nothing affects a patient more positively than a visit from family or friends." Depending on their condition, she recommends that you keep appointments short—fifteen to thirty minutes, with an hour being the longest. In addition, take photos along with you to share and to leave there, if you can. "It's a good idea to place a memo book or journal in your loved one's room, too," Elizabeth suggests. "That way, family members can sign in, write who visited and when, and jot a few words about how the patient was feeling and responding. Then, everyone who comes can catch up by reading the daily log." You can also record changes in medications, testing dates, and other important information in this journal.

If you can't stop by, phone the nurse's station or facility and ask them to tell the patient you called, even if they're unable to take the call.

Elizabeth offers one last tip. "Don't send money to nursing home occupants because often patients will lose it." (It's best to give the monetary gift directly to the office administrator—or mail it to her—who can deposit it in your family member's account.)

Sunday Fun

For one reason or probably several, the week slips away, leaving you with a gnawing feeling that time is passing your family by. You think the chance for making memories has escaped—again. While Sunday afternoons might not be the ideal time for your family to create lasting memories, you can follow these tips on any day of the week that's right for you.

- For outside in those colder climates, slip on the snowsuits and pull out the sleds and camera for good-old traditional sledding fun. You can even bake cookies ahead of time (the ones available in the dairy case will work just fine) and make sure you have hot chocolate on hand.
- Take the family to an outdoor ice skating rink. When ankles are weary and feet are sore, order hot chocolate and cozy up near the fire, if there is one. Some rinks even allow you to roast marshmallows, so inquire before you go. Think how disappointed the kids would be if you forgot the puffy stuff.
- Hike through a state park or wooded area near home. Collect rocks, pinecones, and other treasures that were covered by greens earlier in the year. Shhh! You might even spot a deer or rabbit (but hopefully no bears).
- For inside fun, pop popcorn over an open fire, then string and hang. Or have the kids make and wear their very own popcorn necklaces.
- Mix up a batch of homemade applesauce cinnamon dough and shape into ornaments, package decorations, or hanging air fresheners. For a simple passed-down recipe, see "A Wee Bit More," part three.
- Remember that powdered hard tac candy your great-aunt made? Now you can stir up a portion yourself using our time-tested recipe in "A Wee Bit More," part three. Collect fancy jars before they hit the recycling bin and allow kids to decorate with paint pens, permanent markers, paint, or stickers. Fill with the homemade confections and top it off with a bow. This candy gift will spark many sweet stories and cozy memories.

☞ ALL ABOUT YOU

Interoffice Memo: Potluck for Work

Organize a gift exchange or holiday luncheon at work—even if it's never been done before. (Be sure to obtain permission from the head honcho beforehand.) Send out a memo or invitation to all staff members in the workplace. Include everybody, even the boss or owner, the guy in the mail room, and the cleaning staff. A potluck lunch and grab-bag exchange on the premises will keep the cost and travel time down.

To ensure a variety of eatin's, have each staff member sign up for what he or she will be providing. Add spice to the meal by asking participants to bring a traditional or ethnic dish they normally prepare at home. Take plastic containers, zippered freezer bags, and foil to split the leftovers into doggie bags.

At the party, place all presents in one area. Draw names from a Santa hat, allowing each person to choose one gift as his name is called. Or number the grab-bag items randomly and have employees draw numbers to find their prizes.

(Note: If you take on the corporate entertaining project this December, pass it along to someone else next year.)

Interoffice Memo: The Commute

Use the travel route to and from work to your advantage. One day a week, make arrangements to shop through the dinner hour when people are scrambling to get home. At this time, you'll have little competition at the checkout counter. You might also want to avoid Monday shopping. Mondays are busier because most people think of what they need over the weekend. This is why many businesses give double punches or percentage-off discounts on Tuesdays and Wednesdays.

Use your lunch hour wisely. Sometimes people fall into a lunchtime routine—chatting with coworkers, eating at the same diner—losing those thirty to sixty minutes without realizing it. And by the end of the week, five hours or so have slipped away from you. What can you do more efficiently with that time? Well, that depends upon where you work. If you're close to a shopping plaza or mall, stop to buy a gift or two, have photos developed, drop off party clothes to be dry-cleaned, or mail packages if there's a post office around. If your place of work is somewhat isolated, tote your greetings container with you and start on that stack of holiday cards (if you didn't finish them in October). Review your to-do list in your Frantic Journal. We're sure there are plenty of tasks remaining to keep you busy.

Take Five: To Thine Own Self Be True

Make a goal or set up a reward for yourself—to be initiated after the holidays, at the start of the New Year. Think of it as an early resolution. For example, you might plan to treat yourself to a weekly or monthly manicure, a more regular dip in the Jacuzzi, or a yoga class. Try anything new from joining a Scrabble group to learning Mandarin Chinese.

For example, as her mini-reward, Mary Carmody decided to do double duty. She spends every Saturday morning at a local bookshop/café with her grandson. While Mary enjoys a large cup of joe and their quiet discussions, Ryan—the oldest of five—sips a slushy drink and relishes the one-on-one time with his grandmother.

Your goal can be as simple as that. Keep it in mind as you scrub, cook, and entertain over the next two months—like a dangling carrot luring you through the season's turbulence.

Don't Miss Out

In our concentrated efforts to accomplish the Norman Rockwell/picture-perfect holiday, we forget to grant our own seasonal wishes. As a consequence, after the bustle, we often feel a sense of disappointment or a void. Before you allow this feeling to creep in, therefore, sit back and give some thought to the things you wanted to do in years past that have remained unfulfilled. Do you miss browsing the glorious window displays? Would you like to take a sleigh ride or visit a crèche? The solution might be easier than you think. Simply schedule your family gatherings, home-tour excursions, or shopping trips now before another holiday season gears up and zooms past.

Take Five: That's Entertainment

Arrange a theater trip as a treat to yourself this season. Go with your spouse or a friend, or take a family member who you know would appreciate it. Present her with a playbill and pay for the ticket. Just think, now you have one less gift to buy. To save money, check into matinees or presentations at local theaters, community colleges, and dance schools. Watch for promotional discounts, senior citizen nights (if taking one of your elders), and AAA rates or coupon book offers. It's show time!

ONE-STEP-AT-A-TIME CHECKLIST

Date completed Or N/A   Task

_____ De-decorate and throw away retired Halloween trimmings.

_____ Winterize your car (second chance).

_____ Check final loan-payment due dates for special purchases bought last year.

_____ Send Hanukkah greetings if the holiday falls this month.

_____ Prepare menu and ingredients list for upcoming parties.

_____ Send Hanukkah and Christmas party invitations early.

_____ Confirm December travel plans with overnight guests and complete whole house scrubbing and company preparations.

_____ Map out a Black Friday marathon-shopping course.

_____ Organize rebate forms and reminders.

_____ Decorate the house inside and out.

_____ Toss or give away worn and broken holiday trappings.

_____ Experiment with holiday blooms.

_____ Try a new way to involve everyone at your Thanksgiving celebration.

_____ While the family is together, plan December gatherings.

_____ Accept family members as they are.

_____ Coordinate and collect holiday wear for all.

_____ Send get-well wishes to those down and out.

_____ Turn Sundays into fun family days.

_____ Start a potluck lunch and gift exchange at work.

_____ Use the commute to cross things off your to-do list.

_____ Draw up a New Year's goal or reward for yourself.

_____ Plan family activities to be enjoyed throughout the jolly season.

_____ Buy theater tickets for you and a special someone.

Entertaining

As we flip another page on our calendars, we realize that what was once the New Year with so many plans has evaporated, leaving behind a residue of goals that still need to be fulfilled. On top of that, the most demanding holiday of the year is before us, bringing many picture-perfect expectations of how it should be celebrated. No wonder we're all frantic. But, hold on to your Santa's cap. We've rustled up a sleighful of suggestions—everything from preplanning your party to shopping the after-holiday sales—just for you. So here goes.

'Twas the Night Before Christmas:
The Frantic Version

Ahh, the stockings were hung by the chimney with care, and not a creature was stirring—until St. Nick rounded the corner and what should appear? But a frantic woman scurrying from worry and fear.

With flour in her hair and gift wrap in her hands,
Her face was distorted. Her clothes were in strands.
The jolly red fellow took one look and said,
"My dear Frantic Woman, you look nearly Dead!
Chug something strong and then step aside,
For you'd never believe it, but help has arrived!"
Then in a wink of an eye, he rolled up his sleeves,
Tossed her an aspirin and trimmed all the eaves.
He gathered the gifts, wrapping all in a jiffy,
Flew through the house, cleaning up—neat and spiffy.
Erasing the mess left behind by her pace,
He turned and saw something new on her face.
"Why that's a smile," he said as she glowed.
Then, he turned with a jerk, and up the chimney he rose.
She heard him exclaim as he drove out of sight,
"Go to bed, Frantic Woman, at least for the night,
For tomorrow when real life comes back into view,
The race starts all over again, anew!"

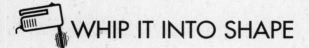 WHIP IT INTO SHAPE

Second Chance:
Ornamenting the Place

December blusters in with Cold Man Winter, fast and furious. If you don't hop to it, you'll be decorating the house and trimming the tree on the night before Christmas, so, here's your second chance. Drop everything for the moment and pull out your stash of trimmings. You can't bury your head in the sand (or snow) any longer. Brew a cup of cider, blast the holiday carols, and trim, trim, trim.

Do you lack time, creativity, and ideas? Interior designer Karen Lantz suggests these quick tips to boost the holiday atmosphere in your home with minimal cost and effort.

- Cut evergreens and holly boughs from your yard. Or leaves, such as from a magnolia tree, can be substituted. Fill outdoor containers with greenery to accent the exterior of your home. Enhance the mantel, dining room centerpiece, and table arrangements with various greens and berries. (Remember: When using fresh greens and berries, keep them out of the reach of pets and children.) If you are low on centerpiece containers, different-sized baskets work nicely. Add a festive bow or an array of colored glass balls.

- Spray-paint magnolia and other leaves, or tall grasses, in gold or silver to finish off your arrangements (insert fresh holiday flowers, if needed). These arrangements will last four weeks or so and your house will be filled with the fragrance of the holidays. Remember to add water to indoor containers on a regular basis.

- Drape your sofas with a red, green, or burgundy throw. Look for small, inexpensive throw pillows in holiday greens, golds, and silvers.

- If you are in need of a holiday covering for your kitchen center island, table, or countertop, consider using felt. Felt is inexpensive and comes in a wide width. Not only is it easy to work with, but it requires no sewing—only cutting. Measure your counter space, and add twelve to fourteen inches on each end. It's also fun to customize your holiday tablecloth by gluing trims or braids to it. Serve buffet style from your kitchen island by dressing it up with this simple tactic.

"All of these decorating ideas require only a little time to prepare," Karen says. "And they'll give your decor the boost it needs this time of year."

✂ SNIPPET: If you're one of the millions who decorate their home using seasonal wreaths, did you ever wonder how the tradition came about? Hanging wreaths at Christmastime is a custom that can be traced back to the crown of thorns worn by Christ when he was crucified. It is believed the crown was made of holly.

Another Second Chance:
Wardrobe and Hair Planning

We're giving you a second chance to plan the party wardrobe for the crew. Don't forget to gather all essentials from hair to heels.

Have you put off making hair appointments for your color touch-up, trim, or elegant updo? And do the kids need some grooming, too?

And One More: Greetings to Go

While you're catching up on second chances, devise the greetings box we mentioned in the October chapter. After all, you can tote this manageable container with you from place to place and jot "Seasons Greetings" to those near and far. With your greetings container in hand, there's no excuse not to pull out the holiday cards, jot a quick note, tuck in a family photo, and x-out the "send cards" entry on your to-do list in your Frantic Journal.

Since the clock is ticking faster than the quickest version of "We Wish You a Merry Christmas" you can sing, involve the kids. Do you have a teen in the house? Assign her the job of making computer-generated labels from your mailing list. Delegate the task of affixing the stamps and return-address labels. Have your 'tweenager slip the pictures inside the cards, then slide them into the pre-addressed envelopes.

To refresh your memory on other greetings pointers, refer back to the October chapter.

In the Mail

Gather Hanukkah and holiday greetings to be mailed early in the month. (For Christmas wishes, you might want to hold off until later or recipients might feel obligated to mail you a card in return. The choice is yours.)

Prepare all long-distance gifts and overseas cards that must be sent. Make it a goal to have these items purchased, wrapped, and in the mail by the 7th of December. Why? Because the closer it gets to the United States Postal Service (USPS) deadline for Christmas Eve delivery, the longer the lines and the crabbier the people tend to become. So, scratch this chore from your list this week.

Skip the trip to the post office altogether and order stamps over the Internet at www.usps.gov. Delivery is free (your friendly postal person brings them right to your mailbox) and you don't have to worry that they'll run out of your favorite choice of stamp. The USPS Web site has a Frequently Asked Questions (FAQ) page and offers tips for preparing packages. It also lists weights in ounces and pounds of an array of items from sheets of paper to CDs in a hard plastic case. For a fee, a pickup service is available, or you can hand your prepaid bundles to your all-weather worker, filling one more pothole in the road between here and your ultimate destination—Christmas.

When mailing packages to foreign lands, check the USPS Web site's page that lists deadlines for getting those packages delivered by Christmas Eve.

Snail-Mail List

As holiday greeting cards come your way from persons not on your list, take a minute to annex them—but don't feel obligated to return a card this year. Also note address changes by saving the envelope and adding the corrections right away. This system will keep your list updated and save you plenty of time next year. (Psst! This is another assignment you can pass along to your teens.)

And Another: Gift-Wrap Station

Okay girls, we've allowed you several second chances this month. And here is another one. Put together the gift-wrapping station we mentioned in "Year Round," part one. Before you wrap another gift, gather all the supplies necessary to create this handy, timesaving device. Once you've customized your gift-wrap station, you'll be scratching your head, wondering why you waited so long to do so.

All Wrapped Up

We're certain you've drawn a line through just about everyone on your gift list by now—especially after hitting the Black Friday sales last month. And now, are you ready to wrap? Here are some strategies to make preparing your surprises for giving a bit easier.

- Host a wrap-it-up party where you and friends, neighbors, or relatives get together to wrap presents, write greeting cards, bake a few cookies, or do whatever remains undone. With a little holiday punch and a few easy hors d'oeuvres, the night becomes a productive escape.

- With your gift-wrapping station in a central location (like on a card table in the living room or a spot on the dining room table), have kids help wrap, tag, and organize. They can package gifts for grandparents, cousins, and each other. As a treat, rent a holiday flick and set out a favorite snack or two for an afternoon of wrapping delight.

- Look for local nonprofit organizations that set up booths in shopping malls for gift wrapping for a minimal donation. Take advantage of this option wherever you find it.

- Wrap as you buy. As soon as you walk in the door from the department store, take your bundle of packages and head straight to your station. Okay, you may take off your coat first.

- If you can enlist the help of your spouse, break the gifts into two categories—either he wraps the boys and you do the girls, or you handle one side of the family and he does the other. Hubby can plop the stuffed animals into gift bags while you figure out how to cover the basketball. It doesn't matter how you divide the task. Just take the help and put the job behind you.

- If you have access to your company's office (or your spouse's) for stashing the goods as you buy them, take advantage of that. Then, one weekend afternoon before the big day, the two of you can go into the office and wrap everything. Who said you needed wine and candlelight to spend quality time together?

- Store the purchased gifts at a friend's or relative's house. Head to your parents' home with merchandise and wrapping station in hand. Spend the evening handling two turtledoves with one stroke by chatting with your mom and wrapping gifts. (Leave the wrapping station as a thank-you.)

- Utilize small waiting periods when they crop up—while preparing dinner, talking on the phone, or watching the news—to whittle away at the mountain of unwrapped presents.
- Make an assembly line when wrapping several "alike" gifts, such as sweatshirts for teens. First, open all the boxes and line with tissue. Then fold the shirts and put in the boxes. Pencil the name on the outside of the box. Next, write out the corresponding name tags. Then, cut a number of sheets of the same-size paper and wrap. Tag each box as you go and add bows.

Recycled Gift Containers

During the jolly season, many food items and some retail merchandise will come in unusual containers or packages. But what does this have to do with gift giving? Think about the wooden crate Clementine oranges are sold in. Or a large plastic jar that holds certain brands of pretzels. Train your eyes and brain to see the potential in each container. Jump-start your ingenuity with these ideas.

- The Clementine crates can be painted, sponged, or stenciled. Then, use them as the foundation for any number of theme gifts such as a home-office supply basket, a stationery or art products collection, or a shower-yourself-in-goodness treat.
- The plastic jug might be used to hold sugar-free snacks and grocery items for that special someone with diabetes or for your favorite dieting family member.
- Popcorn, candy, juice boxes, chips, and a family video or theater gift certificates tucked inside a bucket will make a great movie theme gift.

Now, as the boxes, containers, and jars come your way, give some thought to what you can do with them.

Bake Ahead

You must start mixing up batches of your family favorites, but you're reluctant to bake too early. After all, you've *tried* freezing cookies, only to have soggy slabs on your hands after thawing a few weeks later. Yet, you understand the consequences of not freezing at all—especially once you've eyed the goodie tray at a party, only to bite into a petrified peanut butter ball that you must nonchalantly ditch somewhere.

Well, fret no longer. We've solicited the help of the seasoned freeze-er, Ruth Wiltman. Here are her simple steps for preserving the freshness of those slaved-over treats.

- Allow cookies to cool on a rack until they reach room temperature.
- Layer cookies in a plastic container that has a good snap-on lid. If the seal is damaged from cracks or melted sections from the dishwasher, discard the container and purchase a new one. And contrary to what you might think, there's no need to separate layers with waxed paper or foil unless, of course, you're stacking thumbprints or iced cutout cookies.
- Place a piece of heavy-duty foil over the opened container full of cookies—now, here comes the real trick—then snap the lid closed over it. The foil addition provides a more airtight seal, allowing less air and moisture in. And because it creates another layer under the lid, it serves to "catch" all the frost buildup (those ice crystals that form on frozen food over time) and keeps it from tainting your cookies.
- Freeze any type of cookie at all, even mini-cheesecakes. (Hint: When freezing cheesecakes, don't add the fruit topping until after you've thawed and are ready to serve.) You can even cheat and freeze bought bakery cookies. If you want to preserve the freshness of brownies, bake them in a pan equipped with a snap-on lid. Freeze right in the pan, and don't forget the layer of foil. If you're going to extract only a few brownies at a time, cut them in squares before freezing.

- To thaw, simply remove the cookies you want to use, place them in an airtight container, and allow them to warm up to room temperature on the counter.
- If you like to arrange a cookie tray using several varieties for your guests, try freezing layers of different kinds of cookies in one plastic container. Then, when you go to make up your party tray, rather than opening and resealing five different containers, for example, you'll only need to grab one or two to create that spectacular plate of sweets. (Note: When freezing cookies together, group similar cookies. It works to freeze spritz with sugar cookies or cutouts, for instance, but by putting aromatic cinnamon cookies in a container with fruit-filled ones, you might end up with a cinnamon-tasting raspberry tart.)

"The key to successful freezing," Ruth says, "is to add the heavy-duty foil seal and to freeze the cookies the day you bake them."

Now that you know the freezing secret, you can bake ahead and still have fresh, delicious treats to serve when guests come knocking at your door.

SNIPPET: Has the flour in your cabinet been there longer than you can remember? Well, white flour can be stored in a cool, dry place for years. Really! But if it isn't kept in a sealed container, the flour might taste stale after several months' time. One more caution is that whole-wheat varieties contain oily grains that can turn rancid in just a few weeks at room temperature—so don't buy such specialty kinds in bulk. Now that you can't use the excuse that your flour is old, get baking!

Entertaining Shortcuts

This is what you've been waiting for—the opportunity to entertain friends and family. But who has the time, energy, or money? For

> **HIDDEN GEM:** For a twist on the traditional cookie exchange, follow Karen Lantz's suggestion and update your swap to an hors d'oeuvres exchange instead. Invite three or four friends to your house. Ask each one to bring the ingredients and recipes (including extra copies for all) to make two or three freezable appetizers in quadruple batches. After you've worked at preparing the treats, serve a light menu of salad, fresh bread, and your choice of beverage. Then, invite the laborers to sample the finished products. After an evening of a little work, lots of chatter, and plenty of good food, send everyone home with a variety of servable snacks to freeze for the holidays. (P.S. With many hands in the pot, the make-it, wrap-it, and cleanup stages don't seem like such drudgery.)

some, panic settles in and springs back up just at the thought. Take comfort in the fact that you're not alone. Entertaining overwhelms even the most organized persons. Frankly, it's a lot of work—even if you love it.

Preplanning your party will make things run more smoothly from beginning to end. Before you send the invitations, devise your guest list in proportion to your house size. Take into consideration the people you're inviting and plan the day and time accordingly. For instance, a late-afternoon party works best for families with young children because it's after the napping hour and well before bedtime.

Think about scheduling back-to-back parties in one weekend. Yes, this is a lot to do all at once, but it will also save wear and tear on your house and your body over the long run. Start with the group that will be most demanding on you—say a Friday evening work party (or a dinner with your supervisor and his family). Then, work your way downward toward the easygoing bunch, ending with a gathering of close friends or family on Sunday. This method is akin to the Tackler (mentioned in "Year Round," part one) who tackles the tough laundry first. All the worry is over in the beginning, leaving nothing but fun in the end. Plus, by having all of your parties in one weekend, you'll only be tidying (or hooey-flooey-ing) between celebrations, rather than doing heavy-duty cleaning for each one. And isn't it easier to prepare three trays of stuffed mushrooms at once than to assemble the appetizers for three weekends in a row?

As an alternative, consider having a holiday open house, inviting one and all to your home on a Sunday from one to eight o'clock. Since guests will be popping in and out all day long, you'll alleviate the worry of not having enough room for everyone and of mixing certain "categories" of guests (like blending coworkers with family with school people or neighbors) for long periods of time. Hors d'oeuvres can be served in the early hours and a buffet offered starting later in the afternoon. Set up a punch bowl with your favorite mix and add to it throughout the day.

HIDDEN GEM: When serving an alcoholic punch, consider mixing it with a noncarbonated beverage. Bubbly club soda or ginger ale in your spiked punch allows the alcohol to be absorbed more quickly into the body (and results in a rowdier crew). Dish up protein-rich and starchy foods to curb the effects of alcohol on the crowd. Why? Because guests with full stomachs drink less, and the food slows the absorption of alcohol into the bloodstream. (We know you know all about designated drivers and hiring taxicabs, so we'll save the lecturing for our young adult children.)

If entertaining families with children, think about sharing the responsibility. How? Try a progressive party. Decide how many courses you will take on, depending upon the number of participating families. Three or four work best. Start off with appetizers (include hot cocoa and fun finger foods such as hot dog wraps, mini-pizzas, or peanut butter and jelly triangles for the kids). Move on to soup and salad, then the entrée. Finish the party with scrumptious desserts. You can add a small activity at each house for the kids like hand-crafting ornaments, cookie decorating, or sponge-designing gift wrap. If you start the party early enough, you can end at a home with a good hill for sledding, provided the weather cooperates. Otherwise, a classic holiday movie—*A Christmas Story*, *How the Grinch Stole Christmas*, or *The Santa Clause*—is a great way to end the party and settle down the kids.

Still need a few ideas? Try these.

- A full Sunday brunch—complete with hot dishes along with the usual continental spread—satisfies everyone's appetite. And for an early Sunday gig, more invitees will probably be able to join you.
- A short evening cocktail party featuring hot and cold hors d'oeuvres invites guests to enjoy a taste of your hospitality, then to continue on to their other commitments. Serve bite-sized appetizers so guests can sip their drinks and nibble as they mingle.
- A game-day home tailgate party with chili, subs (or hoagies), snacks, and of course, TV football provides just the right backdrop to enjoy family and friends. See the "Football Time-Out" section in our January chapter to further the idea.

Once the party type, time, and menu planning are complete, what else is there? How about some fun? Did you ever wonder why some parties flow better, keep the kids under control, or provide more fun than others? Entertainment. Though socializing happens to be what parties are all about, you do need to "stir the soup" occasionally by cranking up the heat. Play a game, concoct a contest, or put a spin on a traditional Christmas carol.

For simple party game suggestions that can be played by young and old alike, see our November chapter. Depending upon the group, you can send out a photocopied coloring page with invitations announcing a contest for the most original creation. Maybe you'd rather devise a guessing game for your company by having them guess the number of ornaments on the tree. Another idea is a "White Elephant Gift Giveaway." Have each guest bring an unwanted item, the ghastlier the better, but make sure it's wrapped. Put names in a basket. When a name is called, that person selects and unwraps the chosen gift. And last, sing some holiday songs with a twist. For "The Twelve Days of Christmas," divide the party people into twelve groups. Then assign each group a day: the partridges, the turtledoves, the French hens, and so forth. When the singing begins, each group will sing and act out their day. Imagine how your friends will perform ten lords a-leaping or six geese a-laying! You'll be surprised how inventive folks can be.

Ah, now you're finished with your party details. Hold it right there! You almost forgot the tail end—sending visitors off with a touch from your home to their home. In plain English, what about the party favor? Kids aren't the only ones who like a special treat. As a pleasant remembrance, snap pictures of each family in front of the fireplace or the tree using an instant or digital camera, if you have one. Hand out the instant photographs complete with pre-made thank-you labels, or e-mail the digitals (including candid shots) to all.

Or purchase clear ornaments and fill the inside with strands of shredded metallic paper or shredded two-sided wrapping paper (kids can help stuff these). On one side of the ball, write "To the Schneiders" with a paint pen or permanent marker. On the other side, write "Happy Holidays, the Rulnicks." Don't forget to include the year. These ornaments can decorate a small tree until friends depart.

Now that you are brimming with creativity, smile. Your party will be what every hostess hopes to accomplish—a chance for your company to have a great time while taking home a remembrance.

HIDDEN GEM: Want a unique, memorable way to capture the spirit of entertaining friends and family? If so, Julie Kloo's got just the tip for you. When Julie has friends over, she covers the dining room table with a plain tablecloth and then asks the guests to sign it in ink. Later, she embroiders their signatures. When more company comes, she pulls out the same tablecloth, asking new visitors for their "John Hancock"s, too. As friends and family inscribe, they read the names of other signers and ask about who they are, what they do, and so forth. Julie recommends this technique to new home owners and brides-to-be to use in place of a guest book.

Dare We Offer Another
Second Chance?
We Must, We Must

Here's your second chance to do the heavy-duty cleaning. Roll up your sleeves and give it your all. Then, the day before your guests arrive, you'll need only to lightly dust, vacuum, and spruce up the bathroom. Don't know where to start? Go directly to our "Spring-Cleaning Checklist" in "A Wee Bit More," part three.

Mattress Reminder

While you're dusting and cleaning, take a moment to flip your bed mattresses. If you don't, you'll find yourself in a rut in no time.

Double Duty

We suggest having an all-day moviethon to solicit help from the family. While your favorite festive flicks are playing, ask family members to help complete menial sit-down chores like wrapping gifts, filling out invitations, putting stamps on envelopes, clipping coupons, making party favors, even folding towels and mating socks. What a productive way to spend holiday time together.

Snowy days are great for this type of activity. If you can't go anywhere due to wintry conditions, why not get something done instead?

Memory Log

While in the spirit of the season, wouldn't it be uplifting to pull out one photo album that encompassed a time line of all your Hanukkahs or Christmases past? You can if you create a holiday memory log through which you can flip, page after page, bringing back toasty memories and, at the same time, recapping the growth and change of your family. Include not only your own pictures, but also seasonal newsletters, event programs, and snapshots from other relatives and friends. Here's how easy it is to create your holiday memory log.

- Aim to make it a family project. Set up a card table with a basket of photos, fun scissors (like pinking shears in various patterns available at craft supply stores), scrapbook cutouts, and permanent markers.
- Gather all snapshots and related materials from holiday seasons of yesteryear.
- Purchase a large photo album that holds four hundred pictures or more. If you're looking to add your personal touch, make sure you buy a book that contains full pages rather than one that has separate sleeves to slip prints inside.
- When placing pictures in the album, start with the oldest and work your way toward the present. Put the date in the corner of each page. You might also want to write "Holiday Memory Log" on the spine of the album with a paint pen or permanent marker for ease of reference. If you feel so inclined, crop the photos into fun shapes or cut out with the fancy-edged shears. Use scrapbook supplies including cutouts and stickers to make each page more fun. Make a customized cover on your computer or hand-create one and place it on the first page or inside cover of your album.
- If you have duplicate shots, start an album for your children or parents as a gift.
- If you're the ultimate procrastinator, don't become overwhelmed with pictures from past celebrations. Start with this year and move into the future.
- If you have keepsake cards, photo cards, playbills, or spiritual event programs boasting your kids' names from past years, insert these, as well. If you travel during the joyous season, add memorabilia from trips, too.
- As photographs come in from other greeters' cards, pull out your memory log and arrange them right away. Or specify a separate album to collect photo cards received from friends and family.

In general, if you can't seem to find the time to update year-round photo albums, the great advantage of the holiday memory log is that it is manageable because it only covers a few weeks of the year. And yet, it succeeds in capturing the tender warmth we all seek and cherish.

Your log can hold a prime spot on your coffee table. Won't your guests be surprised to see their mug shots featured from past years? Keep a pen and some colored paper cutouts handy for friends and relatives to jot a quick note to be inserted near their smiling faces for a personalized touch from all.

DARLING LITTLE ANGELS (AND THE WHOLE BLISSFUL BUNCH)

Kid Klutter

Give the kids' rooms one more de-cluttering sweep before new packages from Santa arrive. Sort through miscellaneous articles stored in closets and toy boxes. And eliminate unwanted items stowed under the bed. Each bag of giveaways you fill is one more tax deduction to claim, so remember to obtain receipts.

December Birthdays

December birthdays have caused many frantic moms to feel a tad of guilt coupled with one more reason to panic. How can you celebrate your offspring's birthday without shortchanging her during this demanding season? Follow Janice Kuczler's lead.

For the past seven years, Janice has eliminated the problem by celebrating her child's half-birthday instead. In June, with the warm weather as a bonus, Janice throws an outdoor party for Morgan. The extended family has come to expect the summer invitation. And as Janice's sister-in-law Amy says, "It's one less commitment during an already hectic period for all of us." Then, on her daughter's real birthday, Janice celebrates by preparing her child's favorite meal and baking an exceptional cake. "Instead of feeling slighted because of a birthday surrounded by so much chaos," Janice says, "Morgan actually feels extra special."

Or, if a summer party is too soon for you, do what Sharon Knobeloch does for her daughter's December 21st birthday. "I host her party the week before Thanksgiving," Sharon says. "Keeping it separate from the rush of the holidays makes it special for her and easier for me."

But, Sue Kolton feels it's a little late to adopt either of these systems for her fourteen-year-old son's December 15th birthday. Still, she doesn't want him to feel shortchanged, so she waits to bake, decorate, and wrap holiday gifts—she holds off the whole seasonal shebang—until after his celebration, making her one frenzied woman.

Hold on, Sue. Maybe it is too late in the game to switch to Janice's half-year idea, but try these tips to lessen your holiday stresses while giving your child the day he deserves.

- To get the baking done, incorporate a family bake-off. Once a week or so, gather ingredients for everyone's favorite cookies. After dinner (or whatever time of day works for you), pull out the supplies and give members the job of mixing up their "faves." Make hot chocolate or milk shakes to go with the fresh-baked yummies. Drop a dozen into the cookie jar and flip the rest into the freezer. That way, you'll have batches of baked goods built up in no time.

- Squeeze in the greeting cards. If you're sending out birthday party invitations, write your holiday greeting cards at the same time. Hold them a day or two after you've mailed the invitations so the envelopes arrive on different days. Use small snatches of time to write the cards as we mentioned in the October chapter. You can always call it an early night, climb into bed with your greetings box, and jot away.

- To gain some time for yourself if you have older kids, offer to take the gang to the mall or to see a movie. While the kids are doing their thing, you can scurry through the shops with their

Santa lists and birthday wishes in hand. Before you meet the kids, stash packages in the trunk of the car or the back of the van and cover with a blanket. After an evening with friends, little will your child know you had an ulterior motive.

Behind the mask of a birthday celebration, you can prepare using these ideas (and a few of your own). Then, jump full force into the decorating, once the party is over. And you won't feel the slightest twinge of guilt, because you won't be rushing through your child's special day or neglecting holiday responsibilities.

Kid Traditions

Take the younger kids to visit Santa and to ride the holiday train in the first week of December, before lines get longer and you get swamped. While you're there, allow them to pick out small gifts for Dad, Grandma, and their friends.

Strive to create new customs for your family. Your adopted idea can be as simple as doing something the same way every holiday season. One year, rather than forfeit displaying her own collector Nativity set, Kathy Criniti took the time to sew a plush, kid-friendly set for her three young children. They were delighted to have a scene of their own, helping them to leave Mom's untouched. As Kathy added more stuffed pieces each year, it became a tradition for her children to play with the set. "It's one of the fond memories the kids share," Kathy says. "In fact, this year, my college-aged daughter is taking the infant Jesus to show her friends. I never knew the simple set would mean so much to them."

Kid Fun

This is a good time of year to remember the kids' friends with a token gift or get-together. If you're a working parent and can take days off, pay back any families who have helped out with car pools, school-related responsibilities, and baby-sitting by taking their children for the afternoon. It doesn't have to be extravagant. A brief outing will thrill the kids while giving Mom a few free hours.

- Plan gatherings including snowman-building competitions, cookie-making get-togethers, and sleepovers.
- If you are feeling pressed for time, try what mother and office administrator Toni Senatore did. She took her children and their friends to a fast-food restaurant with a playland. She allowed them to eat, amuse themselves, and exchange gifts there. For Toni, this was an easy solution that got the job done and spread good cheer. And you better believe that while she was there, Toni was updating her gift list and finishing off those greeting cards.
- Because Christmas is fast approaching, use this last chance to window-shop, see a holiday movie, or visit the light displays. Take friends along and call it a celebration.

Holiday Happenings: Ringing in the New Year

Whether you spend New Year's Eve doing the same thing every year or you're ready to implement a new plan, take a moment to look beyond the holiday at hand and give ringing in the New Year some thought. Do you need to make reservations, call a few guests, or R.S.V.P. to an invitation? Decide what you'll wear and what you'll make—putting the plans behind you, for now.

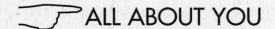 ALL ABOUT YOU

Nibbling Tidbits

After all our hard work and effort during this busy season, the one thing we frantic women think we deserve is to nibble a few tasty treats at parties. And, of course, we want to sample the nut rolls and appetizers we make. But before we know it, we've gained our usual holiday ten pounds or more.

Not this year! These words of advice from personal trainer Kim White will help keep your mouth closed and your jeans loose this season. "What causes the problem is not one piece of cake on the day of your party," Kim says. "Rather it's eating the whole cake (and cookies and snacks, too) for the rest of the week that does you in." Kim recommends you allow yourself to eat the foods you want, but only in moderation. Help yourself to a reasonable portion and know when to say that's enough. "Don't allow one small bite to erupt into a binge," Kim says. On the other hand, if you deprive yourself completely of what it is that you want, you'll be distracted by cravings all day long. So go ahead. Eat nachos at a baseball game or a small plate of sweets at a holiday party. That's what it's all about.

Kim uses herself as an example. She says it's the comfort of good food and the familiar company that make the holidays special. "I love to bake," Kim admits. But rather than bake enough for the next two months, she bakes a dozen or two cookies, shares them with her husband and children, and that's the end of it.

Here are a few concise tips that Kim instills in her sessions with clients and in her own life, as well.

- *Break bad habits.* You've heard it before, but it's true—it takes thirty days or more to change a habit. If you usually eat four cookies after lunch, then limit yourself to one or two. And though it might be difficult at first, tell yourself that in just a few weeks, your new habit will be to eat cookies in smaller portions. To help yourself, try changing the way you go about your day. If you regularly eat a doughnut with coffee at your desk in the morning at work, try to have a cup of coffee and a piece of toast at home instead. Similarly, if you head straight for the dessert table at a party, tell yourself to have a small plate of hot food first. Then treat yourself to one choice dessert.
- *Set goals.* If you know you'll be eating out on Friday evening, say at a party or a restaurant, let it be your goal to watch your intake of sweets all week, so you can splurge on a super-gooey wonder on Friday.

- *Forgive yourself.* If you do overindulge one day, don't beat yourself up over it. Don't look at such a breakdown as a failure—and don't quit altogether. Keep in mind that adopting better eating habits is a lifelong thing, and that one day won't make a difference in the overall picture. If it happens, just be sure to make it end right there.

Take Five: Nothing but the Truth

We're not going to pull any punches here. Personal time during the month of December is a passing whim, so you're best off to admit this to yourself up front. If you're lucky, you'll be able to grab a cup of tea and watch *It's a Wonderful Life* or a televised holiday special. And most likely if you do snatch a little leisure time, you'll be pulling double duty, working as you watch, wrapping as you chat, checking off as you go.

Interoffice Memo: Festive Theme Day

Organize a theme day when coworkers wear blue for Hanukkah. Have another day on which everyone wears red or green to celebrate Christmas.

Interoffice Memo: Business Holiday Greetings

Send cards to business acquaintances, clients, and coworkers. This personal touch goes a long way. Be sure to pick up a card with a greeting that reads "Happy Holidays" or "Season's Greetings" so you can send the same one to all on your list, regardless of religious affiliation.

To eliminate the prolonged task of finding and addressing the envelopes, prepare a separate computer-generated business mailing list.

Interoffice Memo: Out with the Old

At your workplace, take the time to clear out old files that have accumulated throughout the year. With many coworkers taking vacation days, you'll have fewer interruptions. So redesign your filing system or worktable if the one you're using is failing you. Ask yourself what you need to do to improve and adapt accordingly.

Take Five: Just for You

Do something spiritual, introspective, or motivational for yourself. Visit a church or temple, or pick up an inspirational book to massage the psyche and soothe the soul.

The Finale: After the Fact

The end is near, but it isn't over until the fat lady (or jolly man) sings. Before you bid farewell to the old and say hello to the new, you have a few more points to cover.

JOTS & THOUGHTS QUIZ
Thanks, but What Is It?

How many times have you opened a gift and said, "Thank you. It's lovely." In your mind, however, your thoughts chime in, "But what *is* it?" Although some unique gifts make interesting conversation pieces, most of them, yes, they need to go.

Evaluate the gifts you and your children have received over the holidays using the following questions as a guide.

1. Is it difficult for you to decide just what your newly received gift is used for or means?
2. Do you already have one or two of these items?
3. Do you have a similar product that you like better?
4. Is the present something you'll never wear or use?
5. Are you short on space and know you don't have the room to store the new gadget?

6. Do you just plain dislike the gift for reasons of color, taste, or style?
7. Can you admit you're in a gift-retaining rut?

If you answered yes to even one of the above questions, then it's time to get rid of the unwelcome package in one of the following ways.

- *Pass the gift along*. Someone else can use it. But *don't* try to pass it off as a present from you. Simply tell the person something like, "Here's an extra mug for you. I received it as a gift, but knowing how much you love coffee, I'm sure you'll get more use out of it than I will."
- *Return it to the store*. Even if you don't have receipts or gift vouchers, return your least favorites to the store for merchandise credit or, better yet, cash. Do so quickly, though, so as not to receive the super-discounted prices.
- *Give the gift to charity*. Offer the items to a nonprofit organization that might be able to use them in auctions, sales, or giveaway fund-raisers they regularly sponsor. Or you might decide to donate it to the local thrift shop or Goodwill store.

Whatever you do, don't allow your new goods to take up space in your closet or drawer. To rephrase the adage—either use them or lose them.

The Show's Not Over . . . Yet

The hustle and bustle has settled down, but it's not completely gone. Not by a long shot. You must return all items you purchased or received for which you do not have a gift voucher or receipt. These returns must be top priority. Go first thing in the morning, during the dinner hour, or just before store closing time to reduce the wait. Keep in mind that if you exchange an article for one of equal value, you're more likely to walk away with what it's actually worth.

While you're returning merchandise, check out the sales for supplies you can use all year long.

- Gold and silver wrapping paper can be used for wedding, anniversary, bar mitzvah, bat mitzvah, communion, and graduation gifts.
- Red and green paper products will take care of your Valentine's Day and St. Patrick's Day necessities, respectively.
- Blue and red work nicely for the patriotic holidays.
- Solids in green, red, blue, gold, or white can be used for school events or graduations, especially if they coordinate with alma mater colors.
- Bags of bows and spools of ribbon can ornament packages of any variety all year long.
- Winter scene products can be utilized for many weeks to come (all the way through February, really) for special occasions or everyday use.
- Miscellaneous stocking stuffers (without a holiday motif) can be stashed away for party favor bags, classroom festivities, get-well tokens, and Easter basket stuffers.
- Nonpatterned table runners, pillows, candles, and other accessories can dot your decor with colorful accents any time of year.

Recycle, Recycle

Don't throw away the decorated tins (the five-gallon type filled with assorted flavors of popcorn) you received this season. Utilize them with the following suggestions.

- Store ornaments, layered and wrapped, to prevent breakage.
- Stock extra greeting card supplies for easy access next October. (A cautionary note: Don't stow greeting cards in the attic where extreme temperatures cause cards to warp and envelope adhesive to dry.)
- Take an empty can room to room while cleaning to toss in misplaced items.
- Stash annoying tiny toy pieces, such as Legos, blocks, or beads— you know, the ones that really hurt to step on.

- Keep a can full of spare hats, gloves, and scarves for when kids are in search of layers for sledding or outdoor play. Before replacing into the bin, make sure accessories are dry to avoid can rust.
- Use as small garbage cans in the laundry room or garage.

De-Decorate

As the end of the year nears, and you're out and about plucking up those fabulous buys, consider investing in sturdy storage containers to pack away your numerous decorations. Most stores mark down the price of storage containers after Christmas. You'll probably need containers for ornaments, wrapping paper, wall hangings, and other decorations. Buy additional ones for the outside trimmings and anything you might have forgotten. Before you shop, write down in your Frantic Journal the size of containers and how many you will need all together. Keep in mind that you'll have to transport the boxes when they're full, so you might opt for several smaller containers instead of just a few large ones.

Once you've gathered your storage cases, pack away decorations according to the room in which you display them, and mark the outside. This will expedite the decorating process next year.

As you're de-decorating, pay attention to what you're packing. Force yourself to toss out gift boxes, unused ends of wrapping paper, and wrinkled tissue. Sometimes we save more than we need to, adding to our household clutter.

What can you do with the countless photograph cards you received from family and friends? You know you'll feel guilty if you throw them away. But you don't want to tuck them into a drawer to be forgotten either. Instead try one of these options.

- Slip the prints into your holiday memory log. Don't forget to write names and dates near each. Or, as we mentioned previously, if you created a separate memory log just for this purpose, break it out and fill it up.
- If all else fails and you can bear it, toss them in hopes of receiving more next year.

Year-End Tax Planning

It wouldn't be a true year-end without a word from our resident tax adviser, Tim Schneider. "If you expect your total income to be significantly higher this year," Tim says, "you want to do what's called 'accelerating deductions.'" In other words, it's smart tax planning to take as many legitimate deductions on your upcoming itemized tax return as you can to offset the increase in income—but you need to fit them in before year-end. And how to do that is easy. You can pay your fourth-quarter state income and local wage taxes, ordinarily due in January, on or before the 31st of December. (Note: You won't receive a deduction for paying federal income taxes early.) At the same time, you can accelerate donations to charities and your favorite college or university—sending them in before the end of the year, as well. This includes both monetary gifts and donations of unwanted items. In fact, if you'll be selling a car in the near future, consider gifting it to a nonprofit organization instead for a whopper of a deduction. So start packing up all those clothes and toys you plan on giving away in January. Doing so now will benefit you come next April 15th.

ONE-STEP-AT-A-TIME CHECKLIST

Date completed Or N/A	Task
_____	Decorate inside and out (second chance).
_____	Plan your family's holiday wardrobe and make hair appointments.
_____	Finish writing greeting cards and send.
_____	Prepare and ship long-distance packages in the first week of the month.
_____	Update your snail-mail address list as you receive greetings.
_____	Set up a wrapping station (second chance).
_____	Wrap gifts.

_____ Recycle containers to be used as the basis for gift baskets you put together yourself.

_____ Bake ahead and freeze.

_____ Plan gatherings using our entertaining shortcuts.

_____ Do heavy-duty cleaning (second chance).

_____ Flip bed mattresses.

_____ Entice family to pitch in during an all-day moviethon.

_____ Create a holiday memory log.

_____ De-clutter the kids' rooms before Santa's sack is emptied
again.

_____ Try our December birthday party variations.

_____ Visit Santa and ride the holiday train early in the month.

_____ Plan casual get-togethers with kids' friends.

_____ Make reservations for New Year's Eve.

_____ Curb your overeating tendencies using our expert's tips.

_____ Admit that personal time will be next to nil this month.

_____ Organize a festive theme day at work.

_____ Send greetings to coworkers and clients.

_____ Clear out the year's old files at work.

_____ Visit a house of worship or read an inspirational book.

_____ Unload unwanted gifts.

_____ Shop the post-holiday sales.

_____ Recycle popcorn tins.

_____ De-decorate.

_____ Donate items and send in monetary gifts before year-
end for smart tax planning.

Part Three

A Wee Bit More

P.S.

Hurrah! You're making it through little by little. Your monthly One-Step-at-a-Time Checklists have more checks than blanks. Whew! Although the frantic race might still be moving a little faster than you'd like, you're making progress and that's all that counts.

But, we're sure there were times along the way when you realized you could've used additional advice or a nudge in the right direction. You just needed a teeny bit more.

So to give you a helping hand, here we are again, in part three appropriately called "A Wee Bit More." In this section, we've created lists for you to photocopy, resources to check out, and recipes to concoct—all with the idea of making your life a tad easier. Let's get moving.

RETRO PARTY DRINKS FOR FUN

The next time you throw a shindig, serve up a couple of these fun drinks from the past. Who knows? You might end up starting a new trend.

✦ Melon Ball ✦

INGREDIENTS

ice cubes
2 ounces Midori melon liqueur
1 ounce vodka
pineapple juice (or orange juice)

Fill a tall glass with ice. Pour in melon liqueur and vodka. Fill with juice.

✦ Moscow Mule ✦

INGREDIENTS

1 ¼ ounces vodka
ginger beer
ice cubes
lime juice

Pour vodka in a copper mug. Fill with ginger beer, add ice, and top off with a squeeze of lime.

✦ Sea Breeze ✦

INGREDIENTS

ice cubes
1 ½ ounces vodka
4 ounces cranberry juice
1 ounce grapefruit juice
lime wedges

Fill glass with ice. Pour in vodka, add juices, and garnish with a wedge of lime.

ETHNIC PIES

➤ *Pierogies* ◆

Whip up a batch of pierogies for your crew, compliments of our dear friend Vel Bongartz.

INGREDIENTS

3 to 5 pounds mashed potatoes
16 ounces cheddar cheese
salt and pepper to taste
3 eggs
½ cup water
1 teaspoon salt
2 cups flour

Step one: Make mashed potatoes. Add cheese while the spuds are hot (before adding milk). Season with salt and pepper to taste.
(Hint: This is a great way to utilize leftover mashed potatoes.)

Step two: Beat eggs, water, and salt. Gradually, add flour. Mix with a fork or dough blender to make a dough-like consistency. The mixture should be blended enough to roll out, but be careful not to overwork it. If the mixture is sticky, add a little more flour. Roll the dough onto a floured surface. Use a 3- to 4-inch-round cookie cutter or the top of a glass to cut out circles.

Step three: Take a rounded teaspoonful of the potato mixture and place into the middle of the pie (circle of dough). Fold over into a crescent shape. Moisten the ends with a little water, and then pinch the edges together with a fork.

Step four: Carefully drop the pierogies into a pot of boiling water. When they float to the top (after only a few minutes), remove them with a slotted spoon. Smother pierogies with melted butter and sautéed sliced onions.

STOCKING THE PANTRY SHELVES

Our frantic woman's pantry list is filled with universal items from baking supplies your grandmother would have had on hand to nonfood products you'll need for everyday meal preparation. Photocopy this list to refer to when writing your grocery list.

Baker's Plus

Baking powder
Baking soda
Biscuit, muffin mixes
Brownie mixes
Cake mixes and canned icing
Chocolate (unsweetened squares, semisweet chips, cocoa powder)
Cooking spray
Cornmeal
Cornstarch
Extracts (almond, lemon, orange, vanilla)
Flour (bleached, cornmeal, wheat)
Gelatin (unflavored, powdered)
Honey
Milk (evaporated, powdered)
Nuts (walnuts, pecans, peanuts)
Sugar (confectioner's, granulated, light and dark brown)
Vegetable shortening
Yeast

Condiments on the Side

Jams and/or jellies
Ketchup
Mayonnaise
Mustard (honey, spiced, yellow)
Oils (canola, olive, peanut)
Olives

Pickles
Relish
Salad dressing
Vinegar (wine, white; balsamic is useful for both cooking and dressings)

The Cold Stuff

Biscuits (canned)
Bread dough (frozen)
Butter, margarine
Cheese
Cookies (slice-and-bake)
Eggs (or egg substitute)
Fish
Fruits (fresh, frozen)
Half-and-half
Juice (fresh, concentrated)
Meat (freeze it)
Milk
Poultry (chicken, Cornish hen, turkey)
Veggies (fresh, frozen)

Nonfood

Aluminum foil
Coffee filters
Drinking straws
Napkins
Paper plates
Paper towels
Plastic plates
Plastic wrap
Waxed paper
Zippered freezer and storage bags

Spices

Allspice
Arrowroot starch
Basil
Bay leaves
Chili powder
Cinnamon (ground, sticks)
Cloves (ground, whole)
Cream of tartar
Cumin
Curry powder
Dill weed
Fennel seeds
Five-spice powder
Garlic powder (minced garlic, garlic salt)
Ginger
Marjoram
Mint
Mustard (ground)
Nutmeg
Onion powder
Oregano
Paprika
Pepper (black, cayenne, red flakes)
Peppercorns
Poppy seeds
Rosemary
Sage
Salt
Sesame seeds
Tarragon
Thyme
Turmeric

Staples

Artichoke hearts

Beans, canned (black, red kidney, white)

Beans, dried (black, lentils, lima, pinto, split pea)

Bread, bread crumbs

Broth (beef, chicken, vegetable)

Cereal (cream of wheat, dry, grits, oatmeal)

Cocoa

Coffee (decaffeinated, flavored, regular)

Crackers

Dried fruits (apricots, pineapples, raisins)

Garlic (fresh and jarred)

Lemons

Limes

Maple syrup

Onions (French fried, fresh)

Pasta (angel hair, egg noodles, fettuccine, lasagna, linguini, pastina, penne, spaghetti)

Peanut butter

Potatoes (white, sweet)

Rice (long-grain, wild)

Risotto

Soup (canned, bouillon cubes)

Tea (Chi, decaffeinated, herbal, regular)

Tomatoes (chopped, crushed, puree, sauce, whole)

Tuna

Veggies (canned carrots, corn, green beans, peas, etc.)

PACK YOUR BAGS AND MORE

You're cruising down the highway, grinning from ear to ear, your destination is within reach—finally. You can feel it, taste it. But wait; did you remember your flight tickets? Reservation confirmation? Wallet? In all the hoopla to get ready, have you forgotten some vital documents? This year, don't get caught empty-handed. Photocopy our "Pack Your Bags and More" list to keep close at hand while preparing and packing.

Don't Leave Home Without

Addresses for sending postcards/e-mail
Airline tickets (paper or e-ticket confirmation)
Auto insurance card
Business cards
Currency converter
Credit/debit cards
Driver's license
Emergency numbers
First aid kit
Foreign language dictionary and phrase book
Frequent flier/frequent guest membership cards
Gift certificates (clubs, restaurants, shops)
Itinerary
Keys (extra set)
Luggage locks, tags
Maps and directions
Medical history (if necessary)
Medicines, prescriptions
Money
Passports, birth certificates, photo IDs
Prepaid phone card
Temporary health insurance information
Temporary insurance card for driving outside the United States
Traveler's checks and receipt (keep separate)
Travel guide(s)
Vacation packing list
Vaccination certificates (if required)
Tickets (amusement parks, concerts, games)
Umbrella

Look Good, Feel Good
    Aloe vera (for sunburn relief)
    Antacids
    Antibiotic cream
    Anti-diarrhea medication
    Bandages (adhesive and Ace)
    Benadryl
    Blow dryer, curling iron (with adapter for overseas, if necessary)
    Body lotion
    Brush, comb, hair pick, hair bands, scrunchies
    Cold and sinus tablets
    Contact lenses, solution
    Cotton balls, swabs
    Deodorant
    Eyeglasses, sunglasses (spare pair of both)
    Feminine protection products
    Insect repellent
    Lip balm (with SPF protection)
    Makeup, makeup remover
    Moisturizer
    Motion sickness medicine
    Pain reliever (non-aspirin)
    Prescription medicines
    Seasickness bands
    Shampoo, conditioner, styling products
    Shaving kit (razor, cream)
    Sunscreen (SPF 15+)
    Swimmer's ear drops
    Toothbrush, toothpaste, floss, mouthwash
    Tweezers

Let's Have Some Fun
    Beach bag, blanket, chairs, towels, umbrella
    Cooler

Playing cards
Reading material
Scented candle
Snacks and drinks
Sports equipment (bike helmets, boogie and skim boards, golf clubs,
     snorkel gear, swim goggles, tennis racquets)
Water bottle
Waterproof ball
Zippered plastic bags (for collecting driftwood, fossils, rocks, shells)

Darling Little Angels' Necessities

Art supplies (colored pencils, coloring book, paper)
Disposable cameras (land, waterproof)
Flotation devices (arm floaties, beach ball, rafts, rings)
Handheld electronic games (spare batteries)
Miniature cars, dolls
Nets (crab, fish, shell catching)
Sand and water toys

Technology to Go

CD player, CDs (spare batteries)
Cell phone (recharger)
Digital camera, batteries, manual
Laptop, pocket PC
Planner (business calls)

P.S. Don't Forget

Bathing suit, cover-up, long-sleeve T-shirt, sarong
Beach or water shoes
Belt
Costume jewelry (bracelets, earrings, necklace, watch)
Robe
Slip, body slimmer
Straw hat, visor
Swim trunks, jockstrap

Before You Depart—With the Whole Bunch

Adjust thermostat.

Arrange pet care.

Check departure times.

Check luggage closures, locks, and tags.

Check stove and oven.

Clean out refrigerator.

Close draperies.

Confirm reservations.

Empty trash.

Inform school, teachers.

Lock house, windows, and screens.

Notify home security company and a trustworthy neighbor.

Obtain traveler's checks, small bills (for tipping).

Run garbage disposal and dishwasher.

Set light timers.

Set security system.

Shut off main water valve.

Stop newspaper, mail (USPS: 1-800-275-8777), and deliveries.

Turn off hot water tank, sprinkler system.

Unplug appliances, computers, and televisions.

Water plants.

Before You Depart—Without the Angels

Buy quick-meal ingredients.

Give itinerary to sitter and neighbor.

Hire sitter or arrange for kids to stay elsewhere.

Leave money for activities, emergencies, and lunches.

Make car pool arrangements.

Notarize emergency health care forms (giving permission to sitter for emergency medical treatment for kids).

Notify school, teachers, coaches with sitter's name and contact information.

Organize kids' clothing and sports equipment.

Prepare contact numbers for emergencies (include appliance, house repair, phone, electric, and cable).

KEEPING YOUR SANITY FOR GREAT VACATIONS

In your mind, you replay this living-color film of the fabulous family vacation you're about to embark on. After a few hours on the road, however, you realize you've landed smack-dab in the middle of *National Lampoon's Vacation* and you're asking, "Who switched the film clips?" To alleviate the problems, we've gathered a list of books and sites—to help stop the insanity from claiming your family vacation.

The Written Word Traveling Resources

52 Fun Things to Do on the Plane (52 Series) by Lynn Gordon (Chronicle Books, 1996).

The Amazing Backseat Booka-Ma-Thing: Thousands of Miles Worth of Hands-On Games and Activities by Kevin Plottner and the Editors of Klutz Press (Klutz, Inc., 1998).

Are We There Yet? Travel Games for Kids by Richard Salter (Random House, 1991).

The Everything Kids' Travel Activity Book: Games to Play, Songs to Sing, Fun Stuff to Do—Guaranteed to Keep You Busy the Whole Ride! by Erik A. Hanson and Jeanne K. Hanson (Adams Media Corporation, 2002).

FamilyFun's Games on the Go by Lisa Stiepock and the Experts at *FamilyFun Magazine* (Hyperion, 1998). (P.S. Check out "Radio Bingo" on page 31, contributed by Mary Jo.)

The License Plate Game Book: 40 Great Travel Games for Fun on the Go! by Michael S. Teitelbaum and James Buckley Jr. (Troll Association, 2000).

Miles of Smiles: 101 Great Car Games & Activities by Carole Terwilliger
Meyers (Carousel Press, 1992).
Miles of Smiles: Backseat Games by Mary Lynn Blasutta (Pleasant Com-
pany Publications, 1999).
Rubber Neckers: Everyone's Favorite Travel Games by Matthew Lore
and Mark Lore (Chronicle Books, 1999).

Travel Resources from the Cyber World

www.amtrak.com/plan/travelingkids.html
www.familyeducation.com (search traveling with kids)
www.family-travels.net
www.flyingwithkids.com
www.freetraveltips.com
www.hotelfun4kids.com
www.makoa.org/travel.htm (for physically challenged travelers)
www.momsminivan.com
www.savvytraveler.com (search traveling with kids)
www.thefamilytravelfiles.com
www.travelingwithkids.com
www.travelwithyourkids.com

OFF TO CAMP WE GO: PACKING LIST

Finally, the time has come to send your darling little angel off to
camp. Whether this is his first time or he's a veteran, the bundle of
stuff you must pack can be mind-boggling. This "have-to-take" list of
essentials will ease your concerns when saying good-bye. (P.S. Remember, some camps might require specific items to make your camper's
experience one he or she will always remember.)

General

Alarm clock
Backpack
Bathing suit, beach towel, sunscreen
Bedding (blanket, fitted sheet, pillow, sleeping bag or mattress cover)
Brush, comb
Camera, film (disposable, underwater disposable)
Drinks, water (if allowed)
Feminine protection products
Flashlight, extra batteries
Hat
Headbands, ponytail holders
Insect repellent (non-aerosol)
Lanyard (for dormitory key)
Laundry bag
Medical care and release form
Money (for vending machines, souvenirs)
Notepaper, pen, stamped envelopes (preaddressed)
Prepaid phone card
Shampoo, conditioner
Shower shoes
Snacks (if permitted)
Sunglasses
Sweatshirt, jacket (for chilly nights), long-sleeve T-shirt
Toothbrush, toothpaste, dental floss
Washcloth, bath towel, hand towel, soap
Water bottle

P.S.

Susan Orr of Girl Scouts of Southwestern Pennsylvania recommends the following supplies (in addition to the general supplies listed) when sending your child to a Scout camp.

Bandanna
Dunk bag (nylon net bag to hold wet dishes)

Mess kit (or equivalent—plate, silverware, and cup)
Raincoat or poncho
Sit-upon or stadium seat
Sleeping bag (make sure it is recommended weight)
Socks (over-the-ankle ones)
Waterproof boots
Water-repellent bed cover (to protect bedding from moisture)

Psst! Don't Forget

For outdoors and/or sports camps, take:

An extra pair of sport shoes
Two pairs of socks per day
Ace bandage
An extra hand towel or two (for wiping sweaty faces)

SUMMER SURVIVAL KIT

To keep your kids stocked with a supply of fun all summer long, store these items in an accessible bin within arm's reach. A rubberized waterproof container, approximately twenty-gallon, prevents moisture and creatures from invading your gang's good time.

Balloons (regular, water)
Balls (play, rubber, super, tennis, Wiffle)
Beach ball
Bubbles, fancy wands
Bucket, handheld hoe, rake, shovel
Bug catcher, bug keeper container
Cards (playing, Old Maid, Crazy Eights)
Chalk (colored and white)
Clay, cookie cutters, miniature rolling pin
Dominoes
Flower leis, grass skirts
Insects (plastic)

Jacks and ball
Jump rope (Chinese and regular)
Kaleidoscope
Marbles
Paddle ball (with ball attached)
Pinwheel
Sailboats (plastic)
Sponges
Squirt guns
Swimmies, raft
Telescope
Tempera paint (for face painting)
Visors (plastic)
Walking sticks (small)
Word search book

BACK-TO-CAMPUS WISH LIST

The college decision has been confirmed, the dormitory assignment received, and the roommate contacted. So what else is there to do? You'll be sorry you asked—as there are about a hundred other things that must be taken care of. Our Back-to-Campus Wish List will provide your college-bound student with just about everything he or she will need to survive campus life.

Don't Leave Home Without

Checkbook
Credit cards
Dormitory assignment
Insurance policy card (auto, dental, medical) or policy name,
    number, contact, and phone number
Money
Social Security card

Day-to-Day Stuff

Address book
Airtight food storage containers
Alarm clock
Answering machine, telephone (cordless is preferred)
Batteries
Bicycle (some students actually use one)
Can and bottle openers
Desk lamp
Dishware (glasses, mugs, plates, silverware)
Drawer and shelf liner
Dry erase or memo board (for door)
Extension cords (at least one with surge protector)
Fan
Flashlight
Hangers
Over-the-door rack (for towels)
Posters, decorations
Prepaid phone cards
Push pins (college usually provides bulletin board)
Quarters (for laundry)
Sewing kit
Snacks, breakfast items, beverages
Stereo sound system
Tape, Fun Tac
Trash can
TV
Umbrella
Under-the-bed containers (check height of bed with college)
Watch
Water bottle

Getting the ZZZs

Bedspread or comforter

Blankets (for bed and to use when watching TV)
Mattress cover
Pillow and cases
Sheets (twin or extra long, flannel for colder weather)

Showering Stuff

Bathrobe
Shower caddy (with holes in the bottom allowing water to escape)
Shower shoes
Towels, washcloths

"Look Good and Feel Good" Must-Haves

Acne control product
Baby powder
Bandages (adhesive, Ace)
Blow dryer, curling iron
Body lotion
Brush, comb, hair bands, hair pick, scrunchies
Cologne, perfume
Contact lenses, solution, eyeglasses, sunglasses
Cotton balls and swabs
Deodorant
Feminine protection products
Fingernail clippers, emery board, hand cream
First aid kit
Lip balm
Makeup
Nail polish, remover
Pain reliever (non-aspirin)
Prescription and over-the-counter medicines (antiseptic cream, cold
        and sinus tablets, cough syrup, throat lozenges)
Shampoo, conditioner, styling spray or gel
Shaving basics
Toothbrush, toothpaste, dental floss, mouthwash
Vitamins and supplements

Making the Grade
Backpack
Binder, paper
Calculator
Calendar, daily planner
Computer CDs, diskettes
Correction fluid, eraser
Dictionary, thesaurus, writing reference guide
Envelopes, stamps, stationery
Folders
Glue
Notebooks
Paper clips
Pencils, pens, highlighters, markers
Printer paper
Rubber bands
Ruler
Scissors
Stapler, staples
Tape

White Glove and More
Broom
Bucket, rags
Detergent (laundry and dish)
Dishcloths, dishpan
Disinfectant
Dryer sheets/fabric softener
Furniture polish
Hamper/laundry bag
Iron, mini-ironing board
Laundry basket
Spot remover

But, Mom, I Need It!
Area carpet, throw rugs
Camera, film
CD player, CDs (extra batteries)
Coffeemaker, filters
Computer or word processor
Hot plate (check the school's regulations)
Micro-fridge or refrigerator
Toaster, toaster oven (check the school's regulations)
Vacuum cleaner
VCR, DVD, movies
(Hints: Make sure bedding, throw rugs, and towels are in the same color family to minimize the number of laundry loads necessary. Also, by keeping the colors in the white family, other light-colored clothing can be tossed in with the towels. Stay with a medium-weight towel for a faster drying time.)

Nourishment Plus: Non-perishables
(Note: Stock up on these items when they go on sale.)
Breakfast bars and drinks
Cereal
Cheddar cheese (canned or jarred)
Chips, nachos, pretzels, etc.
Coffee, cappuccino mixes, hot chocolate, tea bags
Cookies
Dried soup, noodle packages (Oodles of Noodles)
Drink mixes (iced tea, lemonade)
Fruit (canned and dried)
Granola bars
Instant oatmeal
Instant mashed potatoes
Pasta lunches (microwavable)
Peanut butter, jarred
Peanut butter and cheese crackers (packaged)

Popcorn, microwavable
Powdered creamer, sugar, sugar substitute
Ravioli (canned)
Salad dressing (small bottles)
Saltines
Single-serve applesauce, fruit cups, gelatin, pudding
Soup (canned and microwavable)
Soup-in-a-cup packages
Toaster pop-ups (Pop Tarts)
Trail mix

Nourishment Plus: Perishables
(Note: Only a week's worth of these should be purchased at one time.)
Bagels
Carrots, baby
Cheese (American, cheddar)
Cream cheese
Jelly, jam
Lunchables
Lunchmeat
Nacho cheese
Pepperoni
Salad (ready-to-eat)

Paper Products
Garbage bags
Napkins
Paper plates
Paper towels
Tissues
Zippered plastic bags

EVERYTHING YOU'LL EVER NEED ON THE GO

Yes, there are days when you seem to spend more time behind the wheel of your taxi than you do in your house. And for those times, you need to stock your vehicle with all the comforts of home.

Activity items (CDs, children's books, colored pencils, flash cards, small toys like Matchbox cars, Barbies)

Cards (playing, Crazy Eights, Old Maid)

Coins, dollar bills (for toll roads, vending machines)

Comb, hairbrush, ponytail holders, scrunchies, spray gel

Drinks (juice boxes, water)

Dust cloth (for wiping dashboard while waiting)

Entertainment book (other coupons, discount cards)

First aid kit (Stash adhesive tape, alcohol wipes, antibiotic cream, antiseptic wipes, bandages, disposable instant cold pack, elastic bandage, emergency numbers—dentist, doctors, health insurance, hospital—first aid manual, gauze, non-aspirin tablets, plastic gloves, scissors, soap, and tweezers in a plastic tackle box.)

Flashlight, extra batteries

Hand towel

Hand wipes, waterless sanitizer

Insect repellent

Keys (extra set for car and house)

Lawn chair (for watching kids' games)

Litter bag

Makeup bag (for days when you're running late)

Map (city and state)

Paper towels

Small envelopes (for receipts, bill payments)

Snacks (the gang's favorites)

Stadium blanket and seat

Stamps

Sunscreen

Sweatshirts, jackets (for unexpected chilly nights)
Tissues
Umbrellas

Cold Weather and Emergencies

Items to stow in your car to handle those unexpected emergencies and Cold Man Winter.

Auto insurance information
Blanket
Bottled water, juice boxes
Brush, scraper
Car owner's manual
Car registration
Cardboard or sand (traction for icy weather)
Coffee can with candle and matches
De-icer (for key lock)
Dry gas
Duct tape
Emergency numbers (auto club, family, friends)
Extra clothing
Flares, reflective triangles, and vest
Flashlight, extra batteries
Food (crackers, dried fruit)
Fuses
Gasoline can (empty, please)
Hand wipes
Jumper cables
Motor oil
Paper, pen
Portable radio, extra batteries
Prepaid phone card
Quarters
Scissors (keep in glove compartment to cut seatbelt)
Small tools (flathead and Phillips screwdrivers, hammer, lug wrench)

Spare tire
Tire jack
Tire pressure gauge
Tire sealant (for small leaks)
Transmission fluid
Washer fluid

BUNCO

Bunco is an old-world dice game dating back to the late 1800s. Today, it is played throughout the country with many variations to the original version. World Bunco Association was chartered in 1996 (1-800-786-9456; www.worldbunco.com) and offers an online newsletter, background information, and rules. We've included one version of the game.

To play you'll need: 2 sets of dice (3 dice at each of 2 tables), 1 bell, 1 paper hole puncher, 8 index cards, 2 tablets, 2 tables (must seat 4 each), 8 frantic women, and prizes. The prizes should include items priced at: $1, $3, $5, $7, and $9.

To achieve Bunco: All three dice thrown must show the same designated number for the round. A Bunco throw is worth 21 points.

To win games: The first team at the high table to reach 21 wins the round. The team with the highest score at the low table wins.

To win prizes: The player with the most Buncos wins the $9 prize. The player with the highest score wins the $7 item. The player with the second-highest score wins the $5 gift. The lowest-score player wins the $3 booby prize. And the last Bunco of the night wins the $1 consolation item. If there is a tie at the end of the night, players roll off. Each rolls one die and the highest number wins the tiebreaker.

To prepare: One table is designated the high table and the other is called the low (four players at each one). The high table controls the bell and the duration of the game. Each table must have a scorekeeper and a switcher. The scorekeeper draws a line down the middle of the tablet with *Us* on one side and *Them* on the other. The switcher starts the game and each new round. The foursome at each table is broken into two teams. Team players sit opposite each other. Each player has an index card and a scorecard with her name on it. A hole will be punched at the top when the player gets Bunco. A hole is punched on the left side of the scorecard when her team wins a game.

To play: The switcher starts the game by throwing the dice. In round one, she continues throwing the dice as long as she has at least one die with a number 1 on each toss. When she doesn't, the dice are passed to the player on the left (from the opposite team), and so on. She receives 1 point for each number 1 thrown. Play continues until one of the teams from the high table scores 21. If all three dice show a number 1, the player has Bunco (this is similar to Yahtzee) and her index card is punched at the top to show a Bunco. When the dice reach the switcher for a second turn, the number switches to 2. Again, when the switcher throws her dice, she must have at least one die with the number 2 on it. This repeats with the other players. Each time the dice return to the switcher, the number switches to the next number and the game continues. When a player at the high table reaches 21, her team wins and the switcher rings the bell to stop the game. The two winning teams get a hole punched at the left side of their cards.

The losers from the high table must move to the low table and the winners from the low table move to the high table. But, players are not allowed to keep the same partner in back-to-back games. Teams must shift seats to change partners.

A predetermined time limit is set, say two hours. Once the time is up, tally the total number of games won and Buncos achieved. Award prizes as previously described. Remember, the very last Bunco wins the dollar prize.

To set up Bunco nights: Store the dice, bell, hole puncher, tablets, pencils, and extra index cards in a box. This Bunco box will be passed to the next hostess in line. Everyone plays hostess by taking turns. Usually Bunco nights run September through May, skipping December. If meeting monthly is too much for your group, consider gathering bimonthly. This way, two women can share the hostess duties, time, and expenses. Refreshments vary from group to group. Some serve a buffet meal; others serve appetizers, wine, and cheese.

The day of the week and time of the gathering should be agreed upon by all members. If someone can't make it to a particular Bunco night, she is responsible for finding a substitute. Or she could ask the hostess if she knows of anyone who would like to fill in.

There are limitless variations to the game, but the whole point is to gather and have fun.

CREATIVE COOKING WITH LIMITED TIME

What can you make for dinner with little preparation time? The answer is found within the pages of these fabulous cookbooks—dishing up menus to please just about everyone. Whether you want to develop a monthly cooking system, whip up a ten-minute dinner, eat cheaply, or satisfy your fast-food craving, we've found a cookbook just for you. Bon appétit!

Make and Freeze Cookbooks

The Freezer Cooking Manual from 30 Day Gourmet: A Month of Meals Made Easy by Tara Wohlenhaus and Nanci Slagle (30 Day Gourmet Press, 1999).

Frozen Assets Lite and Easy: How to Cook for a Day and Eat for a Month by Deborah Taylor-Hough (Champion Press, 2001).

Once-A-Month Cooking: A Proven System for Spending Less Time in the Kitchen and Enjoying Delicious, Homemade Meals Everyday by Mimi Wilson and Mary Beth Lagerborg (St. Martin's Press, 1999).

Fast-Food Addictions Cookbooks

The Copycat Cookbook by Gloria Pitzer (Gloria Pitzer, 2001).

Even More Top Secret Recipes: More Amazing Kitchen Clones of America's Favorite Brand-Name Foods by Todd Wilbur (Plume, 2003).

In a Flash Cookbooks

Better than Take-Out (and Faster, Too): Quick and Easy Cooking for Busy Families by Pamela Marx (Perspective Publishing, 2001).

Beyond Macaroni & Cheese edited by Mary Beth Lagerborg and Karen J. Parks (Zondervan Publishing House, 1998).

Busy Woman's Cookbook: 3 & 4 Ingredient Recipes by Sharon and Gene McFall (P & P Publishing, 2000).

The Can Opener Gourmet: More Than 200 Quick & Delicious Recipes Using Ingredients from Your Pantry by Laura Karr (Hyperion, 2002).

Cooking Out of the Box: The Easy Way to Turn Prepared Convenience Foods into Delicious Family Meals by Bev Bennett (Prima Publishing, 2002).

Desperation Dinners! Home-Cooked Meals for Frantic Families in 20 Minutes Flat and *Desperation Entertaining!* both by Beverly Mills and Alicia Russ (Workman Publishing, 1997 and 2002, respectively).

A Dinner a Day by Sally Sandheim and Suzannah Sloan (Warner Books, 1996).

The Minimalist Cooks Dinner by Mark Bittman (Broadway Books, 2001).

Minutemeals: 3 Ways to Dinner edited by Evie Righter (John Wiley & Sons, 2002).

Monday to Friday Cookbook by Michele Urvater (Workman Publishing, 1991).

Quick Meals for Healthy Kids and Busy Parents: Wholesome Family Recipes in 30 Minutes or Less from Three Leading Child Nutrition Experts by Sandra K. Nissenberg, Margaret L. Bogle, and Audrey C. Wright (John Wiley & Sons, 1995).

Cheap Eats

Cookmiser by R. J. Lavigne (Scrypt Publishing, 2000).

Miserly Meals: Healthy, Tasty Recipes Under 75 Cents Per Serving by Jonni McCoy (Bethany House, 2002).

Not Just Beans: 50 Years of Frugal Family Favorites by Tawra Jean Kellam (Not Just Beans, 1999).

Enticing the Kids

Clueless in the Kitchen: A Cookbook for Teens by Evelyn Raab (Firefly Books, 1998).

Cooking with Justin: Recipes for Kids (and Parents) by the World's Youngest Chef by Justin Miller (Andrews McMeel Publishing, 1997).

Take Five: Just for Fun

Bobby Flay Cooks American: Great Regional Recipes with Sizzling New Flavors by Bobby Flay (Theia, 2001).

The Farallon Cookbook: The Very Best of San Francisco Cuisine by Mark Franz and Lisa Weiss (Chronicle Books, 2001).

Gale Gand's Just a Bite: 125 Luscious, Little Desserts by Gale Gand and Julia Moskin (Clarkson N. Potter, 2001).

Passionate Vegetarian by Crescent Dragonwagon (Workman Publishing, 2002).

TBS Superstation Dinner and a Movie Cookbook by Kimberlee Carlson and Heather Johnson, with recipes by Claud Mann (Andrews McMeel Publishing, 2000).

Three Rivers Cookbook III (Child Health Association of Sewickley, 1990).

ONE EASY TEMPLATE, MANY COSTUMES

With one easy template, you can whip up a number of creative costumes for everyone. Just let your imagination run wild. If you need a few suggestions, consider an eight ball, baseball, basketball, cloud, orange, apple, lemon, or a Christmas tree ornament.

To determine how much fabric to buy, measure from the child's shoulder to the top of her knee (for length) and the widest part of her body (for width). Then, triple the measurement for the width. Next, purchase the amount of felt or material you'll need per costume. If you can't figure out the yardage, take the measurements with you. If entering a fabric store for you is like garlic for Dracula, head straight to the nearest sales associate for assistance. And during the fall, the clerks are accustomed to once-a-year shoppers.

Eight Ball Basic Costume

Supplies: felt, elastic, drawstring cording, glue (fabric or hot glue gun), safety pin, thread, needle, sewing machine. (P.S. If you do not have a sewing machine, you can hand-stitch the costume.)

1. Cut felt according to your length and width measurements.
2. Stitch the two short ends together making a cylinder, leaving a 5-inch opening at the top for ease of taking it off.
3. On a piece of white felt, trace a circle around the bottom of a lampshade, lid of a pot, or a large mixing bowl, and cut out. From black felt, cut out a number eight. Glue the number to the middle of the white felt circle. Glue the white felt circle to the front middle of the cylinder. (If you're making a variation of this costume, adjust this step to fit your needs.)
4. Fold the top of the cylinder down 1 inch and stitch to make a casing. Do the same on the bottom, leaving a 3-inch opening in the seam for the drawstring.
5. Thread a 20-inch drawstring cord (longer if the child is bigger) through the top of the casing. (Attach a safety pin into one end of the cord to make it easier to push the cord through the casing.)
6. Measure the width across the bottom of the child's thighs (or wherever the bottom of the costume will be). Add 5 inches to the measurement and cut a piece of elastic this length. Thread the elastic through the casing at the bottom of the cylinder. (Again, use the safety pin.) Stitch the two ends of the elastic together and stitch the opening closed. (An elastic casing at the bottom will help keep the stuffing from slipping out and will afford the child easier movement.)
7. Slip the costume over the child's head. Pull the drawstring and tie closed. Make a mark for armholes where the child's arms are on the outside of the costume. Slip the costume off, then cut two openings (where marked) for arms to slide through comfortably.
8. Have your child wear a long-sleeved shirt and pants or tights to match the felt color.
9. Once the costume is on, stuff it with fiberfill, tissue paper, or crumpled newspaper.

Variation: You can have a drawstring at the top and bottom of the costume, if preferred.

Condiment Basic Costume

Supplies: felt, ribbon, coordinating felt, thread, needle, glue (fabric or hot glue gun), sewing machine.

With this template, you can whip up a jar of mayo, relish, mustard, steak sauce, or jelly. The measurements for this are slightly different from the eight ball costume. Before you hit the fabric store, you'll need to measure from under the child's armpit to the top of his knee to get the length. Next, measure the largest part of the child's body (hip area or tummy) and add 20 inches for the width.

1. Cut felt according to the measurements obtained.
2. Stitch the two ends together, leaving 5 inches unstitched as a slit for an opening at the top of the cylinder. (The opening makes it easier for kids to get the costume on and off.)
3. Add one 8-inch piece of ribbon to each side of the opening (5-inch unstitched ends). This will make a tie to close the opening.
4. Have the child slip cylinder on. Measure from the top edge of the front over the shoulders to the top edge of the back. Add 3 inches and cut out two straps this length by 3 inches wide. Stitch each strap to top and back of the cylinder.
5. Cut out a piece of white felt for a label.
6. Cut out specific letters needed to spell the condiment. Glue letters to the label. Add a design or trim (paint or make from felt) to label, if desired.
7. Glue label to front of cylinder.
8. Take an old baseball hat the same color as the costume (or spray paint one to match) and cut off the bill to make the bottle cap.

QUICK-AND-EASY FAMILY NEWSLETTER

Follow these easy steps to write a snappy, memorable newsletter your family and friends will love to read. Who knows? Other folks might follow your example next year, turning the holiday newsletter into a tradition.

- *First, outline what you want to say.* Feature each family member in order from oldest to youngest or vice versa. Be sure to include good news and accomplishments, but keep it to one high point per member so it doesn't sound like bragging. If your child has won several awards, focus on one that was especially meaningful. If a family member has health problems, a brief update is acceptable and encouraged. If someone close to you has recently passed away, a simple way of informing others would be to add a quote or thought from him. Underneath his favorite aspect of the holiday season, write the name of the deceased and the birth and death dates. Highlight that dream trip taken or that special wedding anniversary celebrated. Include status changes like the birth of a baby, acquiring a new pet, or sending a child off to college. If you want to mention a recent separation or divorce, something straightforward like "Since Bob and I have parted ways, we're all adjusting. We are hopeful for a peaceful holiday celebration."
- *Open with a heart-warmer.* Use your child's "What Christmas Means to Me" poem, a relevant quote from a classic like Charles Dickens's *A Christmas Carol*, or a line from a traditional holiday movie or song, such as "Have Yourself a Merry Little Christmas." (Always attribute all written material to the creator whether the quote was pulled from a book or the Internet.)
- *Write briefly and in a light, humorous tone, when appropriate.* Avoid extensive detail by limiting the description of each event to one or two sentences and one short paragraph per family member. You might write, "One TV/VCR, one micro-fridge, and fourteen boxes

later, we arrived at Deanna's dormitory room without the aid of modern technology. The two-hour wait for the elevator forced us to tote, lug, and trudge up seven flights in a narrow stairwell."

- *Make it reader-friendly.* Use the same font, 12-point pitch or larger, throughout the text. Control the urge to overuse the bold and underline commands. Too much of this can be hard on the eyes. For the same reason, save the loopy, scripty, or **condensed** fonts for the headings and signature. If you need to emphasize a word or phrase, use all CAPITAL letters or *italicize* it.

- *Conclude on a positive note.* Finish with a wish for good cheer, good health, a wonderful New Year, or by sending your blessings to convey an upbeat message.

- *Customize your newsletter.* Use graphics or a border to ornament the top or bottom, in the middle to break up the text, or all around the outside edge. Or you might try scanning in a snapshot. If you don't have a scanner, photocopy the picture instead or reduce a copy of your child's holiday drawing as a separate enclosure.

- *Decide what type of paper you want.* You can print the newsletter on plain, colored, or specialty paper that comes with coordinating envelopes, sold in office and stationery stores. If you're using one with a border, print a copy of your newsletter on plain paper first. By placing the letter under the bordered paper and holding up to a window, you'll be able to see whether you need to change your margins in order for the body of the letter to clear the image or border. A holiday trifold is a smidgen heavier in weight and can be folded in threes. Add a sticker to close the letter and mail the trifold just like that, without an envelope. This helps cut your costs as it replaces traditional holiday cards. Be sure to leave the middle third of the back side open for addressing.

- *Check for grammar and spelling errors.* It's a good idea to ask someone else to read the newsletter before making additional copies.

- *Add a finishing touch.* Punch two holes about 2 inches apart at the top or bottom of your newsletter. Weave the two ends of an 8-inch piece of satin ribbon from back to front, one end through each hole. Cross the ribbons in the back and come up through the opposite hole. This adds a festive touch. (To use less ribbon, move the holes to about ¼ inch apart.) Enhance a computer-generated graphic by adding move-able eyes with a bit of glue to a reindeer or by gluing a small, satin bow to a package in Santa's sleigh. Or affix button eyes to a snowman.

Now you're ready to tuck your newsletter into your greeting cards and mail them off.

BE PREPARED: MEDICAL PROVISIONS

Winter, spring, summer, or fall—don't be caught off guard when maladies strike your household. Prepare your infirmary by stocking your shelves with these medical provisions.

Adhesive-strip bandages (fingertip, large, small)
Allergy and sinus tablets
Antacids
Antibiotic cream
Anti-diarrhea medicine
Anti-nausea liquid
Antiseptic spray
Aspirin, non-aspirin product
Benadryl (liquid and cream for internal or external allergic reactions)
Burn ointment
Cold and cough medicine, cough drops
Cotton swabs
Decongestants
Drawing salve
Eye wash and cup
First aid book
Gel cold pack (keep in freezer)
Heating pad, hot-water bottle
Hydrocortisone cream
Hydrogen peroxide
Insect repellent

Latex gloves
Lip balm
Motion sickness pills
Plastic gloves
Poison ivy lotion or spray
Rubbing alcohol
Scissors
Small splints
Sterile bandage tape
Sterile gauze bandages or pads (nonstick, assorted sizes)
Sterile rolled bandage
Sunscreen
Swimmer's ear drops
Syrup of ipecac
Thermometer
Tissues (with lotion)
Toothbrushes
Tweezers
Vaporizer
Vapor rub cream
Vitamins (daily, vitamin C, calcium supplements)
Zinc tablets

MORE RECIPES

❧ Applesauce Cinnamon Dough ❧

To create holiday ornaments, this easy-to-make, fragrant dough can be rolled out and cut with cookie cutters.

INGREDIENTS

½ cup cinnamon
½ cup applesauce
1 plastic zippered bag

Step one: Dump cinnamon and applesauce into the zippered bag and seal. Knead five minutes or so until the mixture has a doughlike texture. Roll out dough onto a floured surface and cut with your choice of cookie-cutter designs. Poke a small hole (big enough to thread a string or ribbon through) toward the top of the cutout using the end of a pencil.

Step two: Allow the ornaments to air-dry for 12 hours or until hard. Run string or ribbon through the hole and knot.

Your applesauce cinnamon dough creations will enhance the Christmas tree, holiday packages, or the car as a whimsical air freshener.

✦ Hard Tac Candy ✦

While Mary Jo and her son were researching his ancestors for a school project, they came across this hard tac candy recipe tucked away by his Grandmother Merilyn.

INGREDIENTS

2 cups sugar
⅔ cup light corn syrup
1 cup water
½ teaspoon lemon oil flavoring
a few drops yellow food coloring
confectioners' sugar

Step one: Place sugar, corn syrup, and water in a saucepan. Cook over low heat, stirring until sugar dissolves. Once sugar has dissolved, stop stirring. Allow the mixture to reach 310 degrees F (called hard crack stage). Then wrap a wet cloth around a fork and wipe crystals from the sides of the pan. Quickly stir in flavoring and coloring (make sure the mixture is still at 310 degrees F).

Step two: Pour immediately onto a greased cookie sheet with sides. Sprinkle with confectioners' sugar. Cool. Break into pieces and store in an airtight container.

Enjoy!

Although Grandma Merilyn made her recipe with lemon flavoring, there are a number of other options. Sue Kolton and friends gather one evening every December to make seventeen different kinds of hard tac candy by varying the oil flavoring. In the past, they've whipped up bits of banana, butterscotch, cherry, cinnamon, clove, grape, lemon, lime, peppermint, spearmint, and watermelon, to name a few. Sue recommends that you match the food coloring to the flavoring, such as pink for watermelon. She warns that you might run out of colors and that adding more drops to the mixture to darken the color doesn't always work. For example, once a friend popped a purple candy in her mouth thinking she had chosen grape, only to experience the taste of clove. So, when making as much as Sue and her friends do, store flavors in families—like cherry with grape and spearmint with wintergreen. The fun part is that no matter what your preference, there's a hard tac candy flavor for you.

(Hint: Sue advises that you throw a plastic tablecloth over your table and spray it with nonstick cooking spray to make cleanup of the sticky mess much easier.)

SPRING-CLEANING CHECKLIST

Use this room-by-room checklist to keep abreast of when and where your dust rag has been lately. Mark the date on the line as you complete each task.

Living Room
_____ Walls washed.
_____ Windows cleaned.
_____ Carpets cleaned.
_____ Baseboards, crevices, and register vents cleaned.
_____ Fireplace cleaned.
_____ Chimney swept.
_____ Upholstery cleaned.
_____ Draperies dry-cleaned/laundered.
_____ Miniblinds dusted/cleaned.
_____ Light fixtures/ceiling fans cleaned.

_____ Lampshades vacuumed.
_____ Artificial/live plants doused in the shower.
_____ Collectibles dusted/cleaned.

Family Room
_____ Walls washed.
_____ Windows cleaned.
_____ Carpets cleaned.
_____ Baseboards, crevices, and register vents cleaned.
_____ Fireplace cleaned.
_____ Chimney swept.
_____ Upholstery cleaned.
_____ Draperies dry-cleaned/laundered.
_____ Miniblinds dusted/cleaned.
_____ Light fixtures/ceiling fans cleaned.
_____ Lampshades vacuumed.
_____ Artificial/live plants doused in the shower.
_____ Collectibles dusted/cleaned.

Kitchen
_____ Walls washed.
_____ Windows cleaned.
_____ Floor stripped, waxed, or buffed.
_____ Baseboards and register vents cleaned.
_____ Draperies dry-cleaned/laundered.
_____ Miniblinds dusted/cleaned.
_____ Cabinets cleaned and polished.
_____ Cabinets de-cluttered.
_____ Drawers de-cluttered.
_____ Pantry de-cluttered.
_____ Oven cleaned.
_____ Refrigerator moved and coils vacuumed.
_____ Refrigerator interior emptied and sanitized.
_____ Microwave filters cleaned.

_____ Dishwasher cleaned (run through cycle while empty).

_____ Light fixtures/ceiling fans cleaned.

_____ Artificial/live plants doused in the shower.

Master Bedroom

_____ Walls washed.

_____ Windows cleaned.

_____ Carpets cleaned.

_____ Baseboards, crevices, and register vents cleaned.

_____ Draperies dry-cleaned/laundered.

_____ Miniblinds dusted/cleaned.

_____ Bedspread dry-cleaned/laundered.

_____ Closets de-cluttered.

_____ Closet walls washed.

_____ Drawers de-cluttered.

_____ Under the bed/furniture cleaned.

_____ Light fixtures/ceiling fans cleaned.

_____ Collectibles dusted/cleaned.

Extra Bedroom

_____ Walls washed.

_____ Windows cleaned.

_____ Carpets cleaned.

_____ Baseboards, crevices, and register vents cleaned.

_____ Draperies dry-cleaned/laundered.

_____ Miniblinds dusted/cleaned.

_____ Bedspread dry-cleaned/laundered.

_____ Closets de-cluttered.

_____ Closet walls washed.

_____ Drawers de-cluttered.

_____ Under the bed/furniture cleaned.

_____ Light fixtures/ceiling fans cleaned.

_____ Collectibles dusted/cleaned.

Guest Room/Den

_____ Walls washed.

_____ Windows cleaned.

_____ Carpets cleaned.

_____ Baseboards, crevices, and register vents cleaned.

_____ Draperies dry-cleaned/laundered.

_____ Miniblinds dusted/cleaned.

_____ Bedspread dry-cleaned/laundered.

_____ Closets de-cluttered.

_____ Closet walls washed.

_____ Drawers de-cluttered.

_____ Under the bed/furniture cleaned.

_____ Light fixtures/ceiling fans cleaned.

_____ Collectibles dusted/cleaned.

_____ Bookcases and/or computer center cleared and cleaned.

Bathroom

_____ Walls washed.

_____ Windows cleaned.

_____ Baseboards and register vents cleaned.

_____ Draperies laundered.

_____ Miniblinds dusted/cleaned.

_____ Medicine cabinet de-cluttered and cleaned.

_____ Under-the-sink cabinet de-cluttered and cleaned.

_____ Light fixtures/ceiling fans cleaned.

_____ Shower curtain/door washed.

_____ Handles and knobs polished/cleaned.

_____ Sink, toilet, and tub scoured.

_____ Waste container washed and disinfected.

_____ Floor scrubbed and sanitized.

Laundry Room

_____ Walls washed.

_____ Windows cleaned.

_____ Floor stripped, waxed, or buffed.

_____ Baseboards cleaned.

_____ Washer cleaned inside (run through cycle while empty).

_____ Washer cleaned outside.

_____ Dryer cleaned inside and outside.

_____ Outside dryer vent cleared of debris.

_____ Cabinets/shelves de-cluttered.

_____ Clothes mended or tossed.

_____ Socks mated or tossed.

Garage

_____ Contents removed.

_____ Excess items tossed/donated.

_____ Similar items grouped together.

_____ Bikes and such hung on walls.

_____ Workbench organized.

_____ Floor swept/hosed down.

_____ Extra refrigerator cleaned inside and out.

_____ Mousetraps set (if needed).

_____ Garage door scrubbed.

_____ Door opener components cleaned.

_____ Lighting cleaned/replaced.

Resources

You know you read something important in a book—like a Web site you want to visit or a book you long to buy—but you can't remember in what chapter it was. Doesn't this happen often to today's frantic woman? So you spend hours flipping through the book saying, "I know it was in the upper left-hand corner somewhere." And still you can't relocate the information.

Well, search no longer.

For a quick, at-your-fingertips reference, we've gathered all the recommendations (from books to Web sites and everything in-between) suggested in parts one and two and categorized them in this section for your convenience.

Books

30-Minute Meals by Rachael Ray and Dan Dinicola (Lake Isle Press, 1999); 212-273-0796; www.lakeislepress.com

101 Spooktacular Party Ideas by Linda Sadler (Creative Kids Products, 2000); www.funpartybooks.com

The Angry Child by Dr. Tim Murphy and Loriann Hoff Oberlin (Three Rivers Press, 2002); 1-800-733-3000; www.randomhouse.com

Bed & Breakfast Getaways from Cleveland by Doris Larson (Gray & Co., 2000); 1-800-915-3609; www.grayco.com

The Big Book of Halloween by Laura Dover Doran (Lark Books, 1999);
1-800-284-3388; www.larkbooks.com

Biggest Book of Slow Cooker Recipes by Better Homes and Gardens
(Meredith Books, 2002); www.meredith.com

The Confident Coach's Guide to Teaching Basketball by Beverly Breton
Carroll (Lyons Press, 2003); www.lyonspress.com

Dare to Change Your Job and Your Life by Carole Kanchier (Jist Works,
2000); 1-800-648-5478; www.jist.com

Fix-It and Forget-It Cookbook: Feasting with Your Slow Cooker and *Fix-It
and Forget-It Recipes for Entertaining: Slow Cooker Favorites for All
the Year Round* both by Dawn J. Ranck and Phyllis Pellman Good
(Good Books, 2001 and 2000, respectively); 1-800-762-7171;
www.goodbks.com

Halloween Crafts: Eerily Elegant Décor by Kasey Rogers and Mark Wood
(Krause Publications, 2001); 1-800-258-0929; www.krause.com

Herbs for All Seasons by Karen Patterson (ACW Press, 1999); 1-800-
931-2665; www.acwpress.com

*It's Deductible Cash for Your Used Clothing and Thousands of Commonly
Donated Items* by Income Dynamics; 1-800-875-5927;
www.ItsDeductible.com

Laying Down the Law: The 25 Laws of Parenting by Dr. Ruth Peters
(Rodale Press, 2002); 610-967-5171; www.rodale.com

Safety and Security for Women Who Travel by Sheila Swan and Peter
Laufer (Travelers' Tales Guides, 1998); 1-800-247-6553;
www.travelerstales.com

Surviving Separation and Divorce by Loriann Hoff Oberlin (Adams
Business Media, 2000); www.loriannoberlin.com

The Vegetarian Slow Cooker by Joanna White (Nitty Gritty Productions, 2001).

Walt Disney World for Cheapskates: 125 Money-Saving Tips by Linda
Johnson Tomsho (Tips2go, 2002); www.Tips2go.com

A Woman's Guide to Hiring a Contractor by Alexandra Sabina (Cat-
Jammies, 2001); 724 Allegheny River Boulevard, Verona, PA
15147; www.CatJammies.com

Working at Home While the Kids Are There, Too by Loriann Hoff Oberlin (Career Press, 1997); 1-800-CAREER-1; www.careerpress.com

Write It Down, Make It Happen by Henriette Anne Klauser (Simon & Schuster, 2001); www.simonsays.com

Associations, Organizations, and Such

American Association of University Women, 1111 Sixteenth Street, NW, Washington, DC 20036; 1-800-326-AAUW; www.aauw.org

American Camp Association, 5000 State Road 67 North, Martinsville, IN 46151; 765-342-8456; www.acacamps.org

American Nurses Association, 600 Maryland Street, SW, Suite 100 West, Washington, DC 20024; 202-554-4444; www.nursingworld.org

American Red Cross, 431 Eighteenth Street, NW, Washington, DC 20006; 1-877-272-7337; 202-639-3520; www.redcross.org

Association for Women in Communications, 780 Ritchie Highway, Suite 28-S, Severna Park, MD 21146; 410-544-7442; www.womcom.org

Boy Scouts of America, P.O. Box 152079, Irving, TX 75015; www.scouting.org

Business and Professional Women, 1900 M Street, NW, Suite 310, Washington, DC 20036; 202-293-1100; www.bpwusa.org

Camp Huff 'N Puff, American Respiratory Alliance Western Pennsylvania, 201 Smith Drive, Suite E, Cranberry Township, PA 16066; 724-772-1750 or in PA 1-800-220-1990; www.healthylungs.org

Department of Veterans Affairs; 1-800-827-1000; www.va.gov

Federal Emergency Management Agency (FEMA), 500 C Street, SW, Washington, DC 20472; 1-800-480-2520; www.fema.gov/areyouready

Girl Scouts of the USA, 420 Fifth Avenue, New York, NY 10018; 1-800-478-7248; www.girlscouts.org

GrownUp Camps, 6421 Congress Avenue, Suite 200, Boca Raton, FL 33487; www.GrownUpCamps.com

Habitat for Humanity International, 121 Habitat Street, Americus, GA 31709; www.habitat.org

Hobby Industry Association, 319 E. 54th Street, Elmwood Park, NJ 07407; 201-794-1133; www.hobby.org

National Craft Association, 2012 E. Ridge Road, No. 120, Rochester, NY 14622; 1-800-715-9594; www.craftassoc.com

Nike Sport Camps, US Sports Camps, Inc., 4470 Redwood Highway, San Rafael, CA 94903; 1-800-645-3226; www.eSportsCamps.com

Susan G. Komen Breast Cancer Foundation Pittsburgh Race for the Cure, National Council of Jewish Women, 1620 Murray Avenue, Pittsburgh, PA 15217; 412-521-CURE; www.pittsburghraceforthecure.org

Todd M. Beamer Foundation, P.O. Box 32, Cranbury, NJ 08512; 1-866-Beamer2; www.beamerfoundation.org

United States Department of Education; 1-800-4-FED-AID; www.fafsa.ed.gov

United States Department of Homeland Security; 1-800-BE-READY; www.ready.gov

Women in Technology International, 6345 Balboa Boulevard, Encino, CA 91316; 1-800-334-WITI; www.witi.org

YWCA of the U.S.A., Empire State Building, 350 Fifth Avenue, Suite 301, New York, NY 10118; www.ywca.org

Software and Web Sites

AAA Motor Club: www.aaa.com

American Botanical Council: www.herbalgram.org

American Commerce Insurance Company: www.acilink.com

American Furniture Manufacturers Association: www.FindYourFurniture.com

Basket of Pittsburgh: www.pghbasket.com

Better Homes and Gardens: www.bhg.com

Car Talk with hosts Click & Clack: http://cartalk.cars.com

Dress for Success: www.dressforsuccess.org

Dutch Bulb: www.dutchbulb.com

Dutch Gardens: www.dutchgardens.com

Evite: www.evite.com

EZ Bill Pay: www.ezbillpay.net

FlipAlbum software: www.flipalbum.com

FLS Furnitureland South: www.furniturelandsouth.com;
     336-841-4328

Frantic Woman: www.franticwoman.com

Halloween Magazine: www.halloweenmagazine.com

HealthCentral.com: www.healthcentral.com

Holiday Organizer: www.holidayorganizer.com

Home & Garden Television: www.hgtv.com

I-craft.com: www.i-craft.com

Internal Revenue Service: www.irs.gov

Kids Camps: www.KidsCamps.com

Look Smart: www.looksmart.com

Main Street Mom: www.mainstreetmom.com

Microsoft Office: www.microsoft.com

Mothers & More: www.mothersandmore.org

Mystery Lovers Bookstore: www.mysterylovers.com

NoPaperBills.com: www.nopaperbills.com

Paytrust: www.paytrust.com

Pittsburgh Snax and Nut Company: www.pghsnax.com

Quickbooks: www.intuit.com

Rose Clearance Center: www.roseclearance.com; 336-886-8525

Rose Furniture: www.rosefurniture.com; 336-886-6050

Transportation Security Administration: www.TSATravelTips.us

United States Postal Service: www.usps.gov

U-promise Inc.: www.upromise.com

Versacheck Premium Plus: www.g7ps.com

Women's Business Network, Inc.: www.wbninc.com

Index

About the Authors

Mary Jo Rulnick, events planner for a major western Pennsylvania corporation, has written extensively about parenting and women's issues in magazines across the United States. She has served on the executive board of seven nonprofit organizations. In addition, she is an avid volunteer in her community and has assisted with everything from hammering nails while building a neighborhood playground to cooking meals for disadvantaged children. She is the founder of Women in History Productions, a company performing dramatic portrayals of amazing women from our past. She also presents motivational workshops entitled "Are You Stuck in First Gear?" Mary Jo's ingenuity and creativity have earned her the title of the Do-It-Yourself Expert. Mary Jo lives the frantic life in Pittsburgh, Pennsylvania, with her husband, daughter, son, and German shepherd.

Judith Burnett Schneider qualifies as a world-class frantic. She left a career in organic chemistry to concentrate on writing full-time, but real life kept intervening. As a wife and mother of three active kids,

Judith realized that meshing her analytical side with her creative core, and mixing in the hectic-ness of her everyday experiences, was a winning combination. She is a lecturer, seminar leader, and teacher who has inspired hundreds of writers to tap the muse. In addition, she runs a successful editing/critiquing service. But what is most important to Judith is her family. While they provide much of the wind that whips her into a frantic frenzy, they are also the balm that soothes her soul.

Judith lives in the Pittsburgh area with her childhood-sweetheart husband and their three children. They are blessed to live in close proximity to both sets of parents/grandparents and many of their siblings, nieces, and nephews—all in all, providing an endless wellspring of frantic inspiration.